Pro Java 7 NIO.2

Anghel Leonard

Pro Java 7 NIO.2

ISBN 978-1-4302-4011-2

ISBN 978-1-4302-4012-9 (eBook)

President and Publisher: Paul Manning
Lead Editor: Matthew Moodie
Technical Reviewer: Michael Turner
Editorial Board: Steve Anglin, Mark Beckner, Ewan Buckingham, Gary Cornell, Morgan Ertel, Jonathan Gennick, Jonathan Hassell, Robert Hutchinson, Michelle Lowman, James Markham, Matthew Moodie, Jeff Olson, Jeffrey Pepper, Douglas Pundick, Ben Renow-Clarke, Dominic Shakeshaft, Gwenan Spearing, Matt Wade, Tom Welsh
Coordinating Editor: Corbin Collins
Copy Editor: Bill McManus, Damon Larson
Compositor: Apress Production (Christine Ricketts)
Indexer: SPI Global
Artist: SPI Global
Cover Designer: Anna Ishchenko

Distributed to the book trade worldwide by Springer Science+Business Media New York, 233 Spring Street, 6th Floor, New York, NY 10013. Phone 1-800-SPRINGER, fax (201) 348-4505, e-mail orders-ny@springer-sbm.com, or visit www.springeronline.com.

For information on translations, please e-mail rights@apress.com, or visit www.apress.com.

Apress and friends of ED books may be purchased in bulk for academic, corporate, or promotional use. eBook versions and licenses are also available for most titles. For more information, reference our Special Bulk Sales–eBook Licensing web page at www.apress.com/bulk-sales.

Any source code or other supplementary materials referenced by the author in this text is available to readers at www.apress.com. For detailed information about how to locate your book's source code, go to www.apress.com/source-code/.

Contents at a Glance

Contents at a Glance iii

Contents iv

About the Author xiii

About the Technical Reviewer xiv

Acknowledgments xv

Preface xvi

Chapter 1: Working with the Path Class 1

Chapter 2: Metadata File Attributes 11

Chapter 3: Manage Symbolic and Hard Links 35

Chapter 4: Files and Directories 43

Chapter 5: Recursive Operations: Walks 77

Chapter 6: Watch Service API 111

Chapter 7: Random Access Files 135

Chapter 8: The Sockets APIs 169

Chapter 9: The Asynchronous Channel API 215

Chapter 10: Important Things to Remember 263

Index 273

Contents

Contents at a Glance iii

Contents iv

About the Author xiii

About the Technical Reviewer xiv

Acknowledgments xv

Preface...xvi

Who This Book Is For xvii

What This Book Covers xvii

Carry out Path class operations.. xvii

Get/set file metadata through the new java.nio.file.attribute API xvii

Manage symbolic and hard links xviii

Deal with files and directories through the new java.nio.fileFiles API......... xviii

Use the FileVisitor API to develop recursive file operations....................... xviii

Explore the Watch Service API and file changed notifications xviii

Use the new SeekableByteChannel API for working with random access file xviii

Develop blocking/non-blocking socket-based applications xviii

Use the jewel in the crown of NIO.2: the Asynchronous Channel API.......... xiv

Work with the Zip File System and write a custom file system provider....... xiv

What You Need to Use This Book xviv

Chapter 1: Working with the Path Class 1

Introducing the Path Class 1

Defining a Path 2

Define an Absolute Path 2

Define a Path Relative to the File Store Root 3

Define a Path Relative to the Working Folder 3

Define a Path Using Shortcuts 3

Define a Path from a URI 4

Define a Path using FileSystems.getDefault().getPath() Method 4

Get the Path of the Home Directory 4

Getting Information About a Path 4

Get the Path File/Directory Name 5

Get the Path Root 5

Get the Path Parent 5

Get Path Name Elements 5

Get a Path Subpath 5

Converting a Path 6

Convert a Path to a String 6

Convert a Path to a URI 6

Convert a Relative Path to an Absolute Path 6

Convert a Path to a Real Path 6

Convert a Path to a File 7

Combining Two Paths 7

Constructing a Path Between Two Locations 8

Comparing Two Paths 9

Iterate over the Name Elements of a Path 10

Summary 10

Chapter 2: Metadata File Attributes 11

Supported Views in NIO.2 11

Determining Views Supported by a Particular File System 12

Basic View 13

Get Bulk Attributes with readAttributes() 13

Get a Single Attribute with getAttribute() 14

Update a Basic Attribute 15

DOS View 16

File Owner View 18

Set a File Owner Using Files.setOwner() 18

Set a File Owner Using FileOwnerAttributeView.setOwner() 18

Set a File Owner Using Files.setAttribute() 19

Get a File Owner Using FileOwnerAttributeView.getOwner() 19

Get a File Owner Using Files.getAttribute() 20

POSIX View 21

POSIX Permissions 22

POSIX Group Owner 22

ACL View 23

Read an ACL Using Files.getFileAttributeView() 23

Read an ACL Using Files.getAttribute() 24

Read ACL Entries 24

Grant a New Access in an ACL 26

File Store Attributes..**27**

Get Attributes of All File Stores...28

Get Attributes of the File Store in Which a File Resides 29

User-Defined File Attributes View...**30**

Check User-Defined Attributes Supportability 30

Operations on User-Defined Attributes 31

Summary **34**

Chapter 3: Manage Symbolic and Hard Links 35

Introducing Links...**35**

Creating Links from the Command Line **36**

Creating a Symbolic Link..**36**

Creating a Hard Link...**38**

Checking a Symbolic Link **39**

Locating the Target of a Link...**40**

Checking If a Link and a Target Point to the Same File..................................**41**

Summary **42**

Chapter 4: Files and Directories... 43

Checking Methods for Files and Directories..**43**

Checking for the Existence of a File or Directory..43

Checking File Accessibility 44

Checking If Two Paths Point to the Same File 46

Checking the File Visibility..47

Creating and Reading Directories..**47**

Listing File System Root Directories...47

Creating a New Directory..48

Listing a Directory's Content..49

Creating, Reading, and Writing Files...**53**

Using Standard Open Options...53

Creating a New File...54

Writing a Small File..54

Reading a Small File...56

Working with Buffered Streams...58

Working with Unbuffered Streams...59

Creating Temporary Directories and Files...**62**

Creating a Temporary Directory...62

Creating Temporary Files...66

Deleting, Copying, and Moving Directories and Files 70

Rename a File..75

Summary..**76**

Chapter 5: Recursive Operations: Walks... 77

The FileVisitor Interface..**78**

FileVisitor.visitFile() Method..78

FileVisitor.preVisitDirectory() Method 78

FileVisitor.postVisitDirectory() Method...79

FileVisitor.visitFileFailed() Method 79

The SimpleFileVisitor Class..**79**

Starting the Recursive Process...**80**

Common Walks **81**

Writing a File Search Application 81

Writing a File Delete Application 102

Writing a Copy Files Application 104

Writing a Move Files Application 107

Summary **110**

Chapter 6: Watch Service API 111

The Watch Service API Classes **112**

Implementing a Watch Service **112**

Creating a WatchService 112

Registering Objects with the Watch Service...112

Waiting for the Incoming Events 114

Getting a Watch Key...114

Retrieving Pending Events for a Key 115

Retrieving the Event Type and Count..116

Retrieving the File Name Associated with an Event 117

Putting the Key Back in Ready State 117

Closing the Watch Service 118

Gluing It All Together 118

Other Examples of Using a Watch Service..**120**

Watching a Directory Tree 120

Watching a Video Camera..125

Watching a Printer Tray System 128

Summary **134**

Chapter 7: Random Access Files 135

Brief Overview of ByteBuffer **135**

ByteBuffer Properties...136

ByteBuffer Ancestor Methods 139

Brief Overview of Channels **140**

Using the SeekableByteChannel Interface for Random Access to Files **140**

Reading a File with SeekableByteChannel 141

Writing a File with SeekableByteChannel..143

SeekableByteChannel and File Attributes..144

Reading a File with the Old ReadableByteChannel Interface...145

Writing a File with the Old WritableByteChannel Interface 146

Playing with SeekableByteChannel Position...146

Working with FileChannel... **152**

Mapping a Channel's File Region Directly into Memory 153

Locking a Channel's File...154

Copying Files with FileChannel 157

Summary **168**

Chapter 8: The Sockets APIs 169

NetworkChannel Overview **170**

Socket Options...171

Writing TCP Server/Client Applications **172**

Blocking vs. Non-Blocking Mechanisms..173

Writing a Blocking TCP Server 173

Writing a Blocking TCP Client 179

Testing the Blocking Echo Application...183

Writing a Non-Blocking TCP Client/Server Application 184

Writing UDP Server/Client Applications..**194**

    Writing a UDP Server 195

    Writing a Connectionless UDP Client 199

    Testing the UDP Connectionless Echo Application 201

    Writing a Connected UDP Client...202

    Testing the UDP Connected Echo Application 204

    Multicasting 205

    Testing the UDP Multicast Application 213

Summary **214**

Chapter 9: The Asynchronous Channel API 215

Synchronous I/O vs. Asynchronous I/O **215**

Asynchronous I/O Big Picture..**216**

    Pending Result and the Future Class 216

    Complete Result and the CompletionHandler Interface 217

    Types of Asynchronous Channels 218

    Groups 220

    ByteBuffer Considerations 223

    Introducing the ExecutorService API 224

Developing Asynchronous Applications **224**

    Asynchronous File Channel Examples 224

    Asynchronous Channel Sockets Examples 240

Summary **261**

Chapter 10: Important Things to Remember.. 263

Refactoring java.io.File Code **263**

Working with the ZIP File System Provider **267**

Considerations on Developing a Custom File System Provider **269**

Creating a Custom File System Provider Class...269

Creating a Custom File System Class 269

Useful Methods **270**

Default File System 270

File Stores...270

Path of a File 270

Path String Separator 270

Summary **271**

Index..**273**

About the Author

Anghel Leonard is a senior Java developer with more than 12 years of experience in Java SE, Java EE, and related frameworks. He has written and published more than 30 articles about Java technologies and more than 200 tips and tricks for JavaBoutique, O'Reilly, DevX, Developer and InformIT. In addition, he wrote two books about XML and Java (one for beginners and one for advanced developers) for Albastra, a Romanian publisher, and three books for Packt: *Jboss Tools 3 Developer Guide*, *JSF 2.0 Cookbook* and *JSF 2.0 Cookbook LITE*. Currently, he is developing web applications using the latest Java technologies on the market (EJB 3.0, CDI, Spring, JSF, Struts, Hibernate, and more). In the past two years, he has focused on developing rich Internet applications for geographic information systems. He can be contacted at leoprivacy@yahoo.com.

About the Technical Reviewer

 **Boris Minkin** is a Senior Technical Architect at a major financial corporation. He has more than 20 years of experience working in various areas of information technology and financial services. Boris achieved his Master's Degree in Information Systems at Stevens Institute of Technology, New Jersey. His professional interests are in Internet technology, service-oriented architecture, enterprise application architecture, multi-platform distributed applications, cloud, distributed caching, Java, grid, and high performance computing. You can contact Boris at bm@panix.com.

Acknowledgments

Thank You, God, because without You nothing is possible. Thank you to the Java 7 Project team for developing NIO.2. Thank you to the Apress team for trust in me to write this book and for the hard work you put in this project. And thank you, Octavia, my dear wife, for your love, patience, and for being next to me all the time.

Preface

This book covers all the important aspects involved in developing NIO.2-based applications. It provides clear instructions for getting the most out of NIO.2 and offers many exercises and case studies to spice up your Java 7 applications with the new I/O capabilities. You will learn to develop NIO.2 applications, beginning with simple but essential stuff and gradually moving on to complex features such as sockets and asynchronous channels.

Who This Book Is For

This book is for both experienced Java programmers who are new to Java 7 and for those who have some experience with Java 7. For the opening chapters (Chapters 1-5), it is enough to be familiar with Java syntax and to know how to open and run NetBeans projects. For Chapters 6-10), having some knowledge about a few fundamental programming concepts such as recursion, multi-threading and concurrency, Internet protocols, and network applications is essential.

What This Book Covers

This section contains a brief summary of what is covered in each chapter.

Carry out Path class operations

Chapter 1: Here you meet the new API for manipulating file paths; you now use the `java.nio.file.Path` class to manipulate a file in any file system. In this chapter I cover such important topics as declaring Path instances and syntactic operations.

Get/set file metadata through the new java.nio.file.attribute API (including POSIX)

Chapter 2: With NIO.2 you can manage more details about files' metadata than ever before. Attributes are divided into categories, and now they cover POSIX systems as well. Chapter 2 deeply explores each of these categories.

Manage symbolic and hard links

Chapter 3: An unexplored territory of Java is now revealed in NIO.2. This chapter shows you how to create, follow, and manipulate symbolic and hard links.

Deal with files and directories through the new java.nio.file.Files API

Chapter 4: Here you learn the most common tasks that involve files/directories, such as create, read, write, update, and more. You learn how to check file status and loop file stores, how to work with temporary files, and how to delete, copy, and move files and directories.

Use the FileVisitor API to develop recursive file operations

Chapter 5: Need to copy, move, or delete an entire directory? You've come to the right place. Chapter 5 shows you how to do all that through the brand new FileVisitor API. You also find out how to develop a Search File tool.

Explore the Watch Service API and file changed notification

Chapter 6: Want to monitor a file/directory for changes such as entries created, deleted, or modified? This is what the Watch Service does best. I also cover watching a print tray and surveying a video camera in this chapter. This is where you discover how flexible and versatile the new Watch Service API is.

Use the new SeekableByteChannel API for working with random access file

Chapter 7: Random access file (RAF) is a powerful tool in the right hands. This chapter introduces the new SeekableByteChannel API and provides plenty of examples that exploit its methods. Practice, practice, practice, and go beyond being a RAF apprentice!

Develop blocking/non-blocking socket-based applications

Chapter 8: Learn how to develop Java network-based applications in blocking and non-blocking styles. I cover both TCP and UDP in detail and sprinkle important aspects of sockets programming throughout the chapter.

Use the jewel in the crown of NIO.2: the Asynchronous Channel API

Chapter 9: This is my own personal favorite chapter. It was a pleasure to write, and I hope you find it as useful as I found it fun. With the Asynchronous Channel API, you can develop asynchronous network-based Java applications with a suite of classes and options. Asynchronous Channel API rocks!

Work with the Zip File System Provider and write a custom file system provider

Chapter 10: This last chapter finishes the book with an example of using the new Zip File System Provider. I address a few considerations about writing a custom file system provider as well. Chapter 10 also contains a table with detailed conversions between `java.io.File` and `java.nio.file.Path` APIs.

CHAPTER 1

■ ■ ■

Working with the Path Class

The recommended entry point to start exploring the NIO.2 API, also known as "JSR 203: More New I/O APIs for the Java Platform" (NIO.2), is the new abstract class `java.nio.file.Path`. This class is a milestone of NIO.2, and every application that involves I/O operations will exploit the powerful facilities of this class. Practically, it is the most commonly used class of NIO.2, since many I/O operations are based on a `Path` resource.

The `Path` class supports two types of operations: *syntactic operations* (almost any operation that involves manipulating paths without accessing the file system; these are logical manipulations done in memory) and *operations over files* referenced by paths. This chapter covers the first type of operations and introduces you to the `Path` API. In Chapter 4, I focus on exploring the second type of operations. The concepts presented in this chapter will be very useful in the rest of the book.

Introducing the Path Class

A path resides in a *file system*, which "stores and organizes files on some form of media, generally one or more hard drives, in such a way that they can be easily retrieved."[1] The file system can be accessed through the `java.nio.file.FileSystems` final class, which is used to get an instance of the `java.nio.file.FileSystem` we want to work on. `FileSystems` contains the following two important methods, as well as a set of `newFileSystem()` methods, for constructing new file systems:

- `getDefault()`: This is a static method that returns the default `FileSystem` to the JVM—commonly the operating system default file system.

---

[1] Oracle, *The Java Tutorials*, "What Is a Path? (And Other File System Facts)," http://download.oracle.com/javase/tutorial/essential/io/path.html.

1

- **getFileSystem(URI uri)**: This is a static method that returns a file system from the set of available file system providers that match the given URI schema. The **Path** class manipulates a file in any file system (**FileSystem**) that can use any storage place (**java.nio.file.FileStore**; this class represents the underlying storage). By default (and commonly), the **Path** refers to files in the default file system (the file system of the computer), but NIO.2 is totally modular—an implementation of **FileSystem** for data in memory, on the network, or on a virtual file system is perfectly agreeable to NIO.2. NIO.2 provides us with all file system functionalities that we may need to perform over a file, a directory, or a link.

The **Path** class is an upgraded version of the well-known **java.io.File** class, but the **File** class has kept a few specific operations, so it is not deprecated and cannot be considered obsolete. Moreover, starting with Java 7, both classes are available, which means programmers can mix their powers to obtain the best of I/O APIs. Java 7 provides a simple API for conversion between them. Remember the days when you had to do the following?

```
import java.io.File;
…
File file = new File("index.html");
```

Well, those days are gone, because with Java 7 you can do this:

```
import java.nio.file.Path;
import java.nio.file.Paths;
…
Path path = Paths.get("index.html");
```

At a closer look, a **Path** is a programmatic representation of a path in the file system. The path string contains the file name, the directory list, and the OS-dependent file delimiter (e.g., backslash "\" on Microsoft Windows and forward slash "/" on Solaris and Linux), which means that a **Path** is not system independent since it is based on a system-dependent string path. Because **Path** is basically a string, the referenced resource might not exist.

Defining a Path

Once you identify the file system and the location of a file or directory, you can create a **Path** object for it. Absolute paths, relative paths, paths defined with the notation "." (indicates the current directory) or ".." (indicates the parent directory), and paths containing only a file/directory name are covered by the **Path** class. The simplest solution for defining a **Path** is to call one of the **get()** methods of the **Paths** helper class. The following subsections present several different ways to define a path to the same file (on Windows)—C:\rafaelnadal\tournaments\2009\BNP.txt.

Define an Absolute Path

An absolute path (also known as a full path or file path) is a path that contains the root directory and all other subdirectories that contain a file or folder. Defining an absolute path in NIO.2 is a one-line-of-code task, as you can see in the following example, which points to the file named BNP.txt in the C:\rafaelnadal\tournaments\2009 directory (the file may not exist for testing this code):

```
Path path = Paths.get("C:/rafaelnadal/tournaments/2009/BNP.txt");
```

`get()` also allows you to split a path into a set of chunks. NIO will reconstruct the path for you, no matter how many chunks there are. Note that if you define a chunk for each component of the path, you can omit the file separator delimiter. The preceding absolute path can be chunked as "follows":

```
Path path = Paths.get("C:/rafaelnadal/tournaments/2009", "BNP.txt");
Path path = Paths.get("C:", "rafaelnadal/tournaments/2009", "BNP.txt");
Path path = Paths.get("C:", "rafaelnadal", "tournaments", "2009", "BNP.txt");
```

Define a Path Relative to the File Store Root

A relative path (also known as a nonabsolute path or partial path) is only a portion of the full path. A relative path is often used in creating a web page. Relative paths are used much more frequently than absolute paths. Defining a path relative to the current file store root should start with the file delimiter. In the following examples, if the current file store root is `C:`, then the absolute path is `C:\rafaelnadal\tournaments\2009\BNP.txt`:

```
Path path = Paths.get("/rafaelnadal/tournaments/2009/BNP.txt");
Path path = Paths.get("/rafaelnadal","tournaments/2009/BNP.txt");
```

Define a Path Relative to the Working Folder

When you define a path relative to the current working folder, the path should *not* start with the file delimiter. If the current folder is `/ATP` under `C:` root, then the absolute path returned by the following snippet of code is `C:\ATP\rafaelnadal\tournaments\2009\BNP.txt`:

```
Path path = Paths.get("rafaelnadal/tournaments/2009/BNP.txt");
Path path = Paths.get("rafaelnadal","tournaments/2009/BNP.txt");
```

Define a Path Using Shortcuts

Defining paths using the notation "." (indicates the current directory) or ".." (indicates the parent directory) is a common practice. These kinds of paths can be processed by NIO.2 to eliminate possible cases of redundancy if you call the `Path.normalize()` method (which removes any redundant elements, including any "." or "*directory/..*" occurrences):

```
Path path = Paths.get("C:/rafaelnadal/tournaments/2009/dummy/../BNP.txt").normalize();
Path path = Paths.get("C:/rafaelnadal/tournaments/./2009/dummy/../BNP.txt").normalize();
```

If you want to see the effect of the `normalize()` method, try to define the same `Path` with and without `normalize()`, as follows, and print the result to the console:

```
Path noNormalize = Paths.get("C:/rafaelnadal/tournaments/./2009/dummy/../BNP.txt");
Path normalize = Paths.get("C:/rafaelnadal/tournaments/./2009/dummy/../BNP.txt").normalize();
```

If you use `System.out.println()` to print the preceding paths, you will see the following results, in which `normalize()` has removed the redundant elements:

```
C:\rafaelnadal\tournaments\.\2009\dummy\..\BNP.txt
```

```
C:\rafaelnadal\tournaments\2009\BNP.txt
```

Define a Path from a URI

In some cases, you may need to create a Path from a Uniform Resource Identifier (URI). You can do so by using the URI.create() method to create a URI from a given string and by using the Paths.get() method that takes a URI object as an argument. This is useful if you need to encapsulate a path string that can be entered into the address bar of a web browser:

```
import java.net.URI;
…
Path path = Paths.get(URI.create("file:///rafaelnadal/tournaments/2009/BNP.txt"));
Path path = Paths.get(URI.create("file:///C:/rafaelnadal/tournaments/2009/BNP.txt"));
```

Define a Path using FileSystems.getDefault().getPath() Method

Another common solution for creating a Path is to use the FileSystems class. First, call the getDefault() method to obtain the default FileSystem—NIO.2 will provide a generic object that is capable of accessing the default file system. Then, you can call the getPath() method as follows (the Paths.get() method in the preceding examples is just shorthand for this solution):

```
import java.nio.file.FileSystems;
…
Path path = FileSystems.getDefault().getPath("/rafaelnadal/tournaments/2009", "BNP.txt");
Path path = FileSystems.getDefault().getPath("/rafaelnadal/tournaments/2009/BNP.txt");
Path path = FileSystems.getDefault().getPath("rafaelnadal/tournaments/2009", "BNP.txt");
Path path = FileSystems.getDefault().
                  getPath("/rafaelnadal/tournaments/./2009","BNP.txt").normalize();
```

Get the Path of the Home Directory

When you need a path that points to the home directory, you can proceed as shown in the following example (the returned home directory is dependent on each machine and each operating system):

```
Path path = Paths.get(System.getProperty("user.home"), "downloads", "game.exe");
```

On my Windows 7 machine, this returns C:\Users\Leo\downloads\game.exe, while on my friend's CentOS system (Linux), this returns /home/simpa/downloads/game.exe.

Getting Information About a Path

After you have defined a Path object, you have access to a set of methods that provide useful information about the path elements. These methods are based on the fact that NIO.2 splits the path string into a set of elements (an *element* is a subpath representing a directory or a file) and assigns index 0 to the highest element and index $n - 1$ to the lowest element, where n is the number of path elements; usually, the highest element is the root folder and the lowest element is a file. This section presents examples that apply these information-obtaining methods to the path C:\rafaelnadal\tournaments\2009\BNP.txt:

```
Path path = Paths.get("C:", "rafaelnadal/tournaments/2009", "BNP.txt");
```

Get the Path File/Directory Name

The file/directory indicated by a path is returned by the getFileName() method, which is the farthest element from the root in the directory hierarchy:

```
//output: BNP.txt
System.out.println("The file/directory indicated by path: " + path.getFileName());
```

Get the Path Root

The root of the path can be obtained with the getRoot() method (if the Path does not have a root, it returns null):

```
//output: C:\
System.out.println("Root of this path: " + path.getRoot());
```

Get the Path Parent

The parent of this path (the path's root component) is returned by the getParent() method (if the Path does not have a parent, it returns null):

```
//output: C:\rafaelnadal\tournaments\2009
System.out.println("Parent: " + path.getParent());
```

Get Path Name Elements

You can get the number of elements in a path with the getNameCount() method and get the name of each element with the getName() method:

```
//output: 4
System.out.println("Number of name elements in path: " + path.getNameCount());
```

```
//output: rafaelnadal  tournaments  2009  BNP.txt
for (int i = 0; i < path.getNameCount(); i++) {
  System.out.println("Name element " + i + " is: " + path.getName(i));
}
```

Get a Path Subpath

You can extract a relative path with the subpath() method, which gets two parameters, the start index and the end index, representing the subsequence of elements:

```
//output: rafaelnadal\tournaments\2009
System.out.println("Subpath (0,3): " + path.subpath(0, 3));
```

Converting a Path

In this section, you will see how to convert a `Path` object into a string, a URI, an absolute path, a real path, and a `File` object. The `Path` class contains a dedicated method for each of these conversions, as shown in the following subsections. The following is the path we are going to work with:

```
Path path = Paths.get("/rafaelnadal/tournaments/2009", "BNP.txt");
```

Convert a Path to a String

String conversion of a path can be achieved by the `toString()` method:

```
//output: \rafaelnadal\tournaments\2009\BNP.txt
String path_to_string = path.toString();
System.out.println("Path to String: " + path_to_string);
```

Convert a Path to a URI

You can convert a `Path` to a web browser format string by applying the `toURI()` method, as shown in the following example. The result is a URI object that encapsulates a path string that can be entered into the address bar of a web browser.

```
//output: file:///C:/rafaelnadal/tournaments/2009/BNP.txt
URI path_to_uri = path.toUri();
System.out.println("Path to URI: " + path_to_uri);
```

Convert a Relative Path to an Absolute Path

Obtaining an absolute path from a relative one is a very common task. NIO.2 can do that with the `toAbsolutePath()` method (notice that if you apply this method to an already absolute path, then the same path is returned):

```
//output: C:\rafaelnadal\tournaments\2009\BNP.txt
Path path_to_absolute_path = path.toAbsolutePath();
System.out.println("Path to absolute path: " + path_to_absolute_path.toString());
```

Convert a Path to a Real Path

The `toRealPath()` method returns the real path of an existing file—this means that the file must exist, which is not necessary if you use the `toAbsolutePath()` method. If no argument is passed to this method and the file system supports symbolic links, this method resolves any symbolic links in the path. If you want to ignore symbolic links, then pass to the method the `LinkOption.NOFOLLOW_LINKS` enum constant. Moreover, if the `Path` is relative, it returns an absolute path, and if the `Path` contains any redundant elements, it returns a path with those elements removed. This method throws an `IOException` if the file does not exist or cannot be accessed.

The following snippet of code returns the real path of a file by not following symbolic links:

```
import java.io.IOException;
...
//output: C:\rafaelnadal\tournaments\2009\BNP.txt
try {
    Path real_path = path.toRealPath(LinkOption.NOFOLLOW_LINKS);
    System.out.println("Path to real path: " + real_path);
} catch (NoSuchFileException e) {
    System.err.println(e);
} catch (IOException e) {
    System.err.println(e);
}
```

Convert a Path to a File

A Path can also be converted to a File object using the toFile() method, as follows. This a great bridge between Path and File since the File class also contains a method named toPath() for reconversion.

```
//output: BNP.txt
File path_to_file = path.toFile();

//output: \rafaelnadal\tournaments\2009\BNP.txt
Path file_to_path = path_to_file.toPath();
System.out.println("Path to file name: " + path_to_file.getName());
System.out.println("File to path: " + file_to_path.toString());
```

Combining Two Paths

Combining two paths is a technique that allows you to define a fixed root path and append to it a partial path. This is very useful for defining paths based on a common part. NIO.2 provides this operation through the resolve() method. The following is an example of how it works:

```
//define the fixed path
Path base = Paths.get("C:/rafaelnadal/tournaments/2009");

//resolve BNP.txt file
Path path_1 = base.resolve("BNP.txt");
//output: C:\rafaelnadal\tournaments\2009\BNP.txt
System.out.println(path_1.toString());

//resolve AEGON.txt file
Path path_2 = base.resolve("AEGON.txt");
//output: C:\rafaelnadal\tournaments\2009\AEGON.txt
System.out.println(path_2.toString());
```

There is also a method dedicated to sibling paths, named resolveSibling(). It resolves the passed path against the current path's parent path. Practically, this method replaces the file name of the current path with the file name of the given path.

The following example clarifies the idea:

```
//define the fixed path
Path base = Paths.get("C:/rafaelnadal/tournaments/2009/BNP.txt");

//resolve sibling AEGON.txt file
Path path = base.resolveSibling("AEGON.txt");
//output: C:\rafaelnadal\tournaments\2009\AEGON.txt
System.out.println(path.toString());
```

Constructing a Path Between Two Locations

When you need to construct a path from one location to another, you can call the `relativize()` method, which constructs a relative path between this path and a given path. This method constructs a path originating from the original path and ending at the location specified by the passed-in path. The new path is relative to the original path. For a better understanding of this powerful facility, consider a simple example. Suppose that you have the following two relative paths:

```
Path path01 = Paths.get("BNP.txt");
Path path02 = Paths.get("AEGON.txt");
```

In this case, it is assumed that `BNP.txt` and `AEGON.txt` are siblings, which means that you can navigate from one to the other by going up one level and then down one level. Applying the `relativize()` method outputs `..\AEGON.txt` and `..\BNP.txt`:

```
//output:  ..\AEGON.txt
Path path01_to_path02 = path01.relativize(path02);
System.out.println(path01_to_path02);

//output:  ..\BNP.txt
Path path02_to_path01 = path02.relativize(path01);
System.out.println(path02_to_path01);
```

Another typical situation involves two paths that contain a root element. Consider the following paths:

```
Path path01 = Paths.get("/tournaments/2009/BNP.txt");
Path path02 = Paths.get("/tournaments/2011");
```

In this case, both paths contain the same root element, `/tournaments`. To navigate from `path01` to `path02`, you will go up two levels and down one level (`..\..\2011`). To navigate from `path02` to `path01`, you will go up one level and down two levels (`..\2009\BNP.txt`). This is exactly how the `relativize()` method works:

```
//output:  ..\..\2011
Path path01_to_path02 = path01.relativize(path02);
System.out.println(path01_to_path02);

//output:  ..\2009\BNP.txt
Path path02_to_path01 = path02.relativize(path01);
System.out.println(path02_to_path01);
```

Note If only one of the paths includes a root element, then a relative path cannot be constructed. Both paths *must* include a root element. Even then, the construction of the relative path is system dependent.

Comparing Two Paths

The equality of two `Paths` can be tested in different ways for different purposes. You can test whether two paths are equal by calling the `Path.equals()` method. This method respects the `Object.equals()` specification. It does not access the file system, so the compared paths are not required to exist, and it does not check if the paths are the same file. In some OS implementations, the paths are compared by ignoring the case, while in other implementations, the comparison is case sensitive—the implementation will specify whether case is considered. Here I show a path relative to the current file store and an absolute path, both representing the same file, but not equals:

```
Path path01 = Paths.get("/rafaelnadal/tournaments/2009/BNP.txt");
Path path02 = Paths.get("C:/rafaelnadal/tournaments/2009/BNP.txt");

if(path01.equals(path02)){
    System.out.println("The paths are equal!");
} else {
    System.out.println("The paths are not equal!"); //true
}
```

Sometimes you'll want to check if two paths are the same file/folder. You can easily accomplish this by calling the `java.nio.File.Files.isSameFile()` method (as shown in the following example), which returns a boolean value. Behind the scenes, this method uses the `Path.equals()` method. If `Path.equals()` returns `true`, the paths are equal, and therefore no further comparisons are needed. If it returns `false`, then the `isSameFile()` method enters into action to double-check. Notice that this method requires that the compared files exist on the file system; otherwise, it throws an `IOException`.

```
try {
    boolean check = Files.isSameFile(path01, path02);
    if(check){
        System.out.println("The paths locate the same file!"); //true
    } else {
        System.out.println("The paths does not locate the same file!");
    }
} catch (IOException e) {
    System.out.println(e.getMessage());
}
```

Since the `Path` class implements the `Comparable` interface, you can compare paths by using the `compareTo()` method, which compares two abstract paths lexicographically. This can be useful for sorting. The method returns zero if the argument is equal to this path, a value less than zero if this path is lexicographically less than the argument, or a value greater than zero if this path is lexicographically greater than the argument. The following is an example of using the `compareTo()` method:

```
//output: 24
int compare = path01.compareTo(path02);
System.out.println(compare);
```

Partial comparison can be accomplished by using the startsWith() and endsWith() methods, as shown in the following example. Using these methods, you can test if the current path starts or ends, respectively, with the given path. Both methods returns bool values.

```
boolean sw = path01.startsWith("/rafaelnadal/tournaments");
boolean ew = path01.endsWith("BNP.txt");
System.out.println(sw);  //output:  true
System.out.println(ew);  //output:  true
```

Iterate over the Name Elements of a Path

Since the Path class implements the Iterable interface, you can obtain an object that enables you to iterate over the elements in the path. You can iterate either by using an explicit iterator or with a foreach loop that returns a Path object for each iteration. The following is an example:

```
Path path = Paths.get("C:", "rafaelnadal/tournaments/2009", "BNP.txt");

for (Path name : path) {
    System.out.println(name);
}
```

This outputs the elements starting with the closest to the root, as follows:

```
rafaelnadal

tournaments

2009

BNP.txt
```

Summary

In this chapter you have taken your first step into the NIO.2 API. In addition to learning about basic NIO.2 concepts, such as file systems and file stores, you received an overview of the Path class, knowledge of which is essential for every developer who wants to learn how to use the NIO.2 API. Knowing how to obtain the default file system and how to define and manipulate file paths is important because the Path class will sustain the examples throughout the book and will usually be the entry point of applications.

CHAPTER 2

■ ■ ■

Metadata File Attributes

If you have questions about a file or a directory, such as whether it is hidden, whether it is a directory, what its size is, and who owns it, you can get answers to those questions (and many others) from the *metadata*, which is data about other data.

NIO.2 associates the notion of metadata with attributes and provides access to them through the `java.nio.file.attribute` package. Since different file systems have different notions about which attributes should be tracked, NIO.2 groups the attributes into *views*, each of which maps to a particular file system implementation. Generally, views provide the attributes in bulk through a common method, `readAttributes()`. In addition, you can extract and set a single attribute with the `getAttribute()` and `setAttribute()` methods, respectively, which are available in the `java.nio.file.Files` class. Depending on the view, other methods are available for additional tasks.

In this chapter you will learn how to use the views provided by NIO.2. You will see how to determine whether a file is read-only or hidden, when it was last accessed or modified, who owns it, and how to take ownership of it. You will also discover how to view the access control list (ACL) of a file and how to set Unix permissions on a file. Moreover, you will explore file store attributes and learn how to define your own attributes.

Supported Views in NIO.2

NIO.2 comes with a set of six views, an overview of which follows:

- `BasicFileAttributeView`: This is a view of basic attributes that must be supported by all file system implementations. The attribute view name is `basic`.

- `DosFileAttributeView`: This view provides the standard four supported attributes on file systems that support the DOS attributes. The attribute view name is `dos`.

- `PosixFileAttributeView`: This view extends the basic attribute view with attributes supported on file systems that support the POSIX (Portable Operating System Interface for Unix) family of standards, such as Unix. The attribute view name is `posix`.

- `FileOwnerAttributeView`: This view is supported by any file system implementation that supports the concept of a file owner. The attribute view name is `owner`.

- **AclFileAttributeView**: This view supports reading or updating a file's ACL. The NFSv4 ACL model is supported. The attribute view name is **acl**.

- **UserDefinedFileAttributeView**: This view enables support of metadata that is user defined.

Determining Views Supported by a Particular File System

Before you attempt to access a view's attributes, make sure that your file system supports the corresponding view. NIO.2 lets you either view the entire list of supported views by name or check if a file store—represented by the **FileStore** class that maps any type of store, such as partitions, devices, volumes, and so on—supports a particular view.

Once you obtain access to the default file system—by calling the **FileSystems.getDefault()** method—you can easily iterate over the supported views returned by the **FileSystem.supportedFileAttributeViews()** method. The following code snippet shows how to do this:

```
import java.nio.file.FileSystem;
import java.nio.file.FileSystems;
import java.util.Set;
...
FileSystem fs = FileSystems.getDefault();
Set<String> views = fs.supportedFileAttributeViews();

for (String view : views) {
    System.out.println(view);
}
```

For example, for Windows 7, the preceding code returned the following results:

```
acl

basic

owner

user

dos
```

> **Note** All file systems support the basic view, so you should get at least the **basic** name in your output.

You can test a particular view on a file store by calling the `FileStore.supportsFileAttributeView()` method. You can pass the desired view as a **String** or as a class name. The following code checks whether the basic view is supported by all the available file stores:

```java
import java.nio.file.FileStore;
import java.nio.file.FileSystem;
import java.nio.file.FileSystems;
import java.nio.file.attribute.BasicFileAttributeView;
...
FileSystem fs = FileSystems.getDefault();
for (FileStore store : fs.getFileStores()) {
    boolean supported = store.supportsFileAttributeView(BasicFileAttributeView.class);
    System.out.println(store.name() + " ---" + supported);
}
```

Moreover, you can check if a file store in which a particular file resides supports a single view, as shown in this example:

```java
import java.io.IOException;
import java.nio.file.FileStore;
import java.nio.file.Files;
import java.nio.file.Path;
import java.nio.file.Paths;
...
Path path = Paths.get("C:/rafaelnadal/tournaments/2009", "BNP.txt");

try {
    FileStore store = Files.getFileStore(path);
    boolean supported = store.supportsFileAttributeView("basic");
    System.out.println(store.name() + " ---" + supported);
} catch (IOException e) {
    System.err.println(e);
}
```

Now that you can determine which views are supported on your file system, it is time to dig deeper and explore each view's attributes, starting with the basic view.

Basic View

Most file system implementations support a set of common attributes (size, creation time, last accessed time, last modified time, etc.). These attributes are grouped into a view named `BasicFileAttributeView` and can be extracted and set as described in the following subsections.

Get Bulk Attributes with readAttributes()

You can extract attributes in bulk using the `readAttributes()` method as follows (the **varargs** argument currently supports the `LinkOption.NOFOLLOW_LINKS` enum—do not follow symbolic links):

```java
import java.io.IOException;
import java.nio.file.Files;
import java.nio.file.Path;
```

```java
import java.nio.file.Paths;
import java.nio.file.attribute.BasicFileAttributes;
...
BasicFileAttributes attr = null;
Path path = Paths.get("C:/rafaelnadal/tournaments/2009", "BNP.txt");

try {
    attr = Files.readAttributes(path, BasicFileAttributes.class);
} catch (IOException e) {
    System.err.println(e);
}

System.out.println("File size: " + attr.size());
System.out.println("File creation time: " + attr.creationTime());
System.out.println("File was last accessed at: " + attr.lastAccessTime());
System.out.println("File was last modified at: " + attr.lastModifiedTime());

System.out.println("Is directory? " + attr.isDirectory());
System.out.println("Is regular file? " + attr.isRegularFile());
System.out.println("Is symbolic link? " + attr.isSymbolicLink());
System.out.println("Is other? " + attr.isOther());
```

Get a Single Attribute with getAttribute()

If you need to extract a single attribute instead of all the attributes in bulk, use the `getAttribute()` method. You need to pass the file path and the attribute name and specify whether or not you need to follow symbolic links. The following code snippet shows how to extract the `size` attribute value. Keep in mind that the `getAttribute()` method returns an `Object`, so you need an explicit conversion depending on the attribute's value type.

```java
import java.io.IOException;
import java.nio.file.Files;
import java.nio.file.Path;
import java.nio.file.Paths;
import static java.nio.file.LinkOption.NOFOLLOW_LINKS;
...
Path path = Paths.get("C:/rafaelnadal/tournaments/2009", "BNP.txt");
try {
    long size = (Long)Files.getAttribute(path, "basic:size", NOFOLLOW_LINKS);
    System.out.println("Size: " + size);
} catch (IOException e) {
    System.err.println(e);
}
```

Basic attribute names are listed here:

- lastModifiedTime

- lastAccessTime

- creationTime

- size

- isRegularFile

- isDirectory

- isSymbolicLink

- isOther

- fileKey

The generally accepted form for retrieving a single attribute is [view-name:]attribute-name. The view-name is basic.

Update a Basic Attribute

Updating any or all of the file's last modified time, last access time, and create time attributes can be accomplished with the setTimes() method, which takes three arguments representing the last modified time, last access time, and create time as instances of FileTime, which is a new class in Java 7 representing the value of a file's timestamp attribute. If any one of lastModifiedTime, lastAccessTime, or creationTime has the value null, then the corresponding timestamp is not changed.

```
import java.io.IOException;
import java.nio.file.Files;
import java.nio.file.Path;
import java.nio.file.Paths;
import java.nio.file.attribute.BasicFileAttributeView;
import java.nio.file.attribute.FileTime;
…
Path path = Paths.get("C:/rafaelnadal/tournaments/2009", "BNP.txt");
long time = System.currentTimeMillis();
FileTime fileTime = FileTime.fromMillis(time);
try {
    Files.getFileAttributeView(path,
    BasicFileAttributeView.class).setTimes(fileTime, fileTime, fileTime);
} catch (IOException e) {
    System.err.println(e);
}
```

Updating the file's last modified time can also be accomplished with the Files.setLastModifiedTime() method:

```
long time = System.currentTimeMillis();
FileTime fileTime = FileTime.fromMillis(time);
try {
    Files.setLastModifiedTime(path, fileTime);
} catch (IOException e) {
    System.err.println(e);
}
```

Updating the file's last modified time can also be accomplished with the `setAttribute()` method. Actually, this method may be used to update the file's last modified time, last access time, or create time attributes as if by invoking the `setTimes()` method:

```
import static java.nio.file.LinkOption.NOFOLLOW_LINKS;
...
try {
    Files.setAttribute(path, "basic:lastModifiedTime", fileTime, NOFOLLOW_LINKS);
    Files.setAttribute(path, "basic:creationTime", fileTime, NOFOLLOW_LINKS);
    Files.setAttribute(path, "basic:lastAccessTime", fileTime, NOFOLLOW_LINKS);
} catch (IOException e) {
    System.err.println(e);
}
```

Obviously, now you have to extract the three attributes' values to see the changes. You can do so by using the `getAttribute()` method:

```
try {
    FileTime lastModifiedTime = (FileTime)Files.getAttribute(path,
                            "basic:lastModifiedTime", NOFOLLOW_LINKS);
    FileTime creationTime = (FileTime)Files.getAttribute(path,
                            "basic:creationTime", NOFOLLOW_LINKS);
    FileTime lastAccessTime = (FileTime)Files.getAttribute(path,
                            "basic:lastAccessTime", NOFOLLOW_LINKS);

    System.out.println("New last modified time: " + lastModifiedTime);
    System.out.println("New creation time: " + creationTime);
    System.out.println("New last access time: " + lastAccessTime);

} catch (IOException e) {
    System.err.println(e);
}
```

DOS View

Specific to the DOS file system (or Samba), the `DosFileAttributeView` view extends the basic view with the DOS attributes (which means that you can access the basic view directly from DOS view). There are four attributes, which are mapped by the following methods:

- `isReadOnly()`: Returns the `readonly` attribute's value (if `true`, the file can't be deleted or updated)

- `isHidden()`: Returns the `hidden` attribute's value (if `true`, the file is not visible to the users)

- `isArchive()`: Returns the `archive` attribute's value (specific to backup programs)

- `isSystem()`: Returns the `system` attribute's value (if `true`, the file belongs to the operating system)

The following listing extracts in bulk the preceding four attributes for a given path:

```
import java.io.IOException;
```

```java
import java.nio.file.Files;
import java.nio.file.Path;
import java.nio.file.Paths;
import java.nio.file.attribute.DosFileAttributes;
...
DosFileAttributes attr = null;
Path path = Paths.get("C:/rafaelnadal/tournaments/2009", "BNP.txt");

try {
    attr = Files.readAttributes(path, DosFileAttributes.class);
} catch (IOException e) {
    System.err.println(e);
}

System.out.println("Is read only ? " + attr.isReadOnly());
System.out.println("Is Hidden ? " + attr.isHidden());
System.out.println("Is archive ? " + attr.isArchive());
System.out.println("Is system ? " + attr.isSystem());
```

Setting an attribute's value and extracting a single attribute by name can be accomplished by the setAttribute() and getAttribute() methods, respectively, as follows (I randomly chose the hidden attribute):

```java
import static java.nio.file.LinkOption.NOFOLLOW_LINKS;

...
//setting the hidden attribute to true
try {
    Files.setAttribute(path, "dos:hidden", true, NOFOLLOW_LINKS);
} catch (IOException e) {
    System.err.println(e);
}

//getting the hidden attribute
try {
    boolean hidden = (Boolean) Files.getAttribute(path, "dos:hidden", NOFOLLOW_LINKS);
    System.out.println("Is hidden ? " + hidden);
} catch (IOException e) {
    System.err.println(e);
}
```

DOS attributes can be acquired with the following names:

- hidden

- readonly

- system

- archive

The generally accepted form is [view-name:]attribute-name. The view-name is dos.

File Owner View

Most file systems accept the concept of *file owner* as an identity used to determine access rights to objects in a file system. NIO.2 maps this concept in an interface named `UserPrincipal` and allows you to get or set the owner of a file through the file owner view, which is represented by the `FileOwnerAttributeView` interface. Actually, as you will see in the following code examples, NIO.2 has multiple ways for setting and getting the file owner.

■ **Note** A principal named "*apress*" is used in the examples in this section, but this principal will not be available on your machine. To test the code without getting a `java.nio.file.attribute.UserPrincipalNotFoundException`, you need to add your principal name (an admin user of your machine or a user with the proper OS privileges).

Set a File Owner Using Files.setOwner()

You can set a file owner by calling the `Files.setOwner()` method. Besides the file path, this method gets a `UserPrincipal` instance that maps a string representing the file owner. The user principal lookup service for the default file system can be obtained by calling the `FileSystem.getUserPrincipalLookupService()` method. Here is a simple example of setting a file owner:

```
import java.io.IOException;
import java.nio.file.Files;
import java.nio.file.Path;
import java.nio.file.Paths;
import java.nio.file.attribute.UserPrincipal;
...
UserPrincipal owner = null;
Path path = Paths.get("C:/rafaelnadal/tournaments/2009", "BNP.txt");
try {
    owner = path.getFileSystem().getUserPrincipalLookupService().
                                    lookupPrincipalByName("apress");
    Files.setOwner(path, owner);
} catch (IOException e) {
    System.err.println(e);
}
```

Set a File Owner Using FileOwnerAttributeView.setOwner()

The `FileOwnerAttributeView` maps a file attribute view that supports reading or updating the owner of a file. The `owner` attribute is identified by the name `owner`, and the value of the attribute is a `UserPrincipal` object. The following code snippet shows you how to set the owner using this interface:

```
import java.io.IOException;
import java.nio.file.Files;
import java.nio.file.Path;
```

```
import java.nio.file.Paths;
import java.nio.file.attribute.FileOwnerAttributeView;
import java.nio.file.attribute.UserPrincipal;
...
UserPrincipal owner = null;
Path path = Paths.get("C:/rafaelnadal/tournaments/2009", "BNP.txt");
FileOwnerAttributeView foav = Files.getFileAttributeView(path,
                                        FileOwnerAttributeView.class);
try {
    owner = path.getFileSystem().getUserPrincipalLookupService().
                            lookupPrincipalByName("apress");

    foav.setOwner(owner);
} catch (IOException e) {
    System.err.println(e);
}
```

Set a File Owner Using Files.setAttribute()

As with most views, the file owner view has access to the setAttribute() method. The complete name of the attribute is owner:owner, as you can see here:

```
import java.io.IOException;
import java.nio.file.Files;
import java.nio.file.Path;
import java.nio.file.Paths;
import java.nio.file.attribute.UserPrincipal;
import static java.nio.file.LinkOption.NOFOLLOW_LINKS;

…
UserPrincipal owner = null;
Path path = Paths.get("C:/rafaelnadal/tournaments/2009", "BNP.txt");
try {
    owner = path.getFileSystem().getUserPrincipalLookupService().
                            lookupPrincipalByName("apress");
    Files.setAttribute(path, "owner:owner", owner, NOFOLLOW_LINKS);
} catch (IOException e) {
    System.err.println(e);
}
```

Get a File Owner Using FileOwnerAttributeView.getOwner()

Reading the owner of a file is a common task when determining access rights to objects in a file system. The getOwner() method returns the owner of a file as a UserPrincipal method—the String representing the file owner can be obtained by calling the UserPrincipal.getName() method:

```
import java.io.IOException;
import java.nio.file.Files;
import java.nio.file.Path;
import java.nio.file.Paths;
import java.nio.file.attribute.FileOwnerAttributeView;

…
```

```
Path path = Paths.get("C:/rafaelnadal/tournaments/2009", "BNP.txt");
FileOwnerAttributeView foav = Files.getFileAttributeView(path,
                                   FileOwnerAttributeView.class);
try {
    String owner = foav.getOwner().getName();
    System.out.println(owner);
} catch (IOException e) {
    System.err.println(e);
}
```

Get a File Owner Using Files.getAttribute()

Last example of this section is involving the `Files.getAttribute()` method. I believe that this method is pretty familiar to you from the above sections therefore here is the code snippet:

```
import java.io.IOException;
import java.nio.file.Files;
import java.nio.file.Path;
import java.nio.file.Paths;
import java.nio.file.attribute.UserPrincipal;
import static java.nio.file.LinkOption.NOFOLLOW_LINKS;
...
Path path = Paths.get("C:/rafaelnadal/tournaments/2009", "BNP.txt");
try {
    UserPrincipal owner = (UserPrincipal) Files.getAttribute(path,
                                    "owner:owner", NOFOLLOW_LINKS);
    System.out.println(owner.getName());
} catch (IOException e) {
        System.err.println(e);
    }
```

▓ **Caution**   If the user principal lookup service for the default file system can't be obtained or an invalid username is specified, then a `java.nio.file.attribute.UserPrincipalNotFoundException` will be thrown.

The file owner attribute can be required with the following name:

- `owner`

The generally accepted form is [`view-name:`]attribute-name. The `view-name` is `owner`.

POSIX View

Good news for Unix fans! POSIX extends the basic view with attributes supported by Unix and its flavors—file owner, group owner, and nine related access permissions (read, write, members of the same group, etc.).

Based on the `PosixFileAttributes` class, you can extract the POSIX attributes as follows:

```
import java.io.IOException;
import java.nio.file.Files;
import java.nio.file.Path;
import java.nio.file.Paths;
import java.nio.file.attribute.PosixFileAttributes;
...
PosixFileAttributes attr = null;
Path path = Paths.get("/home/rafaelnadal/tournaments/2009/BNP.txt");
try {
    attr = Files.readAttributes(path, PosixFileAttributes.class);
} catch (IOException e) {
    System.err.println(e);
}

 System.out.println("File owner: " + attr.owner().getName());
 System.out.println("File group: " + attr.group().getName());
 System.out.println("File permissions: " + attr.permissions().toString());
```

Or you can use the "long way" by calling the `Files.getFileAttributeView()` method:

```
import java.nio.file.attribute.PosixFileAttributeView;
...
try {
    attr = Files.getFileAttributeView(path,
                    PosixFileAttributeView.class).readAttributes();
} catch (IOException e) {
    System.err.println(e);
}
```

POSIX attributes can be required with the following names:

- group

- permissions

The generally accepted form is [`view-name:`]attribute-name. The `view-name` is `posix`.

POSIX Permissions

The `permissions()` method returns a collection of `PosixFilePermissions` objects. `PosixFilePermissions` is a permissions helper class. One of the most useful methods of this class is `asFileAttribute()`, which accepts a `Set` of file permissions and constructs a file attribute that can be passed to the `Path.createFile()` method or the `Path.createDirectory()` method. For example, you can extract the POSIX permissions of a file and create another file with the same attributes as follows (this example uses the `attr` object from the previous examples):

```java
import java.io.IOException;
import java.nio.file.Files;
import java.nio.file.Path;
import java.nio.file.Paths;
import java.nio.file.attribute.FileAttribute;
import java.nio.file.attribute.PosixFileAttributes;
import java.nio.file.attribute.PosixFilePermission;
import java.nio.file.attribute.PosixFilePermissions;
import java.util.Set;
…
Path new_path = Paths.get("/home/rafaelnadal/tournaments/2009/new_BNP.txt");
FileAttribute<Set<PosixFilePermission>> posixattrs =
                        PosixFilePermissions.asFileAttribute(attr.permissions());
try {
    Files.createFile(new_path, posixattrs);
} catch (IOException e) {
    System.err.println(e);
}
```

Moreover, you can set a file's permissions as a hard-coded string by calling the `fromString()` method:

```java
Set<PosixFilePermission> permissions = PosixFilePermissions.fromString("rw-r--r--");
try {
    Files.setPosixFilePermissions(new_path, permissions);
} catch (IOException e) {
    System.err.println(e);
}
```

POSIX Group Owner

The file group owner can be set with the POSIX attribute named `group`. The `setGroup()` method gets the file path and a `GroupPrincipal` instance that maps a string representing the group owner—this class extends the `UserPrincipal` interface:

```java
import java.io.IOException;
import java.nio.file.Files;
import java.nio.file.Path;
import java.nio.file.Paths;
import java.nio.file.attribute.GroupPrincipal;
import java.nio.file.attribute.PosixFileAttributeView;
…
Path path = Paths.get("/home/rafaelnadal/tournaments/2009/BNP.txt");
```

```
try {
    GroupPrincipal group = path.getFileSystem().
                    getUserPrincipalLookupService().lookupPrincipalByGroupName("apressteam");
    Files.getFileAttributeView(path, PosixFileAttributeView.class).setGroup(group);
} catch (IOException e) {
    System.err.println(e);
}
```

> **Note** A group principal named "*apressteam*" is used in the preceding example, but this group will not be available on your machine. To test the preceding code without getting a java.nio.file.attribute.UserPrincipalNotFoundException, you need to add your group principal name (an admin group of your machine or a group with the proper OS privileges).

You can easily find out the group by calling the `Files.getAttribute()` method:

```
import static java.nio.file.LinkOption.NOFOLLOW_LINKS;
...
try {
    GroupPrincipal group = (GroupPrincipal) Files.getAttribute(path, "posix:group",
                                                        NOFOLLOW_LINKS);
    System.out.println(group.getName());
} catch (IOException e) {
    System.err.println(e);
}
```

> **Note** You can gain access to owners by calling `FileOwnerAttributeView.getOwner()` and `FileOwnerAttributeView.setOwner()`, which are inherited in the POSIX view.

ACL View

An access control list (ACL) is a collection of permissions meant to enforce strict rules regarding access to a file system's objects. In ACL controls the owners, permissions, and different kinds of flags for each object. NIO.2 provides control over the ACL through the ACL view represented by the `AclFileAttributeView` interface, a file attribute view that supports reading or updating a file's ACL or file owner attributes.

Read an ACL Using Files.getFileAttributeView()

If you've never seen the content of an ACL, then try out the following code, which uses `Files.getFileAttributeView()` to extract the ACL as a `List<AclEntry>`:

```
import java.io.IOException;
import java.nio.file.Files;
import java.nio.file.Path;
import java.nio.file.Paths;
import java.nio.file.attribute.AclEntry;
import java.nio.file.attribute.AclFileAttributeView;
import java.util.List;
...
List<AclEntry> acllist = null;
Path path = Paths.get("C:/rafaelnadal/tournaments/2009", "BNP.txt");

AclFileAttributeView aclview = Files.getFileAttributeView(path, AclFileAttributeView.class);
try {
    acllist = aclview.getAcl();
} catch (IOException e) {
    System.err.println(e);
}
```

Read an ACL Using Files.getAttribute()

You can also use the getAttribute() method to read an ACL:

```
import static java.nio.file.LinkOption.NOFOLLOW_LINKS;
...
List<AclEntry> acllist = null;
Path path = Paths.get("C:/rafaelnadal/tournaments/2009", "BNP.txt");

try {
    acllist = (List<AclEntry>) Files.getAttribute(path, "acl:acl", NOFOLLOW_LINKS);
} catch (IOException e) {
    System.err.println(e);
}
```

ACL attributes can be required with the following names:

- acl

- owner

The generally accepted form is [view-name:]attribute-name. The view-name is acl.

Read ACL Entries

The previous two examples showed you how to extract the ACL for a specified path. The result was a list of AclEntry—a class that maps an entry from an ACL. Each entry has four components:

- Type: Determines if the entry grants or denies access. It can be ALARM, ALLOW, AUDIT, or DENY.

- Principal: The identity to which the entry grants or denies access. This is mapped as a UserPrincipal.

- Permissions: A set of permissions. Mapped as Set<AclEntryPermission>.

- Flags: A set of flags to indicate how entries are inherited and propagated. Mapped as Set<AclEntryFlag>.

You can iterate over the list and extract each entry's components as follows—this is the list extracted in the previous sections:

```
for (AclEntry aclentry : acllist) {
        System.out.println("++++++++++++++++++++++++++++++++++++++++++++++++++++++");
        System.out.println("Principal: " + aclentry.principal().getName());
        System.out.println("Type: " + aclentry.type().toString());
        System.out.println("Permissions: " + aclentry.permissions().toString());
        System.out.println("Flags: " + aclentry.flags().toString());
}
```

The following is example output of this code (tested on Windows 7):

```
++++++++++++++++++++++++++++++++++++++++++++++++++++

Principal: BUILTIN\Administrators

Type: ALLOW

Permissions: [WRITE_OWNER, READ_ACL, EXECUTE, WRITE_NAMED_ATTRS, READ_ATTRIBUTES,
READ_NAMED_ATTRS, WRITE_DATA, WRITE_ACL, READ_DATA, WRITE_ATTRIBUTES, SYNCHRONIZE, DELETE,
DELETE_CHILD, APPEND_DATA]

Flags: []

++++++++++++++++++++++++++++++++++++++++++++++++++++

Principal: NT AUTHORITY\SYSTEM

Type: ALLOW

Permissions: [WRITE_OWNER, READ_ACL, EXECUTE, WRITE_NAMED_ATTRS, READ_ATTRIBUTES,
READ_NAMED_ATTRS, WRITE_DATA, WRITE_ACL, READ_DATA, WRITE_ATTRIBUTES, SYNCHRONIZE, DELETE,
DELETE_CHILD, APPEND_DATA]

Flags: []

++++++++++++++++++++++++++++++++++++++++++++++++++++

Principal: NT AUTHORITY\Authenticated Users

Type: ALLOW
```

```
Permissions: [READ_ACL, EXECUTE, READ_DATA, WRITE_ATTRIBUTES, WRITE_NAMED_ATTRS,
SYNCHRONIZE, DELETE, READ_ATTRIBUTES, READ_NAMED_ATTRS, WRITE_DATA, APPEND_DATA]

Flags: []

+++++++++++++++++++++++++++++++++++++++++++++++++++++++

Principal: BUILTIN\Users

Type: ALLOW

Permissions: [READ_ACL, EXECUTE, READ_DATA, SYNCHRONIZE, READ_ATTRIBUTES, READ_NAMED_ATTRS]

Flags: []
```

Grant a New Access in an ACL

ACL entries are created using an associated `AclEntry.Builder` object by invoking its `build()` method. For example, if you want to grant a new access to a principal, then you must follow this process:

1. Look up the principal by calling the `FileSystem.getUserPrincipalLookupService()` method.

2. Get the ACL view (as previously described).

3. Create a new entry by using the `AclEntry.Builder` object.

4. Read the ACL (as previous described).

5. Insert the new entry (recommended before any `DENY` entry).

6. Rewrite the ACL by using `setAcl()` or `setAttribute()`.

Following these steps, you can write a code snippet for granting read data access and append data access to a principal named apress:

```java
import java.io.IOException;
import java.nio.file.Files;
import java.nio.file.Path;
import java.nio.file.Paths;
import java.nio.file.attribute.AclEntry;
import java.nio.file.attribute.AclEntryPermission;
import java.nio.file.attribute.AclEntryType;
import java.nio.file.attribute.AclFileAttributeView;
import java.nio.file.attribute.UserPrincipal;
import java.util.List;
import static java.nio.file.LinkOption.NOFOLLOW_LINKS;
...
try {
    //Lookup for the principal
    UserPrincipal user = path.getFileSystem().getUserPrincipalLookupService()
```

```
                                                    .lookupPrincipalByName("apress");

        //Get the ACL view
        AclFileAttributeView view = Files.getFileAttributeView(path,
                                         AclFileAttributeView.class);

        //Create a new entry
        AclEntry entry = AclEntry.newBuilder().setType(AclEntryType.ALLOW).
                setPrincipal(user).setPermissions(AclEntryPermission.READ_DATA,
                AclEntryPermission.APPEND_DATA).build();

        //read ACL
        List<AclEntry> acl = view.getAcl();

        //Insert the new entry
        acl.add(0, entry);

        //rewrite ACL
        view.setAcl(acl);
        //or, like this
        //Files.setAttribute(path, "acl:acl", acl, NOFOLLOW_LINKS);

} catch (IOException e) {
    System.err.println(e);
}
```

■ **Note** The principal named "*apress*" used in the preceding example will not be available on your machine. To test the code without getting a `java.nio.file.attribute.UserPrincipalNotFoundException`, add your principal name (an admin user of your machine or a user with the proper OS privileges).

The preceding code adds a new entry in an ACL of an existing file. In common cases, you will probably do that when you create a new file.

■ **Note** You can gain access to owners by calling `FileOwnerAttributeView.getOwner()` and `FileOwnerAttributeView.setOwner()`, which are inherited in the ACL view.

File Store Attributes

If you think of a computer as a file storage container, then you can easily identify more types of stores, such as partitions, devices, volumes, and so on. NIO.2 can obtain information about each type of store through the `FileStore` abstract class. For a particular store, you can obtain its name, its type, total space, used space, and available free space. In the following subsections you will see how to obtain that information for all the stores in the default file system and for the store that contains a specified file.

Get Attributes of All File Stores

Once you obtain access to the default file system—by calling the FileSystems.getDefault() method—you can easily iterate over the file stores list provided by the FileSystem.getFileStores() method. Since each instance (name, type, total space, used space, and available free space) is a FileStore object, you can call the corresponding dedicated methods such as name(), type(), getTotalSpace(), and so on. The following code snippet prints information about your stores:

```java
import java.io.IOException;
import java.nio.file.FileStore;
import java.nio.file.FileSystem;
import java.nio.file.FileSystems;
…
FileSystem fs = FileSystems.getDefault();
for (FileStore store : fs.getFileStores()) {
  try {
        long total_space = store.getTotalSpace() / 1024;
        long used_space = (store.getTotalSpace() - store.getUnallocatedSpace()) / 1024;
        long available_space = store.getUsableSpace() / 1024;
        boolean is_read_only = store.isReadOnly();

        System.out.println("--- " + store.name() + " --- " + store.type());
        System.out.println("Total space: " + total_space);
        System.out.println("Used space: " + used_space);
        System.out.println("Available space: " + available_space);
        System.out.println("Is read only? " + is_read_only);

  } catch (IOException e) {
     System.err.println(e);
  }
}
```

The following is example output of this code:

```
--- --- NTFS

Total space: 39070048

Used space: 31775684

Available space: 7294364


--- --- NTFS
```

Total space: 39070048

Used space: 8530348

Available space: 30539700

--- SAMSUNG DVD RECORDER VOLUME --- UDF

Total space: 2936192

Used space: 2936192

Available space: 0

▓ **Note** As you can see in the preceding example, if a store does not have a name, a blank string is returned. In addition, the values returned for the amount of disk space are expressed in bytes, so you will probably want to convert those numbers to kilobytes, megabytes, or gigabytes to make them easier for humans to read.

Get Attributes of the File Store in Which a File Resides

Based on the `FileStore` class, you can get attributes of a file store in which a particular file resides. This task can be accomplished by calling the `Files.getFileStore()` method, which gets a single argument representing the file (a `Path` object). NIO.2 determines the file store for you and provides access to the information. The following code shows a possible approach:

```
import java.io.IOException;
import java.nio.file.FileStore;
import java.nio.file.Files;
import java.nio.file.Path;
import java.nio.file.Paths;
...
Path path = Paths.get("C:/rafaelnadal/tournaments/2009", "BNP.txt");
try {
    FileStore store = Files.getFileStore(path);

    long total_space = store.getTotalSpace() / 1024;
    long used_space = (store.getTotalSpace() - store.getUnallocatedSpace()) / 1024;
    long available_space = store.getUsableSpace() / 1024;
    boolean is_read_only = store.isReadOnly();

    System.out.println("--- " + store.name() + " --- " + store.type());
    System.out.println("Total space: " + total_space);
```

```
    System.out.println("Used space: " + used_space);
    System.out.println("Available space: " + available_space);
    System.out.println("Is read only? " + is_read_only);
} catch (IOException e) {
    System.err.println(e);
}
```

Example output of this code follows:

```
--- --- NTFS

Total space: 39070048

Used space: 8530348

Available space: 30539700

Is read only? false
```

A file store may support one or more `FileStoreAttributeView` classes that provide a read-only or updatable view of a set of file store attributes, as follows:

```
FileStoreAttributeView fsav =
        store.getFileStoreAttributeView(FileStoreAttributeView.class);
```

▪ **Note** In addition, you can read the value of a file store attribute by using the `getAttribute()` method.

User-Defined File Attributes View

If you find that there are not enough built-in attributes for your needs or if you have some unique metadata (meaningful to the file system) that you want to associate with a file, you can define your own attributes. NIO.2 offers the user-defined file attributes view—extended attributes—through the `UserDefinedFileAttributeView` interface. This facility allows you to associate to a file any attribute that you consider to be useful for your use cases. For example, this may be useful if you develop a distributed file system. For instance, you could add a boolean attribute that verifies whether or not the file is replicated or distributed to other locations.

Check User-Defined Attributes Supportability

Before you attempt to create your own attributes, check whether your file system supports this facility. Since this is checked over a file store, not over a file itself, first you need to obtain the desired file store. Then, you can call the `supportsFileAttributeView()` method, which takes a `String` argument representing the name of file attribute view or the view as `UserDefinedFileAttributeView.class`. It returns a boolean value, as you can see here:

```
import java.io.IOException;
import java.nio.file.FileStore;
import java.nio.file.Files;
import java.nio.file.Path;
import java.nio.file.Paths;
import java.nio.file.attribute.UserDefinedFileAttributeView;
...
Path path = Paths.get("C:/rafaelnadal/tournaments/2009", "BNP.txt");

try {
    FileStore store = Files.getFileStore(path);
    if (!store.supportsFileAttributeView(UserDefinedFileAttributeView.class)) {
      System.out.println("The user defined attributes are not supported on: " + store);
    } else {
      System.out.println("The user defined attributes are supported on: " + store);
    }
} catch (IOException e) {
    System.err.println(e);
}
```

■ **Note** You can do this check over all file stores, or a set of file stores, by getting them directly from the default file system. It is not required to get the file store from where a file resides.

Operations on User-Defined Attributes

If your file system supports user-defined attributes, then you are all set to create your own. Next, you will see how to define an attribute, how to list the user-defined attributes, and how to delete a user-defined attribute. Your focus in this section should be on the life cycle of user-defined attributes.

Define a User Attribute

To start, you will define an attribute named file.description that has the value "This file contains private information!". After you get the view by calling Files.getFileAttributeView(), you can write this user-defined attribute as follows:

```
import java.io.IOException;
import java.nio.charset.Charset;
import java.nio.file.Files;
import java.nio.file.Path;
import java.nio.file.Paths;
import java.nio.file.attribute.UserDefinedFileAttributeView;
...
Path path = Paths.get("C:/rafaelnadal/tournaments/2009", "BNP.txt");
UserDefinedFileAttributeView udfav = Files.getFileAttributeView(path,
                                      UserDefinedFileAttributeView.class);

try {
```

```
    int written = udfav.write("file.description", Charset.defaultCharset().
            encode("This file contains private information!"));
} catch (IOException e) {
    System.err.println(e);
}
```

The `write()` method writes the value of the attribute from a given buffer as a sequence of bytes. It receives two arguments: the attribute name and the buffer containing the attribute value. If an attribute of the given name already exists, then its value is replaced. As you can see, the method returns an `int`, which represents the number of bytes written, possibly zero.

■ **Note** In addition, you can write an attribute using the `setAttribute()` method. You can write it from a buffer or byte array (`byte[]`).

List User-Defined Attribute Names and Value Sizes

At any moment, you can see the list of user-defined attribute names and value sizes by calling the `UserDefinedFileAttributeView.list()` method. The returned list is a collection of strings that represents the attribute names. Passing their names to the `UserDefinedFileAttributeView.size()` method will result in the sizes of the attribute values.

```
import java.io.IOException;
import java.nio.file.Files;
import java.nio.file.Path;
import java.nio.file.Paths;
import java.nio.file.attribute.UserDefinedFileAttributeView;
...
Path path = Paths.get("C:/rafaelnadal/tournaments/2009", "BNP.txt");
UserDefinedFileAttributeView udfav = Files.getFileAttributeView(path,
                                UserDefinedFileAttributeView.class);

try {
    for (String name : udfav.list()) {
        System.out.println(udfav.size(name) + "        " + name);
    }
} catch (IOException e) {
    System.err.println(e);
}
```

Get the Value of a User-Defined Attribute

Reading the value of a user-defined attribute is accomplished by using the `UserDefinedFileAttributeView.read()` method. You pass to it the attribute name and the destination buffer, and it returns the value in the specified buffer. The following code snippet shows you how to do it:

```
import java.io.IOException;
```

```
import java.nio.ByteBuffer;
import java.nio.charset.Charset;
import java.nio.file.Files;
import java.nio.file.Path;
import java.nio.file.Paths;
import java.nio.file.attribute.UserDefinedFileAttributeView;
...
Path path = Paths.get("C:/rafaelnadal/tournaments/2009", "BNP.txt");
UserDefinedFileAttributeView udfav = Files.getFileAttributeView(path,
                                    UserDefinedFileAttributeView.class);

try {
    int size = udfav.size("file.description");
    ByteBuffer bb = ByteBuffer.allocateDirect(size);
    udfav.read("file.description", bb);
    bb.flip();
    System.out.println(Charset.defaultCharset().decode(bb).toString());
} catch (IOException e) {
    System.err.println(e);
}
```

■ **Note** Using the UserDefinedFileAttributeView.size() method, you can easily set the correct size of the buffer that represents the value of the user-defined attribute.

■ **Note** You can also read an attribute by using the getAttribute() method. The value is returned as byte array (byte[]).

Delete a File's User-Defined Attribute

When a user-defined attribute is no longer useful, you can easily delete it by calling the UserDefinedFileAttributeView.delete() method. You only need to supply the attribute's name to the method and it will do the rest of the work for you. The following shows how to delete the attribute defined earlier:

```
import java.io.IOException;
import java.nio.file.Files;
import java.nio.file.Path;
import java.nio.file.Paths;
import java.nio.file.attribute.UserDefinedFileAttributeView;
...
Path path = Paths.get("C:/rafaelnadal/tournaments/2009", "BNP.txt");
UserDefinedFileAttributeView udfav = Files.getFileAttributeView(path,
                                    UserDefinedFileAttributeView.class);
```

```
try {
    udfav.delete("file.description");
} catch (IOException e) {
    System.err.println(e);
}
```

Summary

In this chapter you have explored the views provided by NIO.2. You saw how to manipulate all kinds of attributes, how to query a file or a file store for different purposes, and how to define your own metadata.

After an introduction to the NIO.2 views and a description of how to determine which views are supported by a particular file system, the chapter introduced the basic and DOS attributes, which should be available for every file. These attributes provide the main metadata, such as size, creation time, last modified time, read-only, and so forth. The chapter next presented the file owner attributes, which provide support for setting and getting a file owner, followed by the POSIX attributes for Unix users and the ACL attributes, which provide access to the collection of permissions that control access to a file system's objects. The chapter wrapped up by discussing file store attributes and user-defined attributes.

CHAPTER 3

■ ■ ■

Manage Symbolic and Hard Links

Linux and Unix users (especially administrators) should be familiar with the concept of links. There is two types of links: symbolic links and hard links. Links commonly reach a file through several names, instead of navigating through a series of directories and subdirectories from the root – think of a link as an entity mapping a file/directory path and identified through a set of names. If you are a dedicated Windows user, you might not be familiar with links, although Windows itself is perfectly aware of them, especially symbolic links, which most resemble Windows shortcuts.

NIO.2 provides support for both hard links and symbolic links. Each method of the Path class knows how to detect a link and will behave in the default manner if no configuration of behavior is specified. In this chapter, you will learn how to manipulate links through the java.nio.file API, including how to create a link and how to find the target of a link. Most operations are implemented through the java.nio.file.Files class, which provides methods such as createLink(), createSymbolicLink(), isSymbolicLink(), and readSymbolicLink(). Each of these methods will be presented in detail in this chapter.

Introducing Links

When you reach a file through a set of names (from command-line, an application, or other ways), you are dealing with a link. A link can be set up either as a hard link (sometimes spelled *hardlink*) or as a symbolic link (also called *symlink* or *softlink*). When a file has two names of equal weight and the inode table (Linux files don't actually live in directories; they are assigned an inode number, which Linux uses to locate them) points directly to the blocks on the disk that contain the data, the link is a hard link. Think of a hard link as a directory reference or pointer to a file. When a file has one main name and an extra entry in the file name table that refers any accesses back to the main name, the link is a symbolic link. Symbolic links are more flexible and used much more often than hard links. The following are the main differences/similarities between the two types of links:

- Hard links can be created only for files, not for directories. Symbolic links can link to a file or a directory.

- Hard links cannot exist across file systems. Symbolic links can exist across file systems.

- The target of a hard link must exist. The target of a symbolic link may not exist.

- Removing the original file that your hard link points to does not remove the hard link itself, and the hard link still provides the content of the underlying file. Removing the original file that your symbolic link points to does not remove the attached symbolic link, but without the original file, the symbolic link is useless.

- If you remove the hard link or the symbolic link itself, the original file stays intact.

- A hard link is the same entity as the original file. All attributes are identical. A symbolic link is not so restrictive.

- A hard link looks, and behaves, like a regular file, so hard links can be hard to find. A symbolic link's target may not even exist, therefore it is much flexible.

Creating Links from the Command Line

Windows users can create symbolic and hard links from the command line by using the `mklink` command. This command gets a set of options, depending on which kind of link you need to create. Some of these options are as follows:

```
/D      Creates a directory symbolic link.  Default is a file symbolic link.
/H      Creates a hard link instead of a symbolic link.
/J      Creates a Directory Junction.
Link    specifies the new symbolic link name.
Target  specifies the path (relative or absolute) that the new link refers to.
```

For instance, if you wanted to make the folder `C:\rafaelnadal\photos` available from `C:\rafaelnadal` as well, you could use the following command:

```
mklink /D C:\rafaelnadal C:\rafaelnadal\photos
```

Now if you look in the `C:\rafaelnadal` directory, you'll also see whatever files were in the `C:\rafaelnadal\photos` directory.

Unix (Linux) users can use the command named `ln` to achieve the same effect achieved in the preceding Windows example (notice that the target file is listed first and the link name is listed second in this case):

```
ln -s /home/rafaelnadal/photos /home/rafaelnadal
```

In addition, in Unix (Linux) you can delete a link using the `rm` command:

```
rm /home/rafaelnadal
```

Creating a Symbolic Link

Creating a symbolic link is very easy to accomplish in NIO.2. You simply call the `Files.createSymbolicLink()` method, which uses the path of the symbolic link to create, the target of the symbolic link, and an array of attributes to set atomically when creating the symbolic link. It returns the path to the symbolic link.

If your file system does not support symbolic links, then an `UnsupportedOperationException` exception will be thrown. In addition, keep in mind that the target of the symbolic link can be absolute or relative (as described in Chapter 1) and might or might not exist.

The following code snippet creates a simple symbolic link with the default attributes. It creates a symbolic link named rafael.nadal.1 for file C:\rafaelnadal\photos\rafa_winner.jpg (the file is recommended to exist and the file system must have permission to create symbolic links).

```
…
Path link = FileSystems.getDefault().getPath("rafael.nadal.1");
Path target= FileSystems.getDefault().getPath("C:/rafaelnadal/photos", "rafa_winner.jpg");

try {
    Files.createSymbolicLink(link, target);
    } catch (IOException | UnsupportedOperationException | SecurityException e) {
      if (e instanceof SecurityException) {
         System.err.println("Permission denied!");
      }
      if (e instanceof UnsupportedOperationException) {
         System.err.println("An unsupported operation was detected!");
      }
      if (e instanceof IOException) {
         System.err.println("An I/O error occurred!");
      }
System.err.println(e);
}
```

When you want to modify the default attributes of the link, you can use the third argument of the createSymbolicLink() method. This argument is an array of attributes of type FileAttribute—the class that encapsulates the value of a file attribute that can be set atomically when creating a new file, directory, or link. The following code snippet reads the attributes of the target file and creates a link, assigning the attributes from the target to the link. It creates a symbolic link named rafael.nadal.2 for file C:\rafaelnadal\photos\rafa_winner.jpg (the file must exist and the file system must have permission to create symbolic links).

```
…
Path link = FileSystems.getDefault().getPath("rafael.nadal.2");
Path target = FileSystems.getDefault().getPath("C:/rafaelnadal/photos", "rafa_winner.jpg");

try {
    PosixFileAttributes attrs = Files.readAttributes(target, PosixFileAttributes.class);
    FileAttribute<Set<PosixFilePermission>> attr =
                       PosixFilePermissions.asFileAttribute(attrs.permissions());

    Files.createSymbolicLink(link, target, attr);
    } catch (IOException | UnsupportedOperationException | SecurityException e) {
      if (e instanceof SecurityException) {
         System.err.println("Permission denied!");
      }
      if (e instanceof UnsupportedOperationException) {
         System.err.println("An unsupported operation was detected!");
      }
      if (e instanceof IOException) {
         System.err.println("An I/O error occured!");
      }
    System.err.println(e);
}
```

In addition, you can use the `setAttribute()` method to modify the link attributes after creation. For example, the following code snippet reads the `lastModifiedTime` and `lastAccessTime` attributes of the target and sets them to the link. It creates a symbolic link named **rafael.nadal.3** for file **C:\rafaelnadal\photos\rafa_winner.jpg** (the file must exist and the file system must have permission to create symbolic links).

```
...
Path link = FileSystems.getDefault().getPath("rafael.nadal.3");
Path target = FileSystems.getDefault().getPath("C:/rafaelnadal/photos", "rafa_winner.jpg");

try {
    Files.createSymbolicLink(link, target);

    FileTime lm = (FileTime) Files.getAttribute(target,
                                    "basic:lastModifiedTime", NOFOLLOW_LINKS);
    FileTime la = (FileTime) Files.getAttribute(target,
                                    "basic:lastAccessTime", NOFOLLOW_LINKS);
    Files.setAttribute(link, "basic:lastModifiedTime", lm, NOFOLLOW_LINKS);
    Files.setAttribute(link, "basic:lastAccessTime", la, NOFOLLOW_LINKS);
} catch (IOException | UnsupportedOperationException | SecurityException e) {
    if (e instanceof SecurityException) {
        System.err.println("Permision denied!");
    }
    if (e instanceof UnsupportedOperationException) {
        System.err.println("An unsupported operation was detected!");
    }
    if (e instanceof IOException) {
        System.err.println("An I/O error occured!");
    }
    System.err.println(e);
}
```

■ **Note** If the symbolic link already exists, then a `FileAlreadyExistsException` exception will be thrown.

Creating a Hard Link

You can create a hard link by calling the `createLink()` method, which uses the link to create and a path to an existing file. It returns the path to the link, which represents the new directory entry. You then can access the file using the link as the path.

If your file system does not support hard links, then an `UnsupportedOperationException` exception will be thrown. In addition, keep in mind that a hard link can be created only for existing files.

The following code snippet creates a hard link named **rafael.nadal.4** for file **C:\rafaelnadal\photos\rafa_winner.jpg** (the file must exist and the file system must have permission to create hard links):

```
import java.io.IOException;
```

```
import java.nio.file.FileSystems;
import java.nio.file.Files;
import java.nio.file.Path;

public class Main {

 public static void main(String[] args) {

  Path link = FileSystems.getDefault().getPath("rafael.nadal.4");
  Path target = FileSystems.getDefault().getPath("C:/rafaelnadal/photos", "rafa_winner.jpg");

  try {
      Files.createLink(link, target);
          System.out.println("The link was successfully created!");
      } catch (IOException | UnsupportedOperationException | SecurityException e) {
        if (e instanceof SecurityException) {
            System.err.println("Permission denied!");
        }
        if (e instanceof UnsupportedOperationException) {
            System.err.println("An unsupported operation was detected!");
        }
        if (e instanceof IOException) {
            System.err.println("An I/O error occured!");
        }
        System.err.println(e);
  }
 }
}
```

▦ **Note** If the hard link already exists, then a `FileAlreadyExistsException` exception will be thrown.

Checking a Symbolic Link

Different instances of `Path` can point to files or links, so you can detect if a `Path` instance points to a symbolic link by calling the `Files.isSymbolicLink()` method. It receives a single argument, representing the `Path` to be tested, and returns a boolean value. The following code snippet is a simple example of testing a `Path` for a symbolic link. It creates a symbolic link named **rafael.nadal.5** for file `C:\rafaelnadal\photos\rafa_winner.jpg` (the file must exist and the file system must have permission to create symbolic links).

```
...
Path link = FileSystems.getDefault().getPath("rafael.nadal.5");
Path target = FileSystems.getDefault().getPath("C:/rafaelnadal/photos", "rafa_winner.jpg");

try {
    Files.createSymbolicLink(link, target);
    } catch (IOException | UnsupportedOperationException | SecurityException e) {
```

```
    ...
}

//check if a path is a symbolic link - solution 1
boolean link_isSymbolicLink_1 = Files.isSymbolicLink(link);
boolean target_isSymbolicLink_1 = Files.isSymbolicLink(target);

System.out.println(link.toString() + " is a symbolic link ? " + link_isSymbolicLink_1);
System.out.println(target.toString() + " is a symbolic link ? " + target_isSymbolicLink_1);
...
```

This code outputs the following result:

```
rafael.nadal.5 is a symbolic link ? true

C:\rafaelnadal\photos\rafa_winner.jpg is a symbolic link ? false
```

As you read in Chapter 2, you can test Path for a symbolic link by using the attribute views. The basic view provides an attribute named isSymbolicLink, which returns true if the specified Path locates a file that is a symbolic link. You can view the isSymbolicLink attribute through the readAttributes() method (not recommended in this case since it returns a bulk list of attributes) or, much more easily, through the getAttribute() method, which can be used as follows:

```
...
try {
    boolean link_isSymbolicLink_2 = (boolean) Files.getAttribute(link,
                                            "basic:isSymbolicLink");
    boolean target_isSymbolicLink_2 = (boolean) Files.getAttribute(target,
                                            "basic:isSymbolicLink");

    System.out.println(link.toString() + " is a symbolic link ? " + link_isSymbolicLink_2);
    System.out.println(target.toString() + " is a symbolic link ? "+ target_isSymbolicLink_2);
} catch (IOException | UnsupportedOperationException e) {
    System.err.println(e);
}
...
```

Again, the output is

```
rafael.nadal.5 is a symbolic link ? true

C:\rafaelnadal\photos\rafa_winner.jpg is a symbolic link ? false
```

Locating the Target of a Link

Starting from a link, you can locate its target (which may not exist) by calling the readSymbolicLink() method. This method receives from the user the link, as a Path, and returns a Path object representing the target of the link. If the passed path is not a link, then a NotLinkException exception will be thrown. The following code snippet uses this method to create a symbolic link named rafael.nadal.6 for file C:\rafaelnadal\photos\rafa_winner.jpg (the file must exist and the file system must have permission to create symbolic links):

```
:

...
Path link = FileSystems.getDefault().getPath("rafael.nadal.6");
Path target = FileSystems.getDefault().getPath("C:/rafaelnadal/photos", "rafa_winner.jpg");...

...
try {
    Path linkedpath = Files.readSymbolicLink(link);
    System.out.println(linkedpath.toString());
} catch (IOException e) {
    System.err.println(e);
}
```

Checking If a Link and a Target Point to the Same File

Sometimes you may need to check if a link and a target point to the same file (location). You can get this information in different ways, but a simple solution is to use the Files.isSameFile() method. This method receives (from the user) the two Paths to be compared and returns a boolean value. The following code snippet creates a target and a symbolic link for the target and then applies the isSameFile() method. It creates a symbolic link named rafael.nadal.7 for file C:\rafaelnadal\photos\rafa_winner.jpg (the file must exist and the file system must have permission to create symbolic links).

```
...
Path link = FileSystems.getDefault().getPath("rafael.nadal.7");
Path target = FileSystems.getDefault().getPath("C:/rafaelnadal/photos", "rafa_winner.jpg");

try {
    Files.createSymbolicLink(link, target);
    } catch (IOException | UnsupportedOperationException | SecurityException e) {

    ...
}

try {
    Path linkedpath = Files.readSymbolicLink(link);
    System.out.println(linkedpath.toString());
    } catch (IOException e) {
      System.err.println(e);
}
```

The output follows:

```
rafael.nadal.7 and C:\rafaelnadal\photos\rafa_winner.jpg point to the same location
```

Summary

In this chapter you saw how NIO.2 deals with symbolic and hard links. After a short overview of these two concepts and some brief examples of how to create them in Windows and Unix (Linux), you saw the NIO.2 approach. You learned how to create symbolic and hard links directly from Java, how to check if a path is a link, how to detect the target of a link, and how to check if a link and a target point to the same file.

■ ■ ■

CHAPTER 4

Files and Directories

Now that you know how to point to a file or directory using the Path class, you are ready to learn how to accomplish the most common tasks for managing files and directories, such as create, read, write, move, delete, and so on. NIO.2 comes with a set of brand new methods to accomplish these tasks, most of which are found in the java.nio.file.Files class.

The chapter starts by exploring some methods dedicated to checking if a Path is readable, writable, executable, regular, or hidden. These checks enable you to determine what kind of file or directory you are dealing with before you apply operations such as write or read. The chapter then focuses on directory operations, showing you how to list, create, and read directories. You will see how to list the file system roots, create directories with methods such as createDirectory() and createTempDirectory(), write directory filters, and list a directory's content using the newDirectoryStream() method. After you are familiar with directory operations, you will explore file operations, such as reading, writing, creating, and opening files. As you will see, there is a wide array of file I/O methods to choose from. In this chapter, you will see at work methods for buffered and unbuffered streams, leaving coverage of the methods for channels for the next chapters, in which you will see the real power of NIO. The chapter ends with the well-known delete, copy, and move operations.

Each of these tasks is detailed presented and, as you will see, many aspects were "redesigned" from previous Java 6, but you will also recognize many of the presented methods from the java.io.File class.

Checking Methods for Files and Directories

The Files class provides a set of is*Something* methods that you can use to perform various kinds of checks before you actually manipulate a file or a directory. Some of these methods were presented in the previous chapters, while the rest are presented here. Taking advantage of these methods is recommended because they can be very useful in helping you to avoid exceptions or other strange behavior in your applications. For example, it is a good idea to check if a file exists before you try to move it to another location. Similarly, it is a good idea to check if a file is accessible to read before you try to read from it. Some of these checks can also be performed through the metadata attributes, as you have seen in Chapter 2.

Checking for the Existence of a File or Directory

As you know from previous chapters, a Path instance is perfectly valid even if the mapped file or directory does not physically exist. Moreover, the syntactic Path methods can be applied with success in such cases because they do not operate on the file or directory itself. But at some point, it is very important to know whether or not a file or directory exists, which is why the Files class provides the following two methods for this type of check:

- exists(): Checks whether a file exists

- notExists(): Checks whether a file does not exist

Both methods receive two arguments, representing the path to the file to test and options indicating how symbolic links are handled. The exists() method returns true if the file exists, and false otherwise (the file does not exist or the checking cannot be performed).

The following code snippet checks if the file AEGON.txt exists in the C:\rafaelnadal\tournaments\2009 directory (in our hypothetical directory structure, this file exists):

```
Path path = FileSystems.getDefault().getPath("C:/rafaelnadal/tournaments/2009","AEGON.txt");
...
boolean path_exists = Files.exists(path, new LinkOption[]{LinkOption.NOFOLLOW_LINKS});
```

If you need to take action only if the file does not exist, then call the notExists() method, which returns true if the file does not exist and false otherwise (the file exists or the checking cannot be performed):

```
Path path = FileSystems.getDefault().getPath("C:/rafaelnadal/tournaments/2009",
"AEGON.txt");
...
boolean path_notexists = Files.notExists(path, new LinkOption[]{LinkOption.NOFOLLOW_LINKS});
```

■ **Note** If both methods are applied to the same Path and both return false, then the checking cannot be performed. For example, if the application does not have access to the file, then the status is unknown and both methods return false. From here, it is easy to draw the conclusion that a file/directory's existence status can be: exist, not exist, or unknown. Immediately after checking this status, the result is outdated, since a file that exists can be deleted just after check, therefore the result must "expire" immediately. If this method indicates the file exists then there is no guarantee that a subsequence access will succeed. In addition, a SecurityException may be thrown if one of these methods does not have permissions to read the file.

■ **Caution**   !Files.exists(…) is not equivalent to Files.notExists(…) and the notExists() method is not a complement of the exists() method.

Checking File Accessibility

Another good practice before you access a file is to check its accessibility level, using the isReadable(), isWritable(), and isExecutable() methods. After you pass the Path to be verified, these methods will check, respectively, if it is a readable Path (the file exists, and JVM has the permissions to open it for reading), a writable Path (the file exists, and JVM has the permissions to open it for writing), and an executable Path (the file exists, and JVM has the permissions to execute it).

In addition, you can check if the Path points to a regular file by calling the isRegularFile() method. *Regular files* are files that have no special characteristics (they are not symbolic links, directories, etc.) and contain real data, such as text or binary files. isReadable(), isWritable(), isExecutable(), and isRegularFile() all return boolean values: true if the file exists and is readable, writable, executable, and regular, or false if either the file does not exist, read, write, execute, and regular access would be denied because the JVM has insufficient permissions, or access cannot be determined.

Putting these methods into a code snippet that checks the accessibility of the AEGON.txt file in the C:\rafaelnadal\tournaments\2009 directory (the file must exist) looks like the following:

```
Path path = FileSystems.getDefault().getPath("C:/rafaelnadal/tournaments/2009","AEGON.txt");

boolean is_readable = Files.isReadable(path);
boolean is_writable = Files.isWritable(path);
boolean is_executable = Files.isExecutable(path);
boolean is_regular = Files.isRegularFile(path, LinkOption.NOFOLLOW_LINKS);

if ((is_readable) && (is_writable) && (is_executable) && (is_regular)) {
    System.out.println("The checked file is accessible!");
} else {
    System.out.println("The checked file is not accessible!");
}
```

Or, you can use this shorter version:

```
boolean is_accessible = Files.isRegularFile(path) & Files.isReadable(path) &
                        Files.isExecutable(path) & Files.isWritable(path);
if (is_accessible) {
    System.out.println("The checked file is accessible!");
} else {
    System.out.println("The checked file is not accessible!");
}
```

▨ **Note** The preceding examples check the accessibility by applying all four methods to a Path, but you can combine these four methods in different ways depending on what level of accessibility you need to get. For example, you may not care whether or not the Path is writable, in which case you can exclude this check.

45

■ **Caution**   Even if these methods confirm the accessibility, there is no guarantee that the file can be accessed. The explanation resides in a well-known software bug, named time-of-check-to-time-of-use (TOCTTOU, pronounced "TOCK too"), which means that in the time between checking and using the checking result, the system may suffer different kinds of changes. Unix fans are probably familiar with this concept, but it is applicable to any other system as well.

Checking If Two Paths Point to the Same File

In the previous chapter, you saw how to check if a symbolic link and a target point to the same file. Another common test that you can perform using the isSameFile() method is to check if two Paths expressed differently point to the same file. For example, a relative Path and an absolute Path may point to the same file, even if it is not quite obvious. Calling the isSameFile() method will reveal this in the following code snippet, which expresses the path to the MutuaMadridOpen.txt file in three different ways (the file must exist in the C:\rafaelnadal\tournaments\2009 directory):

```
Path path_1 = FileSystems.getDefault().getPath("C:/rafaelnadal/tournaments/2009",
                                                "MutuaMadridOpen.txt");
Path path_2 = FileSystems.getDefault().getPath("/rafaelnadal/tournaments/2009",
                                                "MutuaMadridOpen.txt");
Path path_3 = FileSystems.getDefault().getPath("/rafaelnadal/tournaments/dummy/../2009",
                                                "MutuaMadridOpen.txt");
try {
    boolean is_same_file_12 = Files.isSameFile(path_1, path_2);
    boolean is_same_file_13 = Files.isSameFile(path_1, path_3);
    boolean is_same_file_23 = Files.isSameFile(path_2, path_3);

    System.out.println("is same file 1&2 ? " + is_same_file_12);
    System.out.println("is same file 1&3 ? " + is_same_file_13);
    System.out.println("is same file 2&3 ? " + is_same_file_23);
} catch (IOException e) {
    System.err.println(e);
}
```

The output is as follows:

```
is same file 1&2 ? true

is same file 1&3 ? true

is same file 2&3 ? true
```

Checking the File Visibility

If you need to find out if a file is hidden, you can call the `Files.isHidden()` method. Keeping in mind that the notion of "hidden" is platform/provider dependent, you just need to pass the `Path` to be checked and get a `true` or `false` response. The following code snippet checks if the `MutuaMadridOpen.txt` file is a hidden file (the file must exist in the `C:\rafaelnadal\tournaments\2009` directory):

```
Path path = FileSystems.getDefault().getPath("C:/rafaelnadal/tournaments/2009",
                                              "MutuaMadridOpen.txt");
...
try {
    boolean is_hidden = Files.isHidden(path);
    System.out.println("Is hidden ? " + is_hidden);
} catch (IOException e) {
    System.err.println(e);
}
```

Creating and Reading Directories

When it comes to creating and reading directories, NIO.2 provides a set of dedicated methods in the `Files` class. In this section, you will discover how to list the file system roots, create directories (including temporary directories), list a directory's content, and write and use filters for directories.

Listing File System Root Directories

In Java 6, the file system root directories were extracted as an array of `File` objects. Starting with Java 7, NIO.2 gets the file system root directories as an `Iterable` of `Path` objects. This `Iterable` is returned by the `getRootDirectories()` method as follows:

```
Iterable<Path> dirs = FileSystems.getDefault().getRootDirectories();
for (Path name : dirs) {
    System.out.println(name);
}
```

A possible output follows:

```
C:\

D:\

E:\
```

You can easily get from `Iterable` into an array as follows:

```
Iterable<Path> dirs = FileSystems.getDefault().getRootDirectories();
ArrayList<Path> list = new ArrayList<Path>();
for (Path name : dirs) {
    // System.out.println(name);
```

47

```
        list.add(name);
}
Path[] arr = new Path[list.size()];
list.toArray(arr);

for(Path path : arr) {
    System.out.println(path);
}
```

If you need to extract the file system root directories as an array of File, use the Java 6 solution:

```
File[] roots = File.listRoots();
for (File root : roots) {
    System.out.println(root);
}
```

Creating a New Directory

Creating a new directory is a common task that you can accomplish by calling the
Files.createDirectory() method. This method gets the directory to create (Path) and an optional list of
file attributes (FileAttribute<?>) to set atomically at creation time. It returns the created directory. The
following code snippet creates a new directory named \2010 under the C:\rafaelnadal\tournaments
directory with the default attributes (the directory must not exist):

```
Path newdir = FileSystems.getDefault().getPath("C:/rafaelnadal/tournaments/2010/");
...
try {
    Files.createDirectory(newdir);
} catch (IOException e) {
    System.err.println(e);
}
```

You can add a set of attributes at creation time as shown in the following example code snippet,
which creates a new directory on a POSIX file system that has specific permissions:

```
Path newdir = FileSystems.getDefault().getPath("/home/rafaelnadal/tournaments/2010/");
...
Set<PosixFilePermission> perms = PosixFilePermissions.fromString("rwxr-x---");
FileAttribute<Set<PosixFilePermission>> attr = PosixFilePermissions.asFileAttribute(perms);
try {
    Files.createDirectory(newdir, attr);
} catch (IOException e) {
        System.err.println(e);
}
```

■ **Note** If the directory exists, then the createDirectory() method will throw an exception.

Sometimes you need to create more than just a single directory. For example, you may need to create a sequence of hierarchical directories, like \statistics\win\prizes. You can call a cascade of createDirectory() methods or, much more elegantly, use the Files.createDirectories() method, which will create the sequence of directories in a single call; the directories are created, as needed, from the top down, with \statistics as the relative root and \prizes as the last leaf. The sequence of directories is passed as a Path instance with or without a list of file attributes to set atomically when creating the directory. The following code snippet shows how to create a sequence of hierarchical directories under the C:\rafaelnadal directory:

```
Path newdir= FileSystems.getDefault().getPath("C:/rafaelnadal/", "statistics/win/prizes");
...
try {
    Files.createDirectories(newdir);
} catch (IOException e) {
    System.err.println(e);
}
```

■ **Note** If in the sequence of directories one or more directories already exist, then the createDirectories() method will not throw an exception, but rather will just "jump" that directory and go to the next one. This method may fail after creation of some directories, but not all of them.

Listing a Directory's Content

Working with directories and files usually involves looping a directory's content for different purposes. NIO.2 provides this facility through an iterable stream named DirectoryStream, which is an interface that implements Iterable. The access to the directory stream is straightforward through the Files.newDirectoryStream() method, which gets the Path to the directory and returns a new and open directory stream.

Listing the Entire Content

The following code snippet will return the entire contents of a directory as links, files, subdirectories, and hidden files (the listed directory is C:\rafaelnadal\tournaments\2009):

```
Path path = Paths.get("C:/rafaelnadal/tournaments/2009");

//no filter applied
System.out.println("\nNo filter applied:");
try (DirectoryStream<Path> ds = Files.newDirectoryStream(path)) {
    for (Path file : ds) {
        System.out.println(file.getFileName());
    }
}catch(IOException e) {
    System.err.println(e);
}
```

A possible output follows (this is the entire content of the `C:\rafaelnadal\tournaments\2009` directory):

No filter applied:

AEGON.txt

BNP.txt

MutuaMadridOpen.txt

supershot.bmp

Tickets.zip

TournamentsCalendar.xls

Videos

...

Listing the Content by Applying a Glob Pattern

Sometimes, you may need to list only the content that meets certain criteria, which requires applying a filter to the directory's content. Commonly, you need to extract only files and subdirectories whose names match a particular pattern. NIO.2 defines this particular pattern as a built-in glob filter. Conforming to NIO.2 documentation, a glob pattern is just a string that is matched against other strings—in this case, directories and files names. Since this is a pattern, it must respect some rules, as follows:

- *: Represent (match) any number of characters, including none.

- **: Similar to *, but cross directories' boundaries.

- ?: Represent (match) exactly one character.

- {}: Represent a collection of subpatterns separated by commas. For example, {A,B,C} matches A, B, or C.

- []: Convey a set of single characters or a range of characters if the hyphen character is present. Some common examples include the following:

  - [0-9]: Matches any digit

  - [A-Z]: Matches any uppercase letter

  - [a-z,A-Z]: Matches any uppercase or lowercase letter

  - [12345]: Matches any of 1, 2, 3, 4, or 5

- Within the square brackets, *, ?, and \ match themselves.

- All other characters match themselves.

- To match *, ?, or the other special characters, you can escape them by using the backslash character, \. For example, \\ matches a single backslash, and \? matches the question mark.

Now that you know how to build a glob pattern, it is time to introduce the `newDirectoryStream()` method that gets the `Path` to the directory and a glob filter to apply. The following example will extract all files of type PNG, JPG, and BMP (regardless of their names) from the `C:\rafaelnadal\tournaments\2009` directory:

```
Path path = Paths.get("C:/rafaelnadal/tournaments/2009");
…
//glob pattern applied
System.out.println("\nGlob pattern applied:");
try (DirectoryStream<Path> ds = Files.newDirectoryStream(path, "*.{png,jpg,bmp}")) {
    for (Path file : ds) {
        System.out.println(file.getFileName());
    }
} catch (IOException e) {
    System.err.println(e);
}
```

The output will be as follows:

```
Glob pattern applied:

supershot.bmp
```

Listing the Content by Applying a User-Defined Filter

If a glob pattern does not satisfy your needs, then is time to write your own filter. This is a simple task that requires implementing the `DirectoryStream.Filter<T>` interface, which has a single method, named `accept()`. A `Path` is accepted or rejected based on your implementation. For example, the following code snippet accepts only directories in the final result:

```
Path path = Paths.get("C:/rafaelnadal/tournaments/2009");
…
//user-defined filter - only directories are accepted
DirectoryStream.Filter<Path> dir_filter = new DirectoryStream.Filter<Path>() {

public boolean accept(Path path) throws IOException {
    return (Files.isDirectory(path, NOFOLLOW_LINKS));
  }
};
```

The created filter is next passed as a parameter to the `newDirectoryStream()` method:

```
System.out.println("\nUser defined filter applied:");
```

```
try (DirectoryStream<Path> ds = Files.newDirectoryStream(path, dir_filter)) {
for (Path file : ds) {
    System.out.println(file.getFileName());
    }
} catch (IOException e) {
    System.err.println(e);
}
```

The output will be as follows:

```
User defined filter applied:

videos
```

The following list presents a set of commonly used filters:

- Filter that accepts only files/directories larger than 200KB:

```
DirectoryStream.Filter<Path> size_filter = new DirectoryStream.Filter<Path>() {

public boolean accept(Path path) throws IOException {
    return (Files.size(path) > 204800L);
  }
};
```

- Filter that accepts only files modified in the current day:

```
DirectoryStream.Filter<Path> time_filter = new DirectoryStream.Filter<Path>() {

public boolean accept(Path path) throws IOException {
    long currentTime = FileTime.fromMillis(System.currentTimeMillis()).to(TimeUnit.DAYS);
    long modifiedTime = ((FileTime) Files.getAttribute(path, "basic:lastModifiedTime",
                                        NOFOLLOW_LINKS)).to(TimeUnit.DAYS);
    if (currentTime == modifiedTime) {
            return true;
        }

    return false;
  }
};
```

- Filter that accepts only hidden files/directories:

```
DirectoryStream.Filter<Path> hidden_filter = new DirectoryStream.Filter<Path>() {

public boolean accept(Path path) throws IOException {
    return (Files.isHidden(path));
  }
};
```

Creating, Reading, and Writing Files

Probably the most common operations with files involve creating, reading, and/or writing actions. NIO.2 comes with numerous dedicated methods for performing these actions at various levels of complexity and performance, from methods for commonly used small files (cases where it is convenient to read all bytes into a byte array) to methods for advanced features such as file locking and memory-mapped I/O. This section starts with methods for small files and finishes with methods for buffered and unbuffered streams.

A *stream* represents an input source or an output destination (it can be anything from disk files to memory arrays). Streams support different kinds of data, as strings, bytes, primitive data types, localized characters, and objects. In an unbuffered stream, each read or write request is handled directly by the underlying operating system, while in a buffered stream, the data is read from a memory area known as a *buffer*, and the native input API is called only when the buffer is empty. Similarly, buffered output streams write data to a buffer, and the native output API is called only when the buffer is full. When a buffer is written out without waiting for it to fill, we say that the buffer is *flushed*.

Using Standard Open Options

Starting with NIO.2, the methods dedicated to creating, reading and writing actions (or any other action that involves opening a file) support an optional parameter, `OpenOption`, which configures how to open or create a file. Actually, the `OpenOption` is an interface from the `java.nio.file` package and it has two implementations: the `LinkOption` class (remember the well-known `NOFOLLOW_LINKS` enum constant) and the `StandardOpenOption` class, which defines the following enums:

READ	Opens file for read access
WRITE	Opens file for write access
CREATE	Creates a new file if it does not exist
CREATE_NEW	Creates a new file, failing with an exception if the file already exists
APPPEND	Appends data to the end of the file (used with WRITE and CREATE)
DELETE_ON_CLOSE	Deletes the file when the stream is closed (used for deleting temporary files)
TRUNCATE_EXISTING	Truncates the file to 0 bytes (used with the WRITE option)
SPARSE	Causes the newly created file to be sparse

SYNC	Keeps the file content and metadata synchronized with the underlying storage device
DSYNC	Keeps the file content synchronized with the underlying storage device

Some of these constants will be shown at work in the upcoming sections, after you take a look at creating a new file.

Creating a New File

Creating a new file is a common task that can be accomplished by calling the `Files.createFile()` method. This method gets the file to create (`Path`) and an optional list of file attributes (`FileAttribute<?>`) to set atomically at creation time. It returns the created file. The following code snippet creates a new file named `SonyEricssonOpen.txt` in the `C:\rafaelnadal\tournaments\2010` directory (the directory must exist) with the default attributes (initially, the file must not exist; otherwise a `FileAlreadyExistsException` exception will be thrown):

```
Path newfile = FileSystems.getDefault().
                          getPath("C:/rafaelnadal/tournaments/2010/SonyEricssonOpen.txt");
...
try {
    Files.createFile(newfile);
} catch (IOException e) {
    System.err.println(e);
}
```

You can add a set of attributes at creation time as shown in the following code snippet. This code creates a new file on a POSIX file system that has specific permissions.

```
Path newfile = FileSystems.getDefault().
                    getPath("/home/rafaelnadal/tournaments/2010/SonyEricssonOpen.txt");

Set<PosixFilePermission> perms = PosixFilePermissions.fromString("rw-------");
FileAttribute<Set<PosixFilePermission>> attr = PosixFilePermissions.asFileAttribute(perms);
try {
    Files.createFile(newfile, attr);
} catch (IOException e) {
    System.err.println(e);
}
```

As you will see soon, this is not the only way to create a new file.

Writing a Small File

NIO.2 comes with an elegant solution for writing small binary/text files. This facility is provided through two `Files.write()` methods. Both of these methods open the file for writing (this can involve creating the file, if it doesn't exist) or initially truncate an existing regular file to a size of 0 bytes. After all bytes or lines are written, the method closes the file (it closes the file even when an I/O error or exception occurs). In short, this method acts as if the `CREATE`, `TRUNCATE_EXISTING`, and `WRITE` options are present—of course, this is applicable by default when no other options are specified.

Writing Bytes with the write() Method

Writing bytes into a file can be accomplished with the `Files.write()` method. This method gets the path to the file, the byte array with the bytes to write, and options specifying how the file is opened. It returns the path of the written file.

The following code snippet writes a byte array (representing a small tennis ball picture) with the default opening options (the file name is `ball.png` and it will be written in the `C:\rafaelnadal\photos` directory):

```
Path ball_path = Paths.get("C:/rafaelnadal/photos", "ball.png");
...
byte[] ball_bytes = new byte[]{
(byte)0x89,(byte)0x50,(byte)0x4e,(byte)0x47,(byte)0x0d,(byte)0x0a,(byte)0x1a,(byte)0x0a,
(byte)0x00,(byte)0x00,(byte)0x00,(byte)0x0d,(byte)0x49,(byte)0x48,(byte)0x44,(byte)0x52,
(byte)0x00,(byte)0x00,(byte)0x00,(byte)0x10,(byte)0x00,(byte)0x00,(byte)0x00,(byte)0x10,
(byte)0x08,(byte)0x02,(byte)0x00,
...
(byte)0x49,(byte)0x45,(byte)0x4e,(byte)0x44,(byte)0xae,(byte)0x42,(byte)0x60,(byte)0x82
};

try {
    Files.write(ball_path, ball_bytes);
} catch (IOException e) {
    System.err.println(e);
}
```

Now, if you check the corresponding path, you will find a small picture representing a tennis ball.

Moreover, if you need to write text (`String`) and you want to use this method, then convert the text to a byte array as follows (the file name is `wiki.txt` and is created in `C:\rafaelnadal\wiki`):

```
Path rf_wiki_path = Paths.get("C:/rafaelnadal/wiki", "wiki.txt");
...
String rf_wiki = "Rafael \"Rafa\" Nadal Parera (born 3 June 1986) is a Spanish professional
tennis " + "player and a former World No. 1. As of 29 August 2011 (2011 -08-29)[update], he is
ranked No. 2 " + "by the Association of Tennis Professionals (ATP). He is widely regarded as
one of the greatest players " + "of all time; his success on clay has earned him the nickname
\"The King of Clay\", and has prompted " + "many experts to regard him as the greatest clay
court player of all time. Some of his best wins are:";

try {
    byte[] rf_wiki_byte = rf_wiki.getBytes("UTF-8");
    Files.write(rf_wiki_path, rf_wiki_byte);
} catch (IOException e) {
    System.err.println(e);
}
```

Even if this works, it is much easier to use the `write()` method, described next, to write text to files.

Writing Lines with the write() Method

Writing lines into a file can be accomplished by using the `Files.write()` method (a "line" is a char sequence). After each line, this method appends the platform's line separator (`line.separator` system property). This method gets the path to the file, an iterable object over the char sequence, a charset to use for encoding, and options specifying how the file is opened. It returns the path to the written file.

The following code snippet writes some lines into a file (actually, it appends some lines to the end of the file `wiki.txt` created in the preceding section):

```
Path rf_wiki_path = Paths.get("C:/rafaelnadal/wiki", "wiki.txt");
...
Charset charset = Charset.forName("UTF-8");
ArrayList<String> lines = new ArrayList<>();
lines.add("\n");
lines.add("Rome Masters - 5 titles in 6 years");
lines.add("Monte Carlo Masters - 7 consecutive titles (2005-2011)");
lines.add("Australian Open - Winner 2009");
lines.add("Roland Garros - Winner 2005-2008, 2010, 2011");
lines.add("Wimbledon - Winner 2008, 2010");
lines.add("US Open - Winner 2010");

try {
    Files.write(rf_wiki_path, lines, charset, StandardOpenOption.APPEND);
} catch (IOException e) {
    System.err.println(e);
}
```

Reading a Small File

NIO.2 provides a quick method to read small byte/text files in a single shot. This facility is provided through the `Files.readAllBytes()` and `Files.readAllLines()` methods. These methods read the entire file's bytes or lines, respectively, into a single read and take care of opening and closing the stream for you after the file has been read or an I/O error or exception has occurred.

Reading with the readAllBytes() Method

The `Files.readAllBytes()` method reads the entire file into a byte array, while the `Files.readAllLines()` method reads the entire file into a collection of `String` (as described in the next section). Focusing on the `readAllBytes()` method, the following code snippet reads the previously created `ball.png` binary file (the file must exist) into a byte array (the file path is passed as an argument):

```
Path ball_path = Paths.get("C:/rafaelnadal/photos", "ball.png");
...
try {
    byte[] ballArray = Files.readAllBytes(ball_path);
} catch (IOException e) {
    System.out.println(e);
}
```

If you want to make sure that the returned byte array contains the picture, you can run (as a test) the following code snippet, which writes the bytes into a file named bytes_to_ball.png in the same directory:

```
...
Files.write(ball_path.resolveSibling("bytes_to_ball.png"), ballArray);
...
```

Or you can use the ImageIO as follows. The line ImageIO.write() will write your bufferedImage data to your disk as a file of type PNG and will store it in the C:\rafaelnadal\photos directory.

```
BufferedImage bufferedImage = ImageIO.read(new ByteArrayInputStream(ballArray));
ImageIO.write(bufferedImage, "png", (ball_path.resolveSibling("bytes_to_ball.png")).toFile());
```

The readAllBytes() method can also read a text file. This time the byte array should be converted to String, as in the following example (you can use any charset that is proper for your text files):

```
Path wiki_path = Paths.get("C:/rafaelnadal/wiki", "wiki.txt");
...
try {
    byte[] wikiArray = Files.readAllBytes(wiki_path);
    String wikiString = new String(wikiArray, "ISO-8859-1");
    System.out.println(wikiString);
} catch (IOException e) {
    System.out.println(e);
}
```

■ **Caution**   If the file is too large (bigger than 2GB), then the size of the array cannot be allocated and a OutOfMemory error will be thrown. This depends on the Xmx parameter on the JVM: for a 32-bit JVM, it can't be larger than 2GB (but is usually smaller by default, 256MB, depending on the platform). For a 64-bit JVM, it can be much larger—tens of gigabytes potentially.

Reading with the readAllLines() Method

In the preceding example you saw how to read a text file through the readAllBytes() method. A more convenient solution is to use the readAllLines() method, since this method will read the entire file and return a List of String, which can be easily looped as follows (pass to this method the Path of the file to read and the charset to use for decoding):

```
Path wiki_path = Paths.get("C:/rafaelnadal/wiki", "wiki.txt");
...
Charset charset = Charset.forName("ISO-8859-1");
try {
    List<String> lines = Files.readAllLines(wiki_path, charset);
    for (String line : lines) {
        System.out.println(line);
    }
} catch (IOException e) {
```

```
        System.out.println(e);
    }
```

Conforming to official documentation, this method recognizes the following as line terminators:

- \u000D followed by \u000A: CARRIAGE RETURN followed by LINE FEED
- \u000A: LINE FEED
- \u000D: CARRIAGE RETURN

Working with Buffered Streams

In most operating systems, a system call to read or write data is an expensive operation. Buffers can fix this issue by providing a memory space between the buffered methods and the operating system. Before calling the native API, these methods get or put the data from/into a buffer between the operating system and the application, which increases the application's efficiency because it reduces the number of system calls—the disk is accessed only when the buffer is full or empty, depending on whether it is a write operation or a read operation. NIO.2 provides two methods for reading and writing files through buffers: `Files.newBufferedReader()` and `Files.newBufferedWriter()`, respectively. Both of these methods get a `Path` instance and return an old JDK 1.1 `BufferedReader` or `BufferedWriter` instance.

Using the newBufferedWriter() Method

The `newBufferedWriter()` method gets the path to the file, a charset used for encoding, and options specifying how the file is opened. It returns a new default buffered writer (this is a `java.io`-specific `BufferedWriter`). The method opens the file for writing (this can involve creating the file, if it doesn't exist) or initially truncates an existing regular file to a size of 0 bytes. In short, this method acts as if the `CREATE`, `TRUNCATE EXISTING`, and `WRITE` options are present (which is applicable by default when no other options are specified).

The following code snippet uses a buffer to append data into the previously created `wiki.txt` file (the file exists; you should find it in the `C:\rafaelnadal\wiki` directory):

```
Path wiki_path = Paths.get("C:/rafaelnadal/wiki", "wiki.txt");
...
Charset charset = Charset.forName("UTF-8");
String text = "\nVamos Rafa!";
try (BufferedWriter writer = Files.newBufferedWriter(wiki_path, charset,
                                          StandardOpenOption.APPEND)) {
    writer.write(text);
} catch (IOException e) {
    System.err.println(e);
}
```

Using the newBufferedReader() Method

The `newBufferedReader()` method can be used to read files through a buffer. The method gets the path to the file and a charset to use for decoding bytes into characters. It returns a new default buffered reader (this is a `java.io`-specific `BufferedReader`).

The following code snippet reads the `wiki.txt` file using the UTF-8 charset:

```
Path wiki_path = Paths.get("C:/rafaelnadal/wiki", "wiki.txt");
...
Charset charset = Charset.forName("UTF-8");
try (BufferedReader reader = Files.newBufferedReader(wiki_path, charset)) {
    String line = null;
    while ((line = reader.readLine()) != null) {
        System.out.println(line);
    }
} catch (IOException e) {
    System.err.println(e);
}
```

If you followed along with the examples in the previous sections and created the entire `wiki.txt` file, then the preceding code will output the following content:

```
Rafael "Rafa" Nadal Parera (born 3 June 1986) is a Spanish professional tennis player and a
former World No. 1. As of 29 August 2011 (2011 -08-29)[update], he is ranked No. 2 by the
Association of Tennis Professionals (ATP). He is widely regarded as one of the greatest
players of all time; his success on clay has earned him the nickname "The King of Clay", and
has prompted many experts to regard him as the greatest clay court player of all time. Some
of his best wins are:

Rome Masters - 5 titles in 6 years

Monte Carlo Masters - 7 consecutive titles (2005-2011)

Australian Open - Winner 2009

Roland Garros - Winnner 2005-2008, 2010, 2011

Wimbledon - Winner 2008, 2010

US Open - Winner 2010



Vamos Rafa!
```

Working with Unbuffered Streams

The unbuffered streams can be obtained through the new NIO.2 methods and either can be used verbatim or can be converted to buffered streams using the wrapping idiom provided by the `java.io` API. The unbuffered streams methods are `Files.newInputStream()` (input stream to read from the file) and `Files.newOutputStream()` (output stream to write to a file).

Using the newOutputStream() Method

The newOutputStream() method gets the path to the file and options specifying how the file is opened. It returns a new default thread-safe unbuffered stream that may be used to write bytes to the file (this is a java.io-specific OutputStream). The method opens the file for writing (this can involve creating the file, if it doesn't exist) or initially truncates an existing regular file to a size of 0 bytes. In short, this method acts as if the CREATE, TRUNCATE_EXISTING, and WRITE options are present (which is applicable by default when no other options are specified).

The following code snippet will write the text line "Racquet: Babolat AeroPro Drive GT" into the file C:\rafaelnadal\equipment\racquet.txt (the file doesn't initially exist, but it will be automatically created because no options are specified):

```
Path rn_racquet = Paths.get("C:/rafaelnadal/equipment", "racquet.txt");
String racquet = "Racquet: Babolat AeroPro Drive GT";

byte data[] = racquet.getBytes();
try (OutputStream outputStream = Files.newOutputStream(rn_racquet)) {
    outputStream.write(data);
} catch (IOException e) {
    System.err.println(e);
}
```

Moreover, if you decide that it is a better idea to use a buffered stream instead of the preceding code, a conversion based on the java.io API is recommended, such as shown in the following code, which appends to the file racquet.txt (the file must exist) the text "String: Babolat RPM Blast 16":

```
Path rn_racquet = Paths.get("C:/rafaelnadal/equipment", "racquet.txt");
String string = "\nString: Babolat RPM Blast 16";

try (OutputStream outputStream = Files.newOutputStream(rn_racquet, StandardOpenOption.APPEND);
    BufferedWriter writer = new BufferedWriter(new OutputStreamWriter(outputStream))) {
        writer.write(string);
} catch (IOException e) {
    System.err.println(e);
}
```

Using the newInputStream() Method

The newInputStream() method gets the path to the file to open and options specifying how to open the file. It returns a new default thread-safe unbuffered stream that may be used to read bytes from the file (this is a java.io-specific InputStream). The method opens the file for read; if no options are present, then it is equivalent to opening the file with the READ option.

The following code snippet reads the content of the file racquet.txt (the file must exist):

```
Path rn_racquet = Paths.get("C:/rafaelnadal/equipment", "racquet.txt");
...
int n;
try (InputStream in = Files.newInputStream(rn_racquet)) {
    while ((n = in.read()) != -1) {
        System.out.print((char)n);
    }
} catch (IOException e) {
```

```
        System.err.println(e);
}
```

As you probably already know from the `java.io` API, the `InputStream` class also provides a `read()` method that fills up a buffer array of type byte. Therefore, you can modify the preceding code as follows (keep in mind that you are still dealing with an unbuffered stream):

```
Path rn_racquet = Paths.get("C:/rafaelnadal/equipment", "racquet.txt");

...
int n;
byte[] in_buffer = new byte[1024];
try (InputStream in = Files.newInputStream(rn_racquet)) {
    while ((n = in.read(in_buffer)) != -1) {
            System.out.println(new String(in_buffer));
    }
} catch (IOException e) {
    System.err.println(e);
}
```

■ **Note** Calling the `read(in_buffer)` method is the same thing as calling the `read(in_buffer,0,in_buffer.length)` method.

Moreover, you can convert the unbuffered stream to a buffered stream by interoperating with the `java.io` API. The following example has the same effect as the preceding example, but it is more efficient:

```
Path rn_racquet = Paths.get("C:/rafaelnadal/equipment", "racquet.txt");

...
try (InputStream in = Files.newInputStream(rn_racquet);
    BufferedReader reader = new BufferedReader(new InputStreamReader(in))) {
    String line = null;
    while ((line = reader.readLine()) != null) {
            System.out.println(line);
    }
} catch (IOException e) {
    System.err.println(e);
}
```

The past three examples will have the same output:

```
Racquet: Babolat AeroPro Drive GT

String: Babolat RPM Blast 16
```

Creating Temporary Directories and Files

A temporary directory is a directory that stores temporary files. The location of the temporary directory depends on the operating system. In Windows, the temporary directory is set through the TEMP environment variable, usually C:\Temp, %Windows%\Temp, or a temporary directory per user in Local Settings\Temp. In Linux/Unix the global temporary directories are /tmp and /var/tmp.

Creating a Temporary Directory

In NIO.2 you can create a temporary directory with the createTempDirectory() method. Creating a temporary directory in the default operating system location can be accomplished by calling the createTempDirectory() method with two parameters: a prefix string to be used in generating the directory's name (it can be null) and an optional list of file attributes to set atomically when creating the directory. The following code snippet creates two temporary directories, one with a prefix and one without a prefix:

```
String tmp_dir_prefix = "nio_";
try {
    //passing null prefix
    Path tmp_1 = Files.createTempDirectory(null);
    System.out.println("TMP: " + tmp_1.toString());

    //set a prefix
    Path tmp_2 = Files.createTempDirectory(tmp_dir_prefix);
    System.out.println("TMP: " + tmp_2.toString());
} catch (IOException e) {
    System.err.println(e);
}
```

The following is possible output:

```
TMP: C:\Users\Leo\AppData\Local\Temp\3238630399269555448

TMP: C:\Users\Leo\AppData\Local\Temp\nio_10975503551199661257
```

■ **Note** If you don't know what the default location for temporary directories is, you can use the following code:

```
//output: C:\Users\Leo\AppData\Local\Temp\
String default_tmp = System.getProperty("java.io.tmpdir");
System.out.println(default_tmp);
```

Going further, you can specify the default directory in which a temporary directory is created by calling another createTempDirectory() method. Besides the temporary directory prefix and optional list of attributes, this method also gets a Path representing the default directory for temporary directories. The following example creates a temporary directory in the C:\rafaelnadal\tmp directory:

```
Path basedir = FileSystems.getDefault().getPath("C:/rafaelnadal/tmp/");
String tmp_dir_prefix = "rafa_";
...
try {
    //create a tmp directory in the base dir
    Path tmp = Files.createTempDirectory(basedir, tmp_dir_prefix);
    System.out.println("TMP: " + tmp.toString());
} catch (IOException e) {
    System.err.println(e);
}
```

The following is possible output:

```
TMP: C:\rafaelnadal\tmp\rafa_1753327229539718259
```

Deleting a Temporary Directory with Shutdown-Hook

Most operating systems will automatically delete the temporary directories (if not, you can use one of several kinds of cleaner software). But, sometimes you may need to programmatically control the delete process. The createTempDirectory() method does only half of the job, because the deletion is your responsibility. For this you can attach a *shutdown-hook* mechanism, a runtime mechanism used to perform any resource cleanup or save that must take place before the JVM shuts down. This hook can be implemented as a Java Thread. The run() method of the Thread will get executed when the hook is executed by the JVM at shutdown. A nice and simple flow design of a shutdown-hook is shown in Figure 4-1.

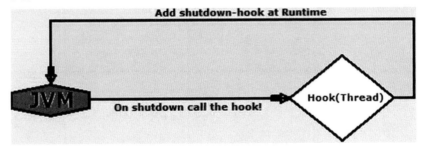

Figure 4-1. The simple flow design of a shutdown-hook

Putting the diagram shown in Figure 4-1 into code lines provide the following skeleton code:

```
Runtime.getRuntime().addShutdownHook(new Thread() {

@Override
public void run() {
```

```
  System.out.println("Shutdown-hook activated ...");

  //… here, cleanup/save resources

  System.out.println("Shutdown-hook successfully executed ...");
  }
});
```

> ▪ **Note** Notice that adding a shutdown-hook as a `Thread` to the `Runtime` can be done as an anonymous inner class, as in the preceding code, or as a separate class that implements the `Runnable` or extends `Thread`.

A shutdown-hook is a nice solution to delete a temporary directory when the JVM shuts down, but, as you probably know, a directory cannot be deleted if it is not empty; therefore, you need to loop through the temporary directory content and delete each entry before deleting the temporary directory itself. At this point, you know how to loop through a directory's content only one level down, so suppose for now that your temporary directory contains only temporary files (as is true in many real-life cases) and other empty temporary directories. Later in this book you will see how to implement recursive operations for navigating through all levels of a hierarchy structure.

The following example combines code from the preceding section for listing directory content with a shutdown-hook:

```
final Path basedir = FileSystems.getDefault().getPath("C:/rafaelnadal/tmp/");
final String tmp_dir_prefix = "rafa_";

try {
//create a tmp directory in the base dir
final Path tmp_dir = Files.createTempDirectory(basedir, tmp_dir_prefix);

Runtime.getRuntime().addShutdownHook(new Thread() {

@Override
public void run() {
  System.out.println("Deleting the temporary folder ...");

  try (DirectoryStream<Path> ds = Files.newDirectoryStream(tmp_dir)) {
      for (Path file : ds) {
              Files.delete(file);
          }
      }

  Files.delete(tmp_dir);

  } catch (IOException e) {
      System.err.println(e);
  }

  System.out.println("Shutdown-hook completed...");
  }
```

```
});

//simulate some I/O operations over the temporary file by sleeping 10 seconds
//when the time expires, the temporary file is deleted
Thread.sleep(10000);
//operations done

} catch (IOException | InterruptedException e) {
    System.err.println(e);
}
```

■ **Note** The preceding example uses a `Thread.sleep()` method to add a delay between the creation time of the temporary directory and the JVM shutdown. Obviously, in place of that, you will provide the business logic that uses the temporary directory for the job for which it was created.

Deleting a Temporary Directory with the deleteOnExit() Method

Another solution for deleting a temporary directory is to call the `deleteOnExit()` method. This method is available in the **java.io.**File class (not specific to NIO.2) and it will delete the passed file or directory when the JVM shuts down. Because this method must be called for each temporary file or directory, it is considered the least attractive choice because it will consume memory for each temporary entity.

■ **Caution**   If your system is active for a long period of time or creates many temporary files or directories in a short period of time, then using `deleteOnExit()` is a bad idea! Before you choose to use `deleteOnExit()`, consider that it can use a lot of memory that will not be released until the JVM terminates.

The following code snippet shows you how to use `deleteOnExit()`:

```
Path basedir = FileSystems.getDefault().getPath("C:/rafaelnadal/tmp/");
String tmp_dir_prefix = "rafa_";

try {
    //create a tmp directory in the base dir
    Path tmp_dir = Files.createTempDirectory(basedir, tmp_dir_prefix);

    File asFile = tmp_dir.toFile();
    asFile.deleteOnExit();

    //simulate some I/O operations over the temporary file by sleeping 10 seconds
    //when the time expires, the temporary file is deleted
    //EACH CREATED TEMPORARY ENTRY SHOULD BE REGISTERED FOR DELETE ON EXIT
    Thread.sleep(10000);
```

```
    //operations done
} catch (IOException | InterruptedException e) {
    System.err.println(e);
}
```

Note Since `deleteOnExit()` applies to `File` instances, not `Path`, you need to convert the `Path` to a `File` by calling the `Path.toFile()` method.

Creating Temporary Files

This section takes a closer look at temporary files and the NIO.2 approach to them. In real-world applications, temporary files often provide very useful help. They work very well when you need files that are not indented to be used outside of the application or the application execution. Known in Java as "work files," they can be placed in any directory chosen from the application or in the default location returned by the Java property `java.io.tmpdir`.

In NIO.2 you can create a temporary file with the `createTempFile()` method. Creating a temporary file in the default operating system location can be accomplished by calling the `createTempFile()` method with three parameters: a prefix string to be concatenated in front of the file's name (it can be `null`), a suffix string to be concatenated at the end of the file's name (it can be `null`; the default is `.tmp`), and an optional list of file attributes to set atomically when creating the file. The following code snippet creates two temporary files, one without a prefix and suffix and one with a specified prefix and suffix:

```
String tmp_file_prefix = "rafa_";
String tmp_file_sufix=".txt";

try {
    //passing null prefix/suffix
    Path tmp_1 = Files.createTempFile(null,null);
    System.out.println("TMP: " + tmp_1.toString());

    //set a prefix and a suffix
    Path tmp_2 = Files.createTempFile(tmp_file_prefix, tmp_file_sufix);
    System.out.println("TMP: " + tmp_2.toString());

} catch (IOException e) {
    System.err.println(e);
}
```

The output will be two empty temporary files in the operating system default location:

```
TMP: C:\Users\Leo\AppData\Local\Temp\6873427319542945524.tmp
```

```
TMP: C:\Users\Leo\AppData\Local\Temp\rafa_6168226983257408796.txt
```

■ **Note** If you don't know what the default location for temporary files is, you can use the following code:

```
//output: C:\Users\Leo\AppData\Local\Temp\
String default_tmp = System.getProperty("java.io.tmpdir");
```

Going further, you can specify the default directory in which a temporary file is created by calling another createTempFile() method. Besides the temporary file prefix and suffix and optional list of attributes, this method also gets a Path representing the default directory for temporary files. The following is an example that creates a temporary file in the C:\rafaelnadal\tmp directory:

```
Path basedir = FileSystems.getDefault().getPath("C:/rafaelnadal/tmp");
String tmp_file_prefix = "rafa_";
String tmp_file_sufix=".txt";

try {
    Path tmp_3 = Files.createTempFile(basedir, tmp_file_prefix, tmp_file_sufix);
    System.out.println("TMP: " + tmp_3.toString());
} catch (IOException e) {
    System.err.println(e);
}
```

The output will be one empty temporary file in the C:\rafaelnadal\tmp directory:

```
TMP: C:\rafaelnadal\tmp\rafa_512352743612949417.txt
```

Deleting a Temporary File with Shutdown-Hook

A temporary file is just a simple file until you make sure that it is truly temporary, which means that an automatic mechanism must delete temporary files periodically or at a specified time. The shutdown-hook mechanism was presented earlier in the chapter in the section "Deleting a Temporary Directory with Shutdown-Hook." The mechanism works in the same way for temporary files, so we will skip that presentation here and go straight to the code example.

The following code snippet will create a temporary file in the C:\rafaelnadal\tmp directory, wait 10 seconds (simulating some file use), and delete the file when the JVM shuts down through the shutdown-hook mechanism:

```
Path basedir = FileSystems.getDefault().getPath("C:/rafaelnadal/tmp");
String tmp_file_prefix = "rafa_";
String tmp_file_sufix = ".txt";

try {
    final Path tmp_file = Files.createTempFile(basedir, tmp_file_prefix, tmp_file_sufix);

    Runtime.getRuntime().addShutdownHook(new Thread() {
```

```
    @Override
    public void run() {
    System.out.println("Deleting the temporary file ...");

    try {
        Files.delete(tmp_file);
    } catch (IOException e) {
        System.err.println(e);
    }

    System.out.println("Shutdown hook completed...");
    }
});

//simulate some I/O operations over the temporary file by sleeping 10 seconds
//when the time expires, the temporary file is deleted
Thread.sleep(10000);
//operations done

} catch (IOException | InterruptedException e) {
    System.err.println(e);
}
```

■ **Note** The preceding code uses a `Thread.sleep()` method to add a delay between the creation time of the temporary file and the JVM shutdown. Obviously, in place of that, you will provide the business logic that uses the temporary file for the job for which it was created.

Deleting a Temporary File with the deleteOnExit() Method

Another solution for deleting a temporary file is to call the `deleteOnExit()` method. This mechanism was detailed in the earlier section "Deleting a Temporary Directory with the deleteOnExit() Method" and works the same way for temporary files, so we will skip it here and to straight to the code example.

The following code snippet will create a temporary file in the `C:\rafaelnadal\tmp` directory, wait 10 seconds (simulating some file use), and delete it when the JVM shuts down through the `deleteOnExit()` mechanism:

```
Path basedir = FileSystems.getDefault().getPath("C:/rafaelnadal/tmp");
String tmp_file_prefix = "rafa_";
String tmp_file_sufix = ".txt";

try {
    final Path tmp_file = Files.createTempFile(basedir, tmp_file_prefix, tmp_file_sufix);

    File asFile = tmp_file.toFile();
    asFile.deleteOnExit();

    //simulate some I/O operations over the temporary file by sleeping 10 seconds
```

```
    //when the time expires, the temporary file is deleted
    Thread.sleep(10000);
    //operations done

} catch (IOException | InterruptedException e) {
    System.err.println(e);
}
```

■ **Note** Since `deleteOnExit()` applies to `File` instances, not `Path`, you need to convert the `Path` to a `File` by calling the `Path.toFile()` method.

Deleting a Temporary File with DELETE_ON_CLOSE

An ingenious solution for deleting a temporary file is to use the DELETE_ON_CLOSE option. As its name suggests, this option deletes the file when the stream is closed. For example, the following code snippet creates a temporary file in the C:\rafaelnadal\tmp directory with the `createTempFile()` method and opens a stream for it with DELETE_ON_CLOSE explicitly specified, so when the stream is closed, the file should be deleted:

```
Path basedir = FileSystems.getDefault().getPath("C:/rafaelnadal/tmp");
String tmp_file_prefix = "rafa_";
String tmp_file_sufix = ".txt";
Path tmp_file = null;

try {
    tmp_file = Files.createTempFile(basedir, tmp_file_prefix, tmp_file_sufix);
} catch (IOException e) {
    System.err.println(e);
}

try (OutputStream outputStream = Files.newOutputStream(tmp_file,
                                 StandardOpenOption.DELETE_ON_CLOSE);
     BufferedWriter writer = new BufferedWriter(new OutputStreamWriter(outputStream))) {

    //simulate some I/O operations over the temporary file by sleeping 10 seconds
    //when the time expires, the temporary file is deleted
    Thread.sleep(10000);
    //operations done
} catch (IOException | InterruptedException e) {
    System.err.println(e);
}
```

Moreover, you can simulate a temporary file even without calling the `createTempFile()` method. Simply define a file name, and use the DELETE_ON_CLOSE option in conjunction with the CREATE option, as shown in the following snippet (the effect is the same as in the preceding example):

```
String tmp_file_prefix = "rafa_";
String tmp_file_sufix = ".txt";
```

```
Path tmp_file = null;

tmp_file = FileSystems.getDefault().getPath("C:/rafaelnadal/tmp", tmp_file_prefix +
                                            "temporary" + tmp_file_sufix);

try (OutputStream outputStream = Files.newOutputStream(tmp_file, StandardOpenOption.CREATE,
                                        StandardOpenOption.DELETE_ON_CLOSE);
    BufferedWriter writer = new BufferedWriter(new OutputStreamWriter(outputStream))) {

    //simulate some I/O operations over the temporary file by sleeping 10 seconds
    //when the time expires, the temporary file is deleted
    Thread.sleep(10000);
    //operations done
} catch (IOException | InterruptedException e) {
    System.err.println(e);
}
```

Deleting, Copying, and Moving Directories and Files

Delete, copy, and move are three of the most common operations used on files and directories. NIO.2 provides dedicated methods to sustain different approaches to these operations. Most of them come from the Files class, as you will see in this section.

Deleting Files and Directories

NIO.2 provides two methods for deleting a file or directory, Files.delete() and Files.deleteIfExits(). Both of them take a single argument representing the Path to delete, but Files.delete() returns void, while Files.deleteIfExits() returns a boolean value representing the success or failure of the deletion process. The delete() method tries to delete the passed Path and, in case of failure, throws one of the following exceptions: NoSuchFileException (if the passed Path does not exist), DirectoryNotEmptyException (if the passed Path is a directory that it is not empty), IOException (if an I/O error occurs), or SecurityException (if the access for deletion is denied).

The following code snippet deletes the file rafa_1.jpg from the C:\rafaelnadal\photos\ directory (the file must exist):

```
Path path = FileSystems.getDefault().getPath("C:/rafaelnadal/photos", "rafa_1.jpg");

//delete the file
try {
    Files.delete(path);
} catch (NoSuchFileException | DirectoryNotEmptyException | IOException |
        SecurityException e) {
    System.err.println(e);
}
```

As the name suggests, the Files.deleteIfExists() method deletes a file only if it exists, which means that the returned boolean value will be false if the file could not be deleted because it did not exist (instead of throwing a NoSuchFileException exception). This is useful when you have multiple threads deleting files and you don't want to throw an exception just because one thread did so first.

Keeping in mind that the preceding code just deleted the `rafa_1.jpg` file, the following code will return `false`:

```
try {
    boolean success = Files.deleteIfExists(path);
    System.out.println("Delete status: " + success);
} catch (DirectoryNotEmptyException | IOException | SecurityException e) {
    System.err.println(e);
}
```

■ **Caution**   If the deleted resource is a directory, then it must be empty. Deleting the entire directory content (which may contain other directories, files, and so on) is a task usually implemented as a recursive operation. This operation is presented in Chapter 5.

■ **Note** If the file is a symbolic link, then the symbolic link itself, not the final target of the link, is deleted.

Copying Files and Directories

Copying files and directories is a piece of cake in NIO.2. It provides three `Files.copy()` methods to accomplish this task and provides a set of options for controlling the copy process—the methods take a `varargs` argument represented by these options. These options are provided under the `StandardCopyOption` and `LinkOption` enums and are listed here:

- `REPLACE_EXISTING`: If the copied file already exists, then it is replaced (in the case of a nonempty directory, a `FileAlreadyExistsException` is thrown). When dealing with a symbolic link, the target of the link it is *not* copied; only the link is copied.

- `COPY_ATTRIBUTES`: Copy a file with its associated attributes (at least, the `lastModifiedTime` attribute is supported and copied).

- `NOFOLLOW_LINKS`: Symbolic links should not be followed.

If you are not familiar with enum types, then you should know that they can be imported into applications as follows. These are called *static imports* and can import any static fields or methods, not just fields from enum types (e.g., methods from `java.lang.Math`).

```
import static java.nio.file.StandardCopyOption.REPLACE_EXISTING;
import static java.nio.file.StandardCopyOption.COPY_ATTRIBUTES;
import static java.nio.file.LinkOption.NOFOLLOW_LINKS;
```

■ **Note** By default, when copying a symbolic link, the target of that link is copied. Copying only the link itself can be accomplished through the REPLACE_EXISTING and NOFOLLOW_LINKS options. Moreover, file attributes are not required to be copied.

■ **Caution** Trying to copy a nonempty directory will result in an empty directory. This is a task usually implemented as a recursive operation, as you will see in Chapter 5. Moreover, copying a file is not an atomic operation, which means that an IOException exception can be thrown and the copy aborted even if the target file is incomplete or the attributes were not totally copied.

Copying Between Two Paths

Usually, when you copy a file, you need a source path (copy from) and a target path (copy to). Based on this simple case, NIO.2 provides a Files.copy() method that takes the path to the file to copy, the path to the target file, and a set of options for controlling the copy process. It returns the path to the target file. If no options are specified, then the copy ends successfully only if the target file does not exist and it is not a symbolic link. Otherwise, an exception will be thrown unless the source and the target are not the same (the isSameFile() method returns true).

The following code snippet will copy the file **draw_template.txt** from C:\rafaelnadal\grandslam\AustralianOpen to C:\rafaelnadal\grandslam\USOpen (the file must exist). It replaces an existing file, copies attributes of the source to the target, and does not follow links.

```
Path copy_from = Paths.get("C:/rafaelnadal/grandslam/AustralianOpen", "draw_template.txt");
Path copy_to= Paths.get("C:/rafaelnadal/grandslam/USOpen",copy_from.getFileName().toString());

try {

    Files.copy(copy_from, copy_to, REPLACE_EXISTING, COPY_ATTRIBUTES, NOFOLLOW_LINKS);

} catch (IOException e) {
    System.err.println(e);
}
```

Copying from an Input Stream to a File

When you need to copy all bytes from an input stream to a file, you can call the Files.copy() method that gets the input stream to read from, the path to the file, and a set of options for controlling the copy process. It returns the number of bytes read or written. By default, the copy fails if the target file already exists or is a symbolic link.

The following code snippet will copy the file **draw_template.txt** from C:\rafaelnadal\grandslam\AustralianOpen to C:\rafaelnadal\grandslam\Wimbledon through an input stream (the file must exist). It will replace an existing file.

```
Path copy_from = Paths.get("C:/rafaelnadal/grandslam/AustralianOpen", "draw_template.txt");
Path copy_to = Paths.get("C:/rafaelnadal/grandslam/Wimbledon", "draw_template.txt");

try (InputStream is = new FileInputStream(copy_from.toFile())) {

    Files.copy(is, copy_to, REPLACE_EXISTING);

} catch (IOException e) {
    System.err.println(e);
}
```

The input stream may be extracted in other ways. For example, the following code snippet will get the input stream from an Internet URL (it will copy the picture indicated by the URL to the C:\rafaelnadal\photos directory only if the file does not exist):

```
Path copy_to = Paths.get("C:/rafaelnadal/photos/rafa_winner_2.jpg");
URI u = URI.create("https://lh6.googleusercontent.com/--
                    udGIidomAM/Tl8KTbYd34I/AAAAAAAAAZw/j2nH24PaZyM/s800/rafa_winner.jpg");

try (InputStream in = u.toURL().openStream()) {

    Files.copy(in, copy_to);

} catch (IOException e) {
    System.err.println(e);
}
```

■ **Caution**   It is strongly recommended that you close the input stream immediately after an I/O error occurs.

Copying from a File to an Output Stream

When you need to copy all bytes from a file to an output stream, you can call the `Files.copy()` method that gets the path to the file and the output stream to write to. It will return the number of bytes read or written.

The following code snippet copies the file draw_template.txt from C:\rafaelnadal\grandslam\AustralianOpen to C:\rafaelnadal\grandslam\RolandGarros. The target file is represented as an output stream (the target will be replaced if exists).

```
Path copy_from = Paths.get("C:/rafaelnadal/grandslam/AustralianOpen", "draw_template.txt");
Path copy_to = Paths.get("C:/rafaelnadal/grandslam/RolandGarros", "draw_template.txt");

try (OutputStream os = new FileOutputStream(copy_to.toFile())) {

    Files.copy(copy_from, os);
```

```
} catch (IOException e) {
    System.err.println(e);
}
```

■ **Caution**   It is strongly recommended that you close the output stream immediately after an I/O error occurs.

Moving Files and Directories

In this section, you will see how to move files and directories using the `Files.move()` method. This method gets the path to the file to move, the path to the target file, and a set of options that controls the moving process. These options are provided under the `StandardCopyOption` enum and are listed here:

- `REPLACE_EXISTING`: If the target file already exists, then the move is still performed and the target is replaced. When dealing with a symbolic link, the symbolic link is replaced but what it points to is not affected.

- `ATOMIC_MOVE`: The file move will be performed as an atomic operation, which guarantees that any process that monitors the file's directory will access a complete file.

Again, these enum types can be imported into an application like this:

```
import static java.nio.file.StandardCopyOption.REPLACE_EXISTING;
import static java.nio.file.StandardCopyOption.ATOMIC_MOVE;
```

By default (when no options are explicitly specified), the `move()` method tries to move the file to the target file, failing if the target file exists (`FileAlreadyExistsException` is thrown) except if the source and target are the same file (the `isSameFile()` method returns `true`), in which case this method has no effect.

■ **Note** By default, when moving a symbolic link, the symbolic link itself is moved, not the target of that link.

■ **Caution**   The `move()` method can also be used to move empty directories. Trying to move a nonempty directory is a task usually implemented as a recursive copy operation, as you will see in Chapter 5. Nevertheless, it is possible to move a directory that it is not empty if it does not require moving the entries in the directory. In some cases a directory has entries for special files (such as links) that are created when the directory is created, and if the directory contains only those entries, it is considered empty.

The following code snippet tries to move the file named rafa_2.jpg (the file must exist) from C:\rafaelnadal to C:\rafaelnadal\photos. If the target already exists, then it is replaced because the REPLACE_EXISITING option is specified.

```
Path movefrom = FileSystems.getDefault().getPath("C:/rafaelnadal/rafa_2.jpg");
Path moveto = FileSystems.getDefault().getPath("C:/rafaelnadal/photos/rafa_2.jpg");

try {
    Files.move(movefrom, moveto, StandardCopyOption.REPLACE_EXISTING);
} catch (IOException e) {
    System.err.println(e);
}
```

You can skip to hard-code the name of the file in the moveto path by using the Path.resolve() method (for more details, see Chapter 1). With this approach, you can move a file by extracting its name directly from the movefrom path (do not forget to restore the rafa_2.jpg file in C:\rafaelnadal before testing this code):

```
Path movefrom = FileSystems.getDefault().getPath("C:/rafaelnadal/rafa_2.jpg");
Path moveto_dir = FileSystems.getDefault().getPath("C:/rafaelnadal/photos");

try {
    Files.move(movefrom, moveto_dir.resolve(movefrom.getFileName()),
                                    StandardCopyOption.REPLACE_EXISTING);
} catch (IOException e) {
    System.err.println(e);
}
```

Rename a File

Finally, with a little trick, you can rename a file using the Files.move() and Path.resolveSibling() methods. The following code snippet renames the file rafa_2.jpg as rafa_renamed_2.jpg in the C:\rafaelnadal\photos directory. If you have tested the preceding code, then rafa_2.jpg should be present in this directory.

```
Path movefrom = FileSystems.getDefault().getPath("C:/rafaelnadal/photos/rafa_2.jpg");

try {
    Files.move(movefrom, movefrom.resolveSibling("rafa_2_renamed.jpg"),
                                    StandardCopyOption.REPLACE_EXISTING);
} catch (IOException e) {
    System.err.println(e);
}
```

Summary

This chapter started by exploring some methods dedicated to checking if a `Path` is readable, writable, regular, or hidden. It then focused on directory operations and how to list, create, and read directories. You saw how to list the file system roots, how to create directories with methods such as `createDirectory()` and `createTempDirectory()`, how to write directory filters, and how to list a directory's content using the `newDirectoryStream()` method. The chapter then explored files operations, such as reading, writing, creating, and opening files. As you saw, there is a wide array of file I/O methods to choose from (for buffered and unbuffered streams). The chapter ended with the well-known delete, copy, and move operations.

CHAPTER 5

■ ■ ■

Recursive Operations: Walks

As you probably know, recursive programming is a debated technique because it usually needs a lot of memory but it simplifies some programming tasks. Basically, a recursive programming is a situation in which a procedure calls itself, passing in a modified value of the parameter or parameters that were passed in to the current iteration of the procedure. Programming tasks such as calculating factorial, Fibonacci numbers, anagrams, and Sierpinski carpet are just a few of the well-known tasks that can be accomplished through the recursive programming technique. The following code snippet uses this technique to calculate the factorial (n! = 1 * 2 * 3* ... *n)—notice how the procedure calls itself:

```
/**
 * Calculate the factorial of n (n! = 1 * 2 * 3 * ... * n).
 *
 * @param n the number to calculate the factorial of.
 * @return n! - the factorial of n.
 */
static int fact(int n) {

    // Base Case:
    // If n <= 1 then n! = 1.
    if (n <= 1) {
        return 1;
    }
    // Recursive Case:
    // If n > 1 then n! = n * (n-1)!
    else {
        return n * fact(n-1);
        }
    }
```

If you are already familiar with this programming technique, then proceed reading this chapter to see how NIO.2 takes advantage of it. Otherwise, it is a good idea before you proceed to read some tutorials dedicated to recursive programming, such as "Mastering Recursive Programming" by Jonathan Bartlett, available at **www.ibm.com/developerworks/linux/library/l-recurs/index.html**.

Many programming tasks that involve working with files require visiting all files in a file tree, which is a good opportunity for using the recursive programming mechanism because every file should be "touched" individually. This is a very common approach when performing tasks such as deleting, copying, or moving a file tree. Based on this mechanism, NIO.2 encapsulates the traversal process of a file tree in an interface, named **FileVisitor**, in the **java.nio.file** package.

This chapter starts by presenting the `FileVisitor`'s scope and methods. Once you are familiar with `FileVisitor`, the chapter will help you to develop a set of applications you can use to perform tasks that involve traversing a file tree, such as finding, copying, deleting, and moving files.

The FileVisitor Interface

As previously mentioned, the `FileVisitor` interface provides the support for recursively traversing a file tree. The methods of this interface represent key points in the traversal process, enabling you to take control when a file is visited, before a directory is accessed, after a directory is accessed, and when a failure occurs; in other words, this interface has hooks for before, during, and after a file is visited, as well as for when failure occurs. Once you have control (at any of these key points), you can choose how to process the visited file and decide what should happen to it next by indicating a visit result through the `FileVisitResult` enum, which contains four enum constants:

- `FileVisitResult.CONTINUE`: This visit result indicates that the traversal process should continue. It can be translated into different actions depending on which `FileVisitor` method is returned. For example, the traversal process may continue by visiting the next file, visiting a directory's entries, or skipping a failure.

- `FileVisitResult.SKIP_SIBLINGS`: This visit result indicates that the traversal process should continue without visiting the siblings of this file or directory.

- `FileVisitResult.SKIP_SUBTREE`: This visit result indicates that the traversal process should continue without visiting the rest of the entries in this directory.

- `FileVisitResult.TERMINATE`: This visit result indicates that the traversal process should terminate.

The constants of this enum type can be iterated as follows:

```
for (FileVisitResult constant : FileVisitResult.values())
    System.out.println(constant);
```

The following subsections discuss how you can control the traversal process by implementing the various `FileVisitor` methods.

FileVisitor.visitFile() Method

The `visitFile()` method is invoked for a file in a directory. Usually, this method returns a `CONTINUE` result or a `TERMINATE` result. For example, when searching for a file, this method should return `CONTINUE` until the file is found (or the tree is completely traversed) and `TERMINATE` after the file is found.

When this method is invoked, it receives a reference to the file and the file's basic attributes. If an I/O error occurs, then it throws an `IOException` exception. The following is the signature of this method:

```
FileVisitResult visitFile(T file, BasicFileAttributes attrs) throws IOException
```

FileVisitor.preVisitDirectory() Method

The `preVisitDirectory()` method is invoked for a directory before visiting its entries. The entries will be visited if the method returns `CONTINUE` and will not be visited if it returns `SKIP_SUBTREE` (the latter visit result is meaningful only when it is returned from this method). Also, you can skip visiting the siblings of this file or directory (and any descendants) by returning the **SKIP_SIBLINGS** result.

When this method is invoked, it gets a reference to the directory and the directory's basic attributes. If an I/O error occurs, then it throws an **IOException** exception. The signature of this method is

```
FileVisitResult preVisitDirectory(T dir, BasicFileAttributes attrs) throws IOException
```

FileVisitor.postVisitDirectory() Method

The **postVisitDirectory()** method is invoked after all entries in the directory (and any descendants) have been visited or the visit has ended suddenly (that is, an I/O error has occurred or the visit has programmatically aborted). When this method is invoked, it gets a reference to the directory and **IOException** object—it will be **null** if no error occurred during the visit or it will return the corresponding error if one occurred. If an I/O error occurs, then it throws an **IOException** exception. The following is the signature of this method

```
FileVisitResult postVisitDirectory(T dir, IOException exc) throws IOException
```

FileVisitor.visitFileFailed() Method

The **visitFileFailed()** method is invoked when the file cannot be accessed for any of several different reasons, such as the file's attributes cannot be read or a directory cannot be opened. When this method is invoked, it gets a reference to the file and the exception that occurred while trying to visit that file. If an I/O error occurs, then it throws an **IOException** exception. The following is the signature of this method:

```
FileVisitResult visitFileFailed(T file, IOException exc) throws IOException
```

The SimpleFileVisitor Class

Implementing the **FileVisitor** interface requires implementing all of its methods, which may be undesirable if you need to implement only one or a few of those methods. In that case, it is much simpler to extend the **SimpleFileVisitor** class, which implements the **FileVisitor** interface. This approach requires overwriting only the desired methods.

For example, you may want to traverse a file tree and list the names of all directories. To accomplish this, it is sufficient to use only the **postVisitDirectory()** and **visitFileFailed()** methods, as shown in the following code snippet (the starting file tree is presented in the next section):

```java
class ListTree extends SimpleFileVisitor<Path> {

    @Override
    public FileVisitResult postVisitDirectory(Path dir, IOException exc) {

        System.out.println("Visited directory: " + dir.toString());

        return FileVisitResult.CONTINUE;
    }

    @Override
    public FileVisitResult visitFileFailed(Path file, IOException exc) {
```

```
        System.out.println(exc);

        return FileVisitResult.CONTINUE;
    }
}
```

As you can see, the **preVisitDirectory()** and **visitFile()** methods were skipped.

Starting the Recursive Process

Once you have created the recursive mechanism (by implementing the **FileVisitor** interface or extending the **SimpleFileVisitor** class), you can start the process by calling one of the two **Files.walkFileTree()** methods. The simplest **walkFileTree()** method gets the starting file (this is usually the file tree root) and the file visitor to invoke for each file (this is an instance of the recursive mechanism class). For example, you can start the code example in the preceding section by calling the **walkFileTree()** method as follows (the passed file tree is **C:\rafaelnadal**):

```
Path listDir = Paths.get("C:/rafaelnadal"); //define the starting file tree
ListTree walk = new ListTree();                //instantiate the walk

try{
    Files.walkFileTree(listDir, walk);         //start the walk
    } catch(IOException e){
      System.err.println(e);
    }
```

The second **walkFileTree()** method gets the starting file, options to customize the walk, the maximum number of directory levels to visit (to ensure that all levels are traversed, you can specify **Integer.MAX_VALUE** for the maximum depth argument), and the walk instance. The accepted options are the constants of the **FileVisitOption** enum. Actually, this enum contains a single constant, named **FOLLOW_LINKS**, indicating that the symbolic links are followed in the walk (by default, they are not followed).

Calling this method for the preceding walk may look like the following:

```
Path listDir = Paths.get("C:/rafaelnadal");              //define the starting file
ListTree walk = new ListTree();                          //instantiate the walk
EnumSet opts = EnumSet.of(FileVisitOption.FOLLOW_LINKS); //follow links

try{
    Files.walkFileTree(listDir, opts, Integer.MAX_VALUE, walk); //start the walk
    } catch(IOException e){
      System.err.println(e);
    }
```

■ **Note** Calling walkFileTree(start, visitor) has the same effect as calling walkFileTree(start, EnumSet.noneOf(FileVisitOption.class), Integer.MAX_VALUE, visitor).

The following lines are the output of the preceding example:

```
Visited directory: C:\rafaelnadal\equipment

Visited directory: C:\rafaelnadal\grandslam\AustralianOpen

Visited directory: C:\rafaelnadal\grandslam\RolandGarros

Visited directory: C:\rafaelnadal\grandslam\USOpen

Visited directory: C:\rafaelnadal\grandslam\Wimbledon

Visited directory: C:\rafaelnadal\grandslam

...

Visited directory: C:\rafaelnadal
```

Common Walks

There is a set of common walks that you can easily implement through the **FileVisitor** interface. This section shows you how to write and implement applications to perform a file search, a recursive copy, a recursive move, and a recursive delete.

Writing a File Search Application

Most operating systems provide a dedicated tool for searching files (for example, Linux has the **find** command, while Windows has the File Search tool). From simple searches to advanced searches, all of the tools generally work in the same way: you specify the search criteria and then wait for the tool to find the matching file(s). But, if you need to accomplish the search programmatically, then **FileVisitor** can help you with the traversal process. Whether you are looking for a file by name, by extension, or by a glob pattern or are looking inside files for some text or code, the approach is always to visit each file in the file store and perform some checks to determine whether the file conforms to your search criteria.

When you write your file search tool based on **FileVisitor**, you need to keep in mind the following:

- The **visitFile()** method is the best place to perform the comparison between the current file and your search criteria. At this point you can extract each file name, its extension, or its attributes or open the file for reading. You can use the file name, extension, and so on for determining whether the visited file is the searched one. Sometimes you will mix these information into complex search criteria. This method does not find directories.

- If you want to find directories, then the comparison must take place in the **preVisitDirectory()** or **postVisitDirectory()** method, depending on case.

- If a file cannot be visited, the **visitFileFailed()** method should return **FileVisitResult.CONTINUE** because this issue does not require the entire search process to be stopped.

- If you search for a file by name and you know that there is a single file with that name in the file tree, then you can return **FileVisitResult.TERMINATE** once the **visitFile()** method finds it. Otherwise, **FileVisitResult.CONTINUE** should be returned.

- The search process can follow symbolic links, which can be a good idea, since following symbolic links may locate the searched file before traversing the symbolic link's target sub-tree. Following symbolic links is not always a good idea; for example, for deleting files it is not advisable.

Searching for Files by Name

The preceding list can be incorporated into the following single code snippet to produce an application that searches for a file by name. This application will search for the file **rafa_1.jpg** in the entire default file system and will stop the search when it finds it.

```java
import java.io.IOException;
import java.nio.file.FileSystems;
import java.nio.file.FileVisitOption;
import java.nio.file.FileVisitResult;
import java.nio.file.FileVisitor;
import java.nio.file.Files;
import java.nio.file.Path;
import java.nio.file.Paths;
import java.nio.file.attribute.BasicFileAttributes;
import java.util.EnumSet;

class Search implements FileVisitor {

    private final Path searchedFile;
    public boolean found;

    public Search(Path searchedFile) {
        this.searchedFile = searchedFile;
        this.found = false;
    }

void search(Path file) throws IOException {
        Path name = file.getFileName();
        if (name != null && name.equals(searchedFile)) {
            System.out.println("Searched file was found: " + searchedFile +
                                            " in " + file.toRealPath().toString());
            found = true;
        }
    }

    @Override
```

```java
    public FileVisitResult postVisitDirectory(Object dir, IOException exc)
                                      throws IOException {
        System.out.println("Visited: " + (Path) dir);
        return FileVisitResult.CONTINUE;
    }

    @Override
    public FileVisitResult preVisitDirectory(Object dir, BasicFileAttributes attrs)
                                      throws IOException {
        return FileVisitResult.CONTINUE;
    }

    @Override
    public FileVisitResult visitFile(Object file, BasicFileAttributes attrs)
                                  throws IOException {
        search((Path) file);
        if (!found) {
            return FileVisitResult.CONTINUE;
        } else {
            return FileVisitResult.TERMINATE;
        }
    }

    @Override
    public FileVisitResult visitFileFailed(Object file, IOException exc)
                                      throws IOException {
        //report an error if necessary
        return FileVisitResult.CONTINUE;
    }
}

class Main {

    public static void main(String[] args) throws IOException {

        Path searchFile = Paths.get("rafa_1.jpg");
        Search walk = new Search(searchFile);
        EnumSet opts = EnumSet.of(FileVisitOption.FOLLOW_LINKS);

        Iterable<Path> dirs = FileSystems.getDefault().getRootDirectories();
        for (Path root : dirs) {
            if (!walk.found) {
                Files.walkFileTree(root, opts, Integer.MAX_VALUE, walk);
            }
        }

        if (!walk.found) {
            System.out.println("The file " + searchFile + " was not found!");
        }
    }
}
```

A fragment of the output may look something like this:

```
…

Visited: C:\Python25\Tools\webchecker

Visited: C:\Python25\Tools

Visited: C:\Python25

…

Visited: C:\rafaelnadal\equipment

Visited: C:\rafaelnadal\grandslam\AustralianOpen

Visited: C:\rafaelnadal\grandslam\RolandGarros

Visited: C:\rafaelnadal\grandslam\USOpen

Visited: C:\rafaelnadal\grandslam\Wimbledon

Visited: C:\rafaelnadal\grandslam

-------------------------------------------------------------

Searched file was found: rafa_1.jpg in C:\rafaelnadal\photos\rafa_1.jpg
```

Searching for Files by Glob Pattern

Sometimes you may have only partial information about the file you want to search for, such as only its name or extension or perhaps even just a chuck of its name or extension. Based on this small piece of information, you can write a glob pattern, as described in the Chapter 4 section "Listing the Content by Applying a Glob Pattern." The search will locate all files in a file store that match the glob pattern, and from the results you'll probably be able to find the file you needed to locate.

The following code snippet searches all files of type *.jpg in the C:\rafaelnadal file tree. The process will stop only after the entire tree has been traversed.

```java
import java.io.IOException;
import java.nio.file.FileSystems;
import java.nio.file.FileVisitOption;
import java.nio.file.FileVisitResult;
import java.nio.file.FileVisitor;
import java.nio.file.Files;
import java.nio.file.Path;
import java.nio.file.PathMatcher;
import java.nio.file.Paths;
```

```java
import java.nio.file.attribute.BasicFileAttributes;
import java.util.EnumSet;


class Search implements FileVisitor {

    private final PathMatcher matcher;

    public Search(String glob) {
        matcher = FileSystems.getDefault().getPathMatcher("glob:" + glob);
    }

    void search(Path file) throws IOException {
        Path name = file.getFileName();
        if (name != null && matcher.matches(name)) {
            System.out.println("Searched file was found: " + name +
                                          " in " + file.toRealPath().toString());
        }
    }

    @Override
    public FileVisitResult postVisitDirectory(Object dir, IOException exc)
                                                            throws IOException {

        System.out.println("Visited: " + (Path) dir);
        return FileVisitResult.CONTINUE;
    }

    @Override
    public FileVisitResult preVisitDirectory(Object dir, BasicFileAttributes attrs)
                                                            throws IOException {

        return FileVisitResult.CONTINUE;
    }

    @Override
    public FileVisitResult visitFile(Object file, BasicFileAttributes attrs)
                                                            throws IOException {

        search((Path) file);
        return FileVisitResult.CONTINUE;
    }

    @Override
    public FileVisitResult visitFileFailed(Object file, IOException exc)
                                                            throws IOException {

        //report an error if necessary
        return FileVisitResult.CONTINUE;
    }
}

class Main {

    public static void main(String[] args) throws IOException {
```

```
        String glob = "*.jpg";
        Path fileTree = Paths.get("C:/rafaelnadal/");
        Search walk = new Search(glob);
        EnumSet opts = EnumSet.of(FileVisitOption.FOLLOW_LINKS);

        Files.walkFileTree(fileTree, opts, Integer.MAX_VALUE, walk);

    }
}
```

A fragment of the output shows the files found:

```
Searched file was found: rafa_1.jpg in C:\rafaelnadal\photos\rafa_1.jpg

Searched file was found: rafa_winner.jpg in C:\rafaelnadal\photos\rafa_winner.jpg

...
```

If you have additional information about the file you are looking for, then you can create a more complex search. For example, besides the small piece of information about the file name and type, perhaps you know that the file size is smaller than a certain number of kilobytes, or perhaps you know a detail such as when the file was created, when the file was last modified, whether the file is hidden or read-only, or who owns it. Additional information may be a part of the file attributes, as shown in the following code snippet that combines the ***.jpg** glob pattern with a size of file smaller then 100KB (as you probably know, the size is a basic attribute):

```java
import java.io.IOException;
import java.nio.file.FileSystems;
import java.nio.file.FileVisitOption;
import java.nio.file.FileVisitResult;
import java.nio.file.FileVisitor;
import java.nio.file.Files;
import java.nio.file.Path;
import java.nio.file.PathMatcher;
import java.nio.file.Paths;
import java.nio.file.attribute.BasicFileAttributes;
import java.util.EnumSet;

class Search implements FileVisitor {

    private final PathMatcher matcher;
    private final long accepted_size;

    public Search(String glob, long accepted_size) {
        matcher = FileSystems.getDefault().getPathMatcher("glob:" + glob);
        this.accepted_size = accepted_size;
    }

    void search(Path file) throws IOException {
        Path name = file.getFileName();
```

```java
        long size = (Long) Files.getAttribute(file, "basic:size");

        if (name != null && matcher.matches(name) && size <= accepted_size) {
            System.out.println("Searched file was found: " + name + " in " +
                                file.toRealPath().toString() + " size (bytes):" + size);
        }
    }

    @Override
    public FileVisitResult postVisitDirectory(Object dir, IOException exc)
                                                        throws IOException {

        System.out.println("Visited: " + (Path) dir);
        return FileVisitResult.CONTINUE;
    }

    @Override
    public FileVisitResult preVisitDirectory(Object dir, BasicFileAttributes attrs)
                                                        throws IOException {

        return FileVisitResult.CONTINUE;
    }

    @Override
    public FileVisitResult visitFile(Object file, BasicFileAttributes attrs)
                                                        throws IOException {

        search((Path) file);
        return FileVisitResult.CONTINUE;
    }

    @Override
    public FileVisitResult visitFileFailed(Object file, IOException exc)
                                                        throws IOException {

        //report an error if necessary
        return FileVisitResult.CONTINUE;
    }
}

class Main {

    public static void main(String[] args) throws IOException {

        String glob = "*.jpg";
        long size = 102400; //100 kilobytes in bytes
        Path fileTree = Paths.get("C:/rafaelnadal/");
        Search walk = new Search(glob, size);
        EnumSet opts = EnumSet.of(FileVisitOption.FOLLOW_LINKS);

        Files.walkFileTree(fileTree, opts, Integer.MAX_VALUE, walk);
    }
}
```

The following is a fragment of the found files output:

```
Searched file was found: rafa_winner.jpg in C:\rafaelnadal\photos\rafa_winner.jpg size
(bytes):77718

...
```

Searching for Files by Content

One of the advanced file searches involves finding files by their content. You pass a sequence of words or sentences and the search returns only files that contain that text. This is the most time-consuming file search task because it requires searching for text inside each visited file, which means opening the file, reading it, and finally closing it. Moreover, there are many file formats that support text, such as PDF, Microsoft Word, Excel, and PowerPoint, simple text files, XML, HTML, XHTML, and so forth. Each of these formats is read differently, which requires dedicated code that is capable of extracting text files from them.

In this section we will develop an application that searches for files by content. The text to search for is passed as a **String** containing a sequence of words or sentences separated by commas; for example: "Rafael Nadal,tennis,winner of Roland Garros,BNP Paribas tournament draws". Using the **StringTokenizer** class, and commas as separators, the following example extracts each word and sentence into an **ArrayList**:

```
...
String words="Rafael Nadal,tennis,winner of Roland Garros,BNP Paribas tournament draws";
ArrayList<String> wordsarray = new ArrayList<>();
...
StringTokenizer st = new StringTokenizer(words, ",");
while (st.hasMoreTokens()) {
        wordsarray.add(st.nextToken());
}
```

The following code loops this **ArrayList** and compares each word and sentence with the text extracted from the visited file. Notice in the **searchText()** method that the extracted text is passed as a parameter.

```
//search text
private boolean searchText(String text) {

    boolean flag = false;
    for (int j = 0; j < wordsarray.size(); j++) {
        if ((text.toLowerCase()).contains(wordsarray.get(j).toLowerCase())) {
            flag = true;
            break;
        }
    }
    return flag;
}
```

The following subsections focus on isolating a set of methods for extracting text from some of the most common file formats and performing the comparison. Since we are not attempting to reinvent the wheel here, we will exploit some third-party libraries that were written especially for understanding a specific file format. We'll then combine each of the methods we develop into a full search program.

Searching in PDFs

For reading PDF files, we will use two of the most popular third-party open source libraries, iText and Apache PDFBox. You can download the iText library from **http://itextpdf.com/** and the PDFBox library from **http://pdfbox.apache.org/**. For purposes of this chapter, I used version 5.1.2 of iText and version 1.6.0 of PDFBox. Based on the iText documentation, I wrote the following method to extract text from a PDF. The first step consists of creating a **PdfReader** over the visited file. Continue by extracting the PDF's number of pages, extracting the text from each page, and passing the extracted text to the **searchText()** method. If one of the tokens is found in the extracted text, then the search in the current file is stopped, the file is considered a valid search result, and its path and name are stored so we can print it out later when the entire search is over.

```
//search in PDF files using iText library
boolean searchInPDF_iText(String file) {

    PdfReader reader = null;
    boolean flag = false;

    try {
        reader = new PdfReader(file);
        int n = reader.getNumberOfPages();

        OUTERMOST:
        for (int i = 1; i <= n; i++) {
            String str = PdfTextExtractor.getTextFromPage(reader, i);

            flag = searchText(str);
            if (flag) {
                break OUTERMOST;
            }
        }

    } catch (Exception e) {
        } finally {
            if (reader != null) {
                reader.close();
            }
            return flag;
        }
}
```

If you are more familiar with PDFBox than iText, then try the following method. Start by creating a **PDFParser** over the PDF file, continue by extracting the number of pages, and finish by extracting the text of each page and passing it to the **searchText()** method.

```
boolean searchInPDF_PDFBox(String file) {

    PDFParser parser = null;
    String parsedText = null;
```

```
    PDFTextStripper pdfStripper = null;
    PDDocument pdDoc = null;
    COSDocument cosDoc = null;
    boolean flag = false;
    int page = 0;

    File pdf = new File(file);

    try {
        parser = new PDFParser(new FileInputStream(pdf));
        parser.parse();

        cosDoc = parser.getDocument();
        pdfStripper = new PDFTextStripper();
        pdDoc = new PDDocument(cosDoc);

        OUTERMOST:
        while (page < pdDoc.getNumberOfPages()) {
            page++;
            pdfStripper.setStartPage(page);
            pdfStripper.setEndPage(page + 1);
            parsedText = pdfStripper.getText(pdDoc);

            flag = searchText(parsedText);
            if (flag) {
                break OUTERMOST;
            }
        }
    } catch (Exception e) {
    } finally {
            try {
                if (cosDoc != null) {
                    cosDoc.close();
                }
                if (pdDoc != null) {
                    pdDoc.close();
                }
            } catch (Exception e) {}
    return flag;
    }
}
```

Searching in Microsoft Word, Excel, and PowerPoint Files

The Microsoft Office suite's files can be manipulated through the Apache POI library, which is the most commonly used Java API for Microsoft documents. You can download this library from http://poi.apache.org/. For purposes of this chapter, I used version 3.7. Based on the developer guide, I wrote the following method for extracting text from a Word document. Apache POI extracts an array of String containing all the paragraphs of a Word document. The array can be looped and each paragraph can be passed to the searchText() method.

```
boolean searchInWord(String file) {

    POIFSFileSystem fs = null;
    boolean flag = false;

    try {
        fs = new POIFSFileSystem(new FileInputStream(file));

        HWPFDocument doc = new HWPFDocument(fs);
        WordExtractor we = new WordExtractor(doc);
        String[] paragraphs = we.getParagraphText();

        OUTERMOST:
        for (int i = 0; i < paragraphs.length; i++) {

                flag = searchText(paragraphs[i]);
                if (flag) {
                    break OUTERMOST;
                }
        }

    } catch (Exception e) {
    } finally {
            return flag;
    }
}
```

We can extract text from Excel files as shown in the following example. After creating an HSSFWorkbook for the Excel document, the basic idea is to iterate over the sheets, then over the rows, and finally over the cells. The cell should contain the specific text that we are looking for.

```
boolean searchInExcel(String file) {

    Row row;
    Cell cell;
    String text;
    boolean flag = false;
    InputStream xls = null;

    try {
        xls = new FileInputStream(file);
        HSSFWorkbook wb = new HSSFWorkbook(xls);

        int sheets = wb.getNumberOfSheets();

        OUTERMOST:
        for (int i = 0; i < sheets; i++) {
            HSSFSheet sheet = wb.getSheetAt(i);

            Iterator<Row> row_iterator = sheet.rowIterator();
            while (row_iterator.hasNext()) {
                row = (Row) row_iterator.next();
```

```
                    Iterator<Cell> cell_iterator = row.cellIterator();
                    while (cell_iterator.hasNext()) {
                        cell = cell_iterator.next();
                        int type = cell.getCellType();
                        if (type == HSSFCell.CELL_TYPE_STRING) {
                            text = cell.getStringCellValue();
                            flag = searchText(text);
                            if (flag) {
                                break OUTERMOST;
                            }
                        }
                    }
                }
            }

        } catch (IOException e) {
        } finally {
            try {
                if (xls != null) {
                    xls.close();
                }
            } catch (IOException e) {}
        return flag;
        }
}
```

Finally, we can extract text from PowerPoint files as shown in the following example; each slide may contain text and notes:

```
boolean searchInPPT(String file) {

    boolean flag = false;
    InputStream fis = null;
    String text;

    try {
        fis = new FileInputStream(new File(file));
        POIFSFileSystem fs = new POIFSFileSystem(fis);
        HSLFSlideShow show = new HSLFSlideShow(fs);

        SlideShow ss = new SlideShow(show);
        Slide[] slides = ss.getSlides();

        OUTERMOST:
        for (int i = 0; i < slides.length; i++) {

            TextRun[] runs = slides[i].getTextRuns();
            for (int j = 0; j < runs.length; j++) {
                TextRun run = runs[j];
                if (run.getRunType() == TextHeaderAtom.TITLE_TYPE) {
                    text = run.getText();
                } else {
```

```
                    text = run.getRunType() + " " + run.getText();
                }

                flag = searchText(text);
                if (flag) {
                        break OUTERMOST;
                }
            }
        }

        Notes notes = slides[i].getNotesSheet();
        if (notes != null) {
            runs = notes.getTextRuns();
            for (int j = 0; j < runs.length; j++) {
                text = runs[j].getText();
                flag = searchText(text);
                if (flag) {
                        break OUTERMOST;
                }
            }
        }
    }
} catch (IOException e) {
} finally {
        try {
            if (fis != null) {
                    fis.close();
            }
        } catch (IOException e) {}
    return flag;
    }
}
```

▓ **Note** I arbitrarily chose the third-party libraries used in the preceding examples. There are many other open source and commercial libraries available for dealing with different kinds of documents. Feel free to use anything that is convenient for your needs. Our search example is not the most efficient way to do the searching. In a worst-case scenario, we would have to walk through an entire array (half of an array in a typical scenario). Perhaps using an indexing search such as the one that Apache Lucene (`http://lucene.apache.org/java/docs/index.html`) provides would be a better way to do it. This as an exercise you can attempt on your own.

Searching in Text Files

Text files (`.txt`, `.html`, `.xml`, etc.) do not require a third-party library. They can be read using pure NIO.2 code as follows:

```
boolean searchInText(Path file) {
```

```
    boolean flag = false;
    Charset charset = Charset.forName("UTF-8");
    try (BufferedReader reader = Files.newBufferedReader(file, charset)) {
        String line = null;

        OUTERMOST:
        while ((line = reader.readLine()) != null) {
            flag = searchText(line);
            if (flag) {
                break OUTERMOST;
            }
        }

    } catch (IOException e) {
    } finally {
        return flag;
    }
}
```

Writing a Complete Search Program

Yes! The pie is ready! Just throw it in the oven! We have the searched text, the text extracted from a set of common file formats, and a method that checks if the extracted text contains the searched text. Put everything in the traversal process and the application is ready:

```
import com.itextpdf.text.pdf.PdfReader;
import com.itextpdf.text.pdf.parser.PdfTextExtractor;
import java.io.BufferedReader;
import java.io.File;
import java.io.FileInputStream;
import java.io.IOException;
import java.io.InputStream;
import java.nio.charset.Charset;
import java.nio.file.FileSystems;
import java.nio.file.FileVisitOption;
import java.nio.file.FileVisitResult;
import java.nio.file.FileVisitor;
import java.nio.file.Files;
import java.nio.file.Path;
import java.nio.file.attribute.BasicFileAttributes;
import java.util.ArrayList;
import java.util.EnumSet;
import java.util.Iterator;
import java.util.StringTokenizer;
import org.apache.pdfbox.cos.COSDocument;
import org.apache.pdfbox.pdfparser.PDFParser;
import org.apache.pdfbox.pdmodel.PDDocument;
import org.apache.pdfbox.util.PDFTextStripper;
import org.apache.poi.hslf.HSLFSlideShow;
import org.apache.poi.hslf.model.Notes;
import org.apache.poi.hslf.model.Slide;
```

```java
import org.apache.poi.hslf.model.TextRun;
import org.apache.poi.hslf.record.TextHeaderAtom;
import org.apache.poi.hslf.usermodel.SlideShow;
import org.apache.poi.hssf.usermodel.HSSFCell;
import org.apache.poi.hssf.usermodel.HSSFSheet;
import org.apache.poi.hssf.usermodel.HSSFWorkbook;
import org.apache.poi.hwpf.HWPFDocument;
import org.apache.poi.hwpf.extractor.WordExtractor;
import org.apache.poi.poifs.filesystem.POIFSFileSystem;
import org.apache.poi.ss.usermodel.Cell;
import org.apache.poi.ss.usermodel.Row;

class Search implements FileVisitor {

    ArrayList<String> wordsarray = new ArrayList<>();
    ArrayList<String> documents = new ArrayList<>();
    boolean found = false;

    public Search(String words) {
        wordsarray.clear();
        documents.clear();

        StringTokenizer st = new StringTokenizer(words, ",");
        while (st.hasMoreTokens()) {
            wordsarray.add(st.nextToken().trim());
        }
    }

    void search(Path file) throws IOException {

        found = false;

        String name = file.getFileName().toString();
        int mid = name.lastIndexOf(".");
        String ext = name.substring(mid + 1, name.length());

        if (ext.equalsIgnoreCase("pdf")) {
            found = searchInPDF_iText(file.toString());
            if (!found) {
                found = searchInPDF_PDFBox(file.toString());
            }
        }

        if (ext.equalsIgnoreCase("doc") || ext.equalsIgnoreCase("docx")) {
            found = searchInWord(file.toString());
        }

        if (ext.equalsIgnoreCase("ppt")) {
            searchInPPT(file.toString());
        }

        if (ext.equalsIgnoreCase("xls")) {
```

```
                searchInExcel(file.toString());
        }

        if ((ext.equalsIgnoreCase("txt")) || (ext.equalsIgnoreCase("xml")
                                        || ext.equalsIgnoreCase("html"))
                || ext.equalsIgnoreCase("htm") || ext.equalsIgnoreCase("xhtml")
                                        || ext.equalsIgnoreCase("rtf")) {
            searchInText(file);
        }

        if (found) {
            documents.add(file.toString());
        }
    }

    //search in text files
    boolean searchInText(Path file) {

        boolean flag = false;
        Charset charset = Charset.forName("UTF-8");
        try (BufferedReader reader = Files.newBufferedReader(file, charset)) {
            String line = null;

            OUTERMOST:
            while ((line = reader.readLine()) != null) {
                flag = searchText(line);
                if (flag) {
                    break OUTERMOST;
                }
            }

        } catch (IOException e) {
        } finally {
            return flag;
        }
    }

    //search in Excel files
    boolean searchInExcel(String file) {

        Row row;
        Cell cell;
        String text;
        boolean flag = false;
        InputStream xls = null;

        try {
            xls = new FileInputStream(file);
            HSSFWorkbook wb = new HSSFWorkbook(xls);

            int sheets = wb.getNumberOfSheets();
```

```
        OUTERMOST:
        for (int i = 0; i < sheets; i++) {
            HSSFSheet sheet = wb.getSheetAt(i);

            Iterator<Row> row_iterator = sheet.rowIterator();
            while (row_iterator.hasNext()) {
                row = (Row) row_iterator.next();
                Iterator<Cell> cell_iterator = row.cellIterator();
                while (cell_iterator.hasNext()) {
                    cell = cell_iterator.next();
                    int type = cell.getCellType();
                    if (type == HSSFCell.CELL_TYPE_STRING) {
                        text = cell.getStringCellValue();
                        flag = searchText(text);
                        if (flag) {
                            break OUTERMOST;
                        }
                    }
                }
            }
        }

    } catch (IOException e) {
    } finally {
        try {
            if (xls != null) {
                xls.close();
            }
        } catch (IOException e) {
        }
        return flag;
    }
}

//search in PowerPoint files
boolean searchInPPT(String file) {

    boolean flag = false;
    InputStream fis = null;
    String text;

    try {
        fis = new FileInputStream(new File(file));
        POIFSFileSystem fs = new POIFSFileSystem(fis);
        HSLFSlideShow show = new HSLFSlideShow(fs);

        SlideShow ss = new SlideShow(show);
        Slide[] slides = ss.getSlides();

        OUTERMOST:
        for (int i = 0; i < slides.length; i++) {
```

```
                    TextRun[] runs = slides[i].getTextRuns();
                    for (int j = 0; j < runs.length; j++) {
                        TextRun run = runs[j];
                        if (run.getRunType() == TextHeaderAtom.TITLE_TYPE) {
                            text = run.getText();
                        } else {
                            text = run.getRunType() + " " + run.getText();
                        }

                        flag = searchText(text);
                        if (flag) {
                            break OUTERMOST;
                        }

                    }

                    Notes notes = slides[i].getNotesSheet();
                    if (notes != null) {
                        runs = notes.getTextRuns();
                        for (int j = 0; j < runs.length; j++) {
                            text = runs[j].getText();
                            flag = searchText(text);
                            if (flag) {
                                break OUTERMOST;
                            }
                        }
                    }
                }

        } catch (IOException e) {
        } finally {
            try {
                if (fis != null) {
                    fis.close();
                }
            } catch (IOException e) {
            }
            return flag;
        }

}

//search in Word files
boolean searchInWord(String file) {

    POIFSFileSystem fs = null;
    boolean flag = false;

    try {
        fs = new POIFSFileSystem(new FileInputStream(file));

        HWPFDocument doc = new HWPFDocument(fs);
```

```
            WordExtractor we = new WordExtractor(doc);
            String[] paragraphs = we.getParagraphText();

            OUTERMOST:
            for (int i = 0; i < paragraphs.length; i++) {

                flag = searchText(paragraphs[i]);
                if (flag) {
                    break OUTERMOST;
                }
            }

        } catch (Exception e) {
        } finally {
            return flag;
        }
    }

    //search in PDF files using PDFBox library
    boolean searchInPDF_PDFBox(String file) {

        PDFParser parser = null;
        String parsedText = null;
        PDFTextStripper pdfStripper = null;
        PDDocument pdDoc = null;
        COSDocument cosDoc = null;
        boolean flag = false;
        int page = 0;

        File pdf = new File(file);

        try {
            parser = new PDFParser(new FileInputStream(pdf));
            parser.parse();

            cosDoc = parser.getDocument();
            pdfStripper = new PDFTextStripper();
            pdDoc = new PDDocument(cosDoc);

            OUTERMOST:
            while (page < pdDoc.getNumberOfPages()) {
                page++;
                pdfStripper.setStartPage(page);
                pdfStripper.setEndPage(page + 1);
                parsedText = pdfStripper.getText(pdDoc);

                flag = searchText(parsedText);
                if (flag) {
                    break OUTERMOST;
                }
            }
```

```java
        } catch (Exception e) {
        } finally {
            try {
                if (cosDoc != null) {
                    cosDoc.close();
                }
                if (pdDoc != null) {
                    pdDoc.close();
                }
            } catch (Exception e) {
            }
            return flag;
        }
    }

    //search in PDF files using iText library
    boolean searchInPDF_iText(String file) {

        PdfReader reader = null;
        boolean flag = false;

        try {
            reader = new PdfReader(file);
            int n = reader.getNumberOfPages();

            OUTERMOST:
            for (int i = 1; i <= n; i++) {
                String str = PdfTextExtractor.getTextFromPage(reader, i);

                flag = searchText(str);
                if (flag) {
                    break OUTERMOST;
                }
            }

        } catch (Exception e) {
        } finally {
            if (reader != null) {
                reader.close();
            }
            return flag;
        }

    }

    //search text
    private boolean searchText(String text) {

        boolean flag = false;
        for (int j = 0; j < wordsarray.size(); j++) {
            if ((text.toLowerCase()).contains(wordsarray.get(j).toLowerCase())) {
                flag = true;
```

```java
                break;
            }
        }

        return flag;
    }

    @Override
    public FileVisitResult postVisitDirectory(Object dir, IOException exc)
                                                    throws IOException {

        System.out.println("Visited: " + (Path) dir);
        return FileVisitResult.CONTINUE;
    }

    @Override
    public FileVisitResult preVisitDirectory(Object dir, BasicFileAttributes attrs)
                                                    throws IOException {

        return FileVisitResult.CONTINUE;
    }

    @Override
    public FileVisitResult visitFile(Object file, BasicFileAttributes attrs)
                                                    throws IOException {

        search((Path) file);
        return FileVisitResult.CONTINUE;
    }

    @Override
    public FileVisitResult visitFileFailed(Object file, IOException exc)
                                                    throws IOException {

        //report an error if necessary

        return FileVisitResult.CONTINUE;
    }
}

class Main {

public static void main(String[] args) throws IOException {

String words = "Rafael Nadal, tennis, winner of Roland Garros, BNP Paribas tournament draws";
Search walk = new Search(words);
EnumSet opts = EnumSet.of(FileVisitOption.FOLLOW_LINKS);

Iterable<Path> dirs = FileSystems.getDefault().getRootDirectories();
for (Path root : dirs) {
    Files.walkFileTree(root, opts, Integer.MAX_VALUE, walk);
}

System.out.println("_____");
for(String path_string: walk.documents){
    System.out.println(path_string);
```

```
        }
        System.out.println("_____");

      }
}
```

Note that sometimes this is a pretty slow process that may take from several seconds to dozens of minutes—the running time will vary based on the file tree size, number of checked files, and the size of those files. In the preceding example, the file tree contains all file stores in the default file system, so each file in any of the supported formats will be opened, read, and explored for our set of search words. Depending on how large and numerous the matching files are, the process may appear to be jammed for a few seconds as the results are returned. You can improve this application by adding more file formats, a progress bar or flag indicating process status, and multiple threads to speed up the process. Moreover, displaying the name of the files as they are found may be a better idea than storing their names and path.

Writing a File Delete Application

Deleting a single file is a simple operation, as you saw in the Chapter 4 section "Deleting Files and Directories." After you call the **delete()** or **deleteIfExists()** method, the file is deleted from your file system. Deleting an entire file tree is an operation based on calling the **delete()** or **deleteIfExists()** method recursively through a **FileVisitor** implementation. Before you see an example, here are a few things you need to keep in mind:

- Before you delete a directory, you must delete all files from it.

- The **visitFile()** method is the best place to perform the deletion of each file.

- Since you can delete a directory only if it is empty, it is recommended to delete directories in the **postVisitDirectory()** method.

- If a file cannot be visited, the **visitFileFailed()** method should return **FileVisitResult.CONTINUE** or **TERMINATE**, depending on your decision.

- The delete process can follow symbolic links, which may be not advisable, since symbolic links may point files outside the deletetion domain. But if you are sure that this case can never happen, or a supplementary condition prevents undesirable deletions, then follow symbolic links.

Our aim in this section is to create an application that deletes an entire file tree. The following code deletes the **C:\rafaelnadal** directory (for further use, make a backup of this directory before you run the following code):

```
import java.io.IOException;
import java.nio.file.FileVisitOption;
import java.nio.file.FileVisitResult;
import java.nio.file.FileVisitor;
import java.nio.file.Files;
import java.nio.file.Path;
import java.nio.file.Paths;
import java.nio.file.attribute.BasicFileAttributes;
import java.util.EnumSet;
```

```
class DeleteDirectory implements FileVisitor {

boolean deleteFileByFile(Path file) throws IOException {
   return Files.deleteIfExists(file);
}

@Override
public FileVisitResult postVisitDirectory(Object dir, IOException exc)
                                                    throws IOException {

    if (exc == null) {
        System.out.println("Visited: " + (Path) dir);
        boolean success = deleteFileByFile((Path) dir);

        if (success) {
             System.out.println("Deleted: " + (Path) dir);
        } else {
             System.out.println("Not deleted: " + (Path) dir);
        }
    } else {
        throw exc;
    }
    return FileVisitResult.CONTINUE;
}

@Override
public FileVisitResult preVisitDirectory(Object dir, BasicFileAttributes attrs)
                                                    throws IOException {

   return FileVisitResult.CONTINUE;
}

@Override
public FileVisitResult visitFile(Object file, BasicFileAttributes attrs)
                                                    throws IOException {

   boolean success = deleteFileByFile((Path) file);

   if (success) {
        System.out.println("Deleted: " + (Path) file);
   } else {
        System.out.println("Not deleted: " + (Path) file);
   }

   return FileVisitResult.CONTINUE;
}

@Override
public FileVisitResult visitFileFailed(Object file, IOException exc)
                                                    throws IOException {

   //report an error if necessary

   return FileVisitResult.CONTINUE;
}
```

```
}
class Main {

  public static void main(String[] args) throws IOException {

    Path directory = Paths.get("C:/rafaelnadal");
    DeleteDirectory walk = new DeleteDirectory();
    EnumSet opts = EnumSet.of(FileVisitOption.FOLLOW_LINKS);

    Files.walkFileTree(directory, opts, Integer.MAX_VALUE, walk);
    }
}
```

■ **Note** Sending the deleted files to the recycle bin can be accomplished by using JNI to invoke Windows API `SHFileOperation()` method. Check out David Shay's post at www.jroller.com/ethdsy/entry/send_to_recycle_bin for more details.

Writing a Copy Files Application

Copying a file tree requires calling the `Files.copy()` method for each traversed file and directory. (For details about copying a file or directory in NIO.2, refer to the Chapter 4 section "Copying Files and Directories.") Before you see an example, here a some pointers to keep in mind:

- Before you copy any files from a directory, you must copy the directory itself. Copying a source directory (empty or not) will result in an empty target directory. This task must be accomplished in the `preVisitDirectory()` method.

- The `visitFile()` method is the perfect place to copy each file.

- When you copy a file or directory, you need to decide whether or not you want to use the `REPLACE_EXISTING` and `COPY_ATTRIBUTES` options.

- If you want to preserve the attributes of the source directory, you need to do that after the files have been copied, in the `postVisitDirectory()` method.

- If you choose to follow links (`FOLLOW_LINKS`) and your file tree has a circular link to a parent directory, the looping directory is reported in the `visitFileFailed()` method with the `FileSystemLoopException` exception.

- If a file cannot be visited, the `visitFileFailed()` method should return `FileVisitResult.CONTINUE` or `TERMINATE`, depending on your decision.

- The copy process can follow symbolic links if you specify the `FOLLOW_LINKS` option.

The following code snippet incorporates the preceding concepts and copies the C:\rafaelnadal subtree to the C:\rafaelnadal_copy file tree:

```
import java.nio.file.FileSystemLoopException;
```

```java
import java.nio.file.attribute.FileTime;
import java.io.IOException;
import java.nio.file.FileVisitOption;
import java.nio.file.FileVisitResult;
import java.nio.file.FileVisitor;
import java.nio.file.Files;
import java.nio.file.Path;
import java.nio.file.Paths;
import java.nio.file.attribute.BasicFileAttributes;
import java.util.EnumSet;
import static java.nio.file.StandardCopyOption.REPLACE_EXISTING;
import static java.nio.file.StandardCopyOption.COPY_ATTRIBUTES;

class CopyTree implements FileVisitor {

    private final Path copyFrom;
    private final Path copyTo;

    public CopyTree(Path copyFrom, Path copyTo) {
        this.copyFrom = copyFrom;
        this.copyTo = copyTo;
    }

    static void copySubTree(Path copyFrom, Path copyTo) throws IOException {
        try {
            Files.copy(copyFrom, copyTo, REPLACE_EXISTING, COPY_ATTRIBUTES);
        } catch (IOException e) {
            System.err.println("Unable to copy " + copyFrom + " [" + e + "]");
        }

    }

    @Override
    public FileVisitResult postVisitDirectory(Object dir, IOException exc)
                                                        throws IOException {
        if (exc == null) {
            Path newdir = copyTo.resolve(copyFrom.relativize((Path) dir));
            try {
                FileTime time = Files.getLastModifiedTime((Path) dir);
                Files.setLastModifiedTime(newdir, time);
            } catch (IOException e) {
                System.err.println("Unable to copy all attributes to: " + newdir+" ["+e+ "]");
            }
        } else {
            throw exc;
        }

        return FileVisitResult.CONTINUE;
    }

    @Override
    public FileVisitResult preVisitDirectory(Object dir, BasicFileAttributes attrs)
```

```java
                                                              throws IOException {
    System.out.println("Copy directory: " + (Path) dir);
    Path newdir = copyTo.resolve(copyFrom.relativize((Path) dir));
    try {
        Files.copy((Path) dir, newdir, REPLACE_EXISTING, COPY_ATTRIBUTES);
    } catch (IOException e) {
        System.err.println("Unable to create " + newdir + " [" + e + "]");
        return FileVisitResult.SKIP_SUBTREE;
    }

    return FileVisitResult.CONTINUE;
}

@Override
public FileVisitResult visitFile(Object file, BasicFileAttributes attrs)
                                                              throws IOException {
    System.out.println("Copy file: " + (Path) file);
    copySubTree((Path) file, copyTo.resolve(copyFrom.relativize((Path) file)));
    return FileVisitResult.CONTINUE;
}

@Override
public FileVisitResult visitFileFailed(Object file, IOException exc)
                                                              throws IOException {
    if (exc instanceof FileSystemLoopException) {
        System.err.println("Cycle was detected: " + (Path) file);
    } else {
        System.err.println("Error occurred, unable to copy:" +(Path) file+" ["+ exc +
"]");
    }

    return FileVisitResult.CONTINUE;
}
}

class Main {

    public static void main(String[] args) throws IOException {

        Path copyFrom = Paths.get("C:/rafaelnadal");
        Path copyTo = Paths.get("C:/rafaelnadal_copy");

        CopyTree walk = new CopyTree(copyFrom, copyTo);
        EnumSet opts = EnumSet.of(FileVisitOption.FOLLOW_LINKS);

        Files.walkFileTree(copyFrom, opts, Integer.MAX_VALUE, walk);
    }
}
```

After running the preceding application, you will find a C:\rafaelnadal_copy target that has the same content and attributes as the C:\rafaelnadal source.

Writing a Move Files Application

Moving a file tree is a task that combines into a single application the steps of copying and deleting the file tree. (For more details about moving files, refer to the Chapter 4 section "Moving Files and Directories.") Actually, there are two approaches commonly used to move a file tree: combine `Files.move()`, `Files.copy()`, and `Files.delete()`, or use only `Files.copy()` and `Files.delete()`. Depending on the approach you choose, `FileVisitor` should be implemented accordingly to accomplish the move file tree task. Before you see an example, here are some items you need to keep in mind:

- Before you move any files from a directory, you must move the directory itself. Since nonempty directories cannot be moved (only empty directories can be moved), you need to use the `Files.copy()` method, which will copy an empty directory instead. This task must be accomplished in the `preVisitDirectory()` method.

- The `visitFile()` method is the perfect place to move each file. For this you can use the `Files.move()` method, or `Files.copy()` combined with `Files.delete()`.

- After all files from a source directory are moved into the target directory, you need to call `Files.delete()` to delete the source directory, which, at this moment, should be empty. This task must be accomplished in the `postVisitDirectory()` method.

- When you copy a file or directory, you need to decide whether or not you want to use the `REPLACE_EXISTING` and `COPY_ATTRIBUTES` options. Moreover, when you move a file or directory, you need to decide if `ATOMIC_MOVE` is needed.

- If you want to preserve the attributes of the source directory, you need to do that after the files have been moved, in the `postVisitDirectory()` method. Some attributes, such as `lastModifiedTime`, should be extracted in the `preVisitDirectory()` method and stored until they are set in `postVisitDirectory()`. The reason is that after you move a file from the source directory, the directory content has changed and the initial last modified time is overwritten by the new date.

- If a file cannot be visited, the `visitFileFailed()` method should return `FileVisitResult.CONTINUE` or `TERMINATE`, depending on your decision.

- The move process can follow symbolic links if you specify the `FOLLOW_LINKS` option. Keep in mind that moving a symbolic link moves the link itself, not the target of that link.

The following code snippet moves the `C:\rafaelnadal` directory content into the `C:\ATP\players\rafaelnafal` directory (before testing, you must manually create the folder `C:\ATP\players\`). In this case the directory and sub-directories are moved using `Files.copy()` and `Files.delete()`, and the files are moved using `Files.move()`.

```java
import java.io.IOException;
import java.nio.file.FileVisitOption;
import java.nio.file.FileVisitResult;
import java.nio.file.FileVisitor;
import java.nio.file.Files;
```

107

```java
import java.nio.file.Path;
import java.nio.file.Paths;
import java.nio.file.attribute.BasicFileAttributes;
import java.nio.file.attribute.FileTime;
import java.util.EnumSet;
import static java.nio.file.StandardCopyOption.REPLACE_EXISTING;
import static java.nio.file.StandardCopyOption.COPY_ATTRIBUTES;
import static java.nio.file.StandardCopyOption.ATOMIC_MOVE;

class MoveTree implements FileVisitor {

    private final Path moveFrom;
    private final Path moveTo;
    static FileTime time = null;

    public MoveTree(Path moveFrom, Path moveTo) {
        this.moveFrom = moveFrom;
        this.moveTo = moveTo;
    }

    static void moveSubTree(Path moveFrom, Path moveTo) throws IOException {
        try {
            Files.move(moveFrom, moveTo, REPLACE_EXISTING, ATOMIC_MOVE);
        } catch (IOException e) {
            System.err.println("Unable to move " + moveFrom + " [" + e + "]");
        }

    }

    @Override
    public FileVisitResult postVisitDirectory(Object dir, IOException exc)
                                                            throws IOException {
        Path newdir = moveTo.resolve(moveFrom.relativize((Path) dir));
        try {
            Files.setLastModifiedTime(newdir, time);
            Files.delete((Path) dir);
        } catch (IOException e) {
            System.err.println("Unable to copy all attributes to: " + newdir+" [" + e + "]");
        }

        return FileVisitResult.CONTINUE;
    }

    @Override
    public FileVisitResult preVisitDirectory(Object dir, BasicFileAttributes attrs)
                                                            throws IOException {
        System.out.println("Move directory: " + (Path) dir);
        Path newdir = moveTo.resolve(moveFrom.relativize((Path) dir));
        try {
            Files.copy((Path) dir, newdir, REPLACE_EXISTING, COPY_ATTRIBUTES);
            time = Files.getLastModifiedTime((Path) dir);
        } catch (IOException e) {
```

```
            System.err.println("Unable to move " + newdir + " [" + e + "]");
            return FileVisitResult.SKIP_SUBTREE;
        }

        return FileVisitResult.CONTINUE;
    }

    @Override
    public FileVisitResult visitFile(Object file, BasicFileAttributes attrs)
                                                    throws IOException {

        System.out.println("Move file: " + (Path) file);
        moveSubTree((Path) file, moveTo.resolve(moveFrom.relativize((Path) file)));
        return FileVisitResult.CONTINUE;
    }

    @Override
    public FileVisitResult visitFileFailed(Object file, IOException exc)
                                                    throws IOException {

        return FileVisitResult.CONTINUE;
    }
}

class Main {

    public static void main(String[] args) throws IOException {

        Path moveFrom = Paths.get("C:/rafaelnadal");
        Path moveTo = Paths.get("C:/ATP/players/rafaelnadal");

        MoveTree walk = new MoveTree(moveFrom, moveTo);
        EnumSet opts = EnumSet.of(FileVisitOption.FOLLOW_LINKS);

        Files.walkFileTree(moveFrom, opts, Integer.MAX_VALUE, walk);
    }
}
```

You can accomplish the same task without using Files.move(), since every move is just a pair of copy and delete operations. For example, you can rewrite the moveSubTree() method to use Files.copy() and Files.delete() to move files also:

```
static void moveSubTree(Path moveFrom, Path moveTo) throws IOException {
        try {
            Files.copy(moveFrom, moveTo, REPLACE_EXISTING, COPY_ATTRIBUTES);
            Files.delete(moveFrom);
        } catch (IOException e) {
            System.err.println("Unable to move " + moveFrom + " [" + e + "]");
        }
    }
```

Summary

This chapter focused on developing recursive operations over files and directories. After a short intro to the recursive programming technique, you learned about the **FileVisitor** interface and **SimpleFileVisitor** implementation. You then saw how to develop a set of applications that that you can use to perform tasks that involve traversing a file tree, such as finding, copying, deleting, and moving files.

CHAPTER 6

■ ■ ■

Watch Service API

The Watch Service API was introduced in Java 7 (NIO.2) as a thread-safe service that is capable of watching objects for changes and events. The most common use is to monitor a directory for changes to its content through actions such as create, delete, and modify. You've probably seen the effect of such a service many times. For example, when you open a text file in an editor (such as GridinSoft Notepad, jEdit, etc.) and the file content is modified outside the editor, you will see a message that asks whether you want to reload the file because it was modified. This means the editor has detected a file change through a watch service and is reporting it accordingly. This is known as the *file change notification* mechanism, and starting with NIO.2, it is available through the Watch Service API.

The Watch Service API is a low-level API that can be used as is or can be customized. You can even write a high-level API on top of it. By default, this API uses the underlying file system functionalities to watch the file system for changes. It allows you to register a directory (or directories) to be monitored for different kinds of notification events that you specify during registration. When one or more of the registered notification events are detected by the watch service, the watch service passes the notification events to the process that is registered to handles them through a separate thread or pool of threads.

Note Starting with NIO.2, you no longer need to poll the file system for changes or use other in-house solutions to monitor the file system changes. In previous Java versions, you have to implement an agent running in a separate thread that keeps track of all the contents of the watched directories, constantly polling the file system to see if anything important has happened. Now, regardless of whether you are running Mac OS X, Linux, Unix, Windows, or some other OS, you have the guarantee that the underlying operating system and file system provide the required functionalities to allow Java to register to receive notification of file system changes.

In this chapter you will see how to develop applications based on the provided Watch Service API. Implementing a functional application isn't easy, so we will start with the simplest case in which the application monitors a single directory for changes. Afterward, you will see how to recursively monitor a directory tree that you have registered to be watched. In addition, we will develop two more applications that are less generic and that encapsulate real-life cases. To get you started, the chapter provides an overview of the main classes involved in writing a Watch Service API–based application.

The Watch Service API Classes

The `java.nio.file.WatchService` interface is the starting point of this API. It has multiple implementations for different file systems and operating systems. You use this interface together with three classes to develop a system that has file system watch capability. These classes are overviewed by the below bullets:

- *Watchable object*: An object is "watchable" if it represents an instance of a class that implements the `java.nio.file.Watchable` interface. In our case, this is the most important class of NIO 2, the well-known `Path` class.

- *Event types*: This is the list of events we are interested in monitoring. Events trigger a notification only if they are specified in the register call. The standard supported events are represented by the `java.nio.file.StandardWatchEventKinds` class and include create, delete, and modify. This class implements the `WatchEvent.Kind<T>` interface.

- *Event modifier*: This qualifies how a `Watchable` is registered with a `WatchService`. As of the time of this writing, NIO.2 does not define any standard modifiers.

- *Watcher*: The watcher watches watchables! In our examples, the watcher is `WatchService` and it monitors the file system changes (the file system is a `FileSystem` instance). As you will see, the `WatchService` will be created through the `FileSystem` class. It will work away silently in the background watching the registered `Path`.

Implementing a Watch Service

Implementing a watch service is a task that requires accomplishing a set of steps. In this section, you will see the main steps for developing a watch service that monitors a given directory for three notification events: delete, create, and modify. Each step is supported by a chunk of code that demonstrates how to practically accomplish the step. At the end, we will glue the chunks together into a complete functional example of a watch service.

Creating a WatchService

We begin our journey by creating a `WatchService` for monitoring the file system. For this we call the `FileSystem.newWatchService()` method:

```
WatchService watchService = FileSystems.getDefault().newWatchService();
```

We now have a watch service at our disposal.

Registering Objects with the Watch Service

Every object that should be watched must be explicitly registered with the watch service. We can register any object that implements the `Watchable` interface. For our example, we will register directories that are instances of the `Path` class. Besides the watched objects, the registration process requires identification of the events for which the service should watch and notify. The supported types of events are mapped under the StandardWatchEventKinds class as constants of type Kind<Path>:

- StandardWatchEventKinds.ENTRY_CREATE: A directory entry is created. An ENTRY_CREATE event is also triggered when a file is renamed or moved into this directory.

- StandardWatchEventKinds.ENTRY_DELETE: A directory entry is deleted. An ENTRY_DELETE event is also triggered when a file is renamed or moved out of this directory.

- StandardWatchEventKinds.ENTRY_MODIFY: A directory entry is modified. Which events constitute a modification is somewhat platform-specific, but actually modifying the contents of a file always triggers a modify event. On some platforms, changing attributes of files can also trigger this event.

- StandardWatchEventKinds.OVERFLOW: Indicates that events might have been lost or discarded. You do not have to register for the OVERFLOW event to receive it.

Since the Path class implements the Watchable interface, it provides the Watchable.register() methods. There are two such methods dedicated for registering objects with the watch service. One of them receives two arguments representing the watch service to which this object is to be registered and the events for which this object should be registered. The second register method receives these two arguments also, and a third argument that specifies modifiers that qualify how the directory is registered. At the time of this writing, NIO.2 does not provide any standard modifiers.

The following code snippet registers the Path C:\rafaelnadal with the watch service (the monitored events will be create, delete, and modify):

```
import static java.nio.file.StandardWatchEventKinds.*;

…
final Path path = Paths.get("C:/rafaelnadal");
WatchService watchService = FileSystems.getDefault().newWatchService();

…
path.register(watchService, StandardWatchEventKinds.ENTRY_CREATE,
              StandardWatchEventKinds.ENTRY_MODIFY, StandardWatchEventKinds.ENTRY_DELETE);

…
watchService.close();
…
```

You receive a WatchKey instance for each directory that you register; this is a token representing the registration of a watchable object with a WatchService. It is your choice whether or not to hang onto this reference, because the WatchService returns the relevant WatchKey to you when an event is triggered. More details about watch keys are provided in the following section.

Waiting for the Incoming Events

Waiting for the incoming events requires an infinite loop. When an event occurs, the watch service is responsible for signaling the corresponding watch key and placing it into the watcher's queue, from where we can retrieve it—we say that the watch key was *queued*. Therefore, our infinite loop may be of the following type:

```
while(true){
//retrieve and process the incoming events
…
}
```

Or it may be of the following type:

```
for(;;){
//retrieve and process the incoming events
…
}
```

Getting a Watch Key

Retrieving a queued key can be accomplished by calling one of the following three methods of the WatchService class. All three methods retrieve the next key and remove it from the queue. They differ in how they respond if no key is available, as described here:

- poll(): If no key is available, it returns immediately a null value.

- poll(long, TimeUnit): If no key is available, it waits the specified time and tries again. If still no key is available, then it returns null. The time period is indicated as a long number, while the TimeUnit argument determines whether the specified time is minutes, seconds, milliseconds, or some other unit of time.

- take(): If no key is available, it waits until a key is queued or the infinite loop is stopped for any of several different reasons.

The following three code snippets show you each of these methods called inside the infinite loop:

```
//poll method, without arguments
while (true) {
        //retrieve and remove the next watch key
        final WatchKey key = watchService.poll();
        //the thread flow gets here immediately with an available key or a null value
…
}

//poll method, with arguments
while (true) {
        //retrieve and remove the next watch key
        final WatchKey key = watchService.poll(10, TimeUnit.SECONDS);
        //the thread flow gets here immediately if a key is available, or after 10 seconds
        //with an available key or null value
…
}
```

```
//take method
while (true) {
        //retrieve and remove the next watch key
        final WatchKey key = watchService.take();
        //the thread flow gets here immediately if a key is available, or it will wait until a
        //key is available, or the loop breaks
...
}
```

Keep in mind that a key always has a state, which can be either ready, signaled, or invalid:

- *Ready*: When it is first created, a key is in the ready state, which means that it is ready to accept events.

- *Signaled*: When a key is in the signaled state, it means that at least one event has occurred and the key was queued, so it is available to be retrieved by poll() or take() methods. (It is analogous to fishing: the key is the float, and the events are the fish. When you have a fish on the hook, the float (key) signals you to pull the line out of the water.) Once signaled, the key remains in this state until its reset() method is invoked to return the key to the ready state. If other events occur while the key is signaled, they are queued without requeuing the key itself (this never happens when fishing).

- *Invalid*: When a key is in the invalid state, it means that it is no longer active. A key remains valid until either it is cancelled by explicitly calling the cancel() method, the directory becomes inaccessible, or the watch service is closed. You can test whether a key is valid by calling the WatchKey.isValid() method, which will return a corresponding boolean value.

Note Watch keys are safe for use by multiple concurrent threads.

Retrieving Pending Events for a Key

When the key is signaled, we have one or more pending events waiting for us to take action. We can retrieve and remove all pending events for a specific watch key by calling the WatchKey.pollEvents() method. It gets no arguments and returns a List containing the retrieved pending events. We can iterate this List to extract and process each pending event individually. The List type is WatchEvent<T>, which represents an event (or repeated event) for an object that is registered with a WatchService:

```
public List<WatchEvent<?>> pollEvents()
```

Note The pollEvents() method does not wait if there are no events pending, which sometimes may result in an empty List.

The following code snippet iterates the pending events for our key:

```
...
while (true) {
        //retrieve and remove the next watch key
        final WatchKey key = watchService.take();

        //get list of pending events for the watch key
        for (WatchEvent<?> watchEvent : key.pollEvents()) {
...
        }
        ...
}
...
```

■ **Note** Watch events are immutable and thread-safe.

Retrieving the Event Type and Count

The WatchEvent<T> interface maps event properties, such as *type* and *count*. The type of an event can be obtained by calling the WatchEvent.kind() method, which returns the event type as a Kind<T> object.

■ **Note** If you ignore the registered event types, it is possible to receive an OVERFLOW event. This kind of event can be ignored or handled, the choice of which is up to you.

The following code snippet will list the type of each event provided by the pollEvents() method:

```
...
//get list of pending events for the watch key
for (WatchEvent<?> watchEvent : key.pollEvents()) {

        //get the kind of event (create, modify, delete)
        final Kind<?> kind = watchEvent.kind();

        //handle OVERFLOW event
        if (kind == StandardWatchEventKinds.OVERFLOW) {
                continue;
        }

        System.out.println(kind);
}
...
```

Besides the event type, we can also get the number of times that the event has been observed (repeated events). This is possible if we call the `WatchEvent.count()` method, which returns an `int`:

```
System.out.println(watchEvent.count());
```

Retrieving the File Name Associated with an Event

When a delete, create, or modify event occurs on a file, we can find out its name by getting the event *context* (the file name is stored as the context of the event). This task can be accomplished by calling the `WatchEvent.context()` method:

```
...
final WatchEvent<Path> watchEventPath = (WatchEvent<Path>) watchEvent;
final Path filename = watchEventPath.context();

System.out.println(filename);
...
```

Putting the Key Back in Ready State

Once signaled, the key remains in this state until its `reset()` method is invoked to return the key to the ready state. It then resumes waiting for events. The `reset()` method returns `true` if the watch key is valid and has been reset, and returns `false` if the watch key could not be reset because it is no longer valid. In some cases, the infinite loop should be broken if the key is no longer valid; for example, if we have a single key, there is no reason to stay in the infinite loop.

Following is the code that is used to break the loop if the key in no longer valid:

```
...
while(true){
    ...
    //reset the key
    boolean valid = key.reset();

    //exit loop if the key is not valid (if the directory was deleted, for example)
    if (!valid) {
            break;
    }
}
...
```

■ **Caution** If you forget or fail to call the `reset()` method, the key will not receive any further events!

Closing the Watch Service

The watch service exits either when the thread exits or when the service is closed. It should be closed by explicitly calling the `WatchService.close()` method, or by placing the creation code in a try-with-resources block, as follows:

```
try (WatchService watchService = FileSystems.getDefault().newWatchService()) {
...
}
```

When the watch service is closed, any current operations are canceled and invalidated. After a watch service is closed, any further attempt to invoke operations upon it will throw `ClosedWatchServiceException`. If this watch service is already closed, then invoking this method has no effect.

Gluing It All Together

In this section, we glue together all the preceding chunks of code, with imports and spaghetti-code, into a single application that watches for create, delete, and modify events for the path `C:\rafaelnadal` and reports the type of event and the file where it occurred. For purposes of testing, try manually to add, delete, or modify a file or directory under this path. Keep in mind that only one level down is monitored (only the `C:\rafaelnadal` directory), *not* the entire directory tree under the `C:\rafaelnadal` directory.

The application code follows:

```
package watch_01;

import java.io.IOException;
import java.nio.file.FileSystems;
import java.nio.file.Path;
import java.nio.file.Paths;
import java.nio.file.StandardWatchEventKinds;
import java.nio.file.WatchEvent;
import java.nio.file.WatchEvent.Kind;
import java.nio.file.WatchKey;
import java.nio.file.WatchService;

class WatchRafaelNadal {

    public void watchRNDir(Path path) throws IOException, InterruptedException {
        try (WatchService watchService = FileSystems.getDefault().newWatchService()) {
            path.register(watchService, StandardWatchEventKinds.ENTRY_CREATE,
                StandardWatchEventKinds.ENTRY_MODIFY, StandardWatchEventKinds.ENTRY_DELETE);

            //start an infinite loop
            while (true) {

                //retrieve and remove the next watch key
                final WatchKey key = watchService.take();

                //get list of pending events for the watch key
                for (WatchEvent<?> watchEvent : key.pollEvents()) {
```

```
                    //get the kind of event (create, modify, delete)
                    final Kind<?> kind = watchEvent.kind();

                    //handle OVERFLOW event
                    if (kind == StandardWatchEventKinds.OVERFLOW) {
                        continue;
                    }

                    //get the filename for the event
                    final WatchEvent<Path> watchEventPath = (WatchEvent<Path>) watchEvent;
                    final Path filename = watchEventPath.context();

                    //print it out
                    System.out.println(kind + " -> " + filename);
                }

                //reset the key
                boolean valid = key.reset();

                //exit loop if the key is not valid (if the directory was deleted, for
example)
                if (!valid) {
                    break;
                }
            }
        }
    }
}

public class Main {

    public static void main(String[] args) {

        final Path path = Paths.get("C:/rafaelnadal");
        WatchRafaelNadal watch = new WatchRafaelNadal();

        try {
            watch.watchRNDir(path);
        } catch (IOException | InterruptedException ex) {
            System.err.println(ex);
        }

    }
}
```

Since this application contains an infinite loop, be careful to manually stop the application, or implement a stop mechanism. The application is provided as a NetBeans project, so you can easily stop it, with no supplementary code, from the Output window.

Other Examples of Using a Watch Service

In this section, we will "play" with the preceding application for coding some scenarios meant to explore the possibilities of the watch service. We will build new applications based on this one for accomplish more complicated tasks that involves a watch service. As in the previous section, following the description of each step, a chunk of code supporting the step is provided. After the steps are described in full, we will pull everything together into the complete application.

■ **Note** For purposes of keeping the code as clean as possible, we will skip the declaration of variables (their names are the same as in the previous application) and code that should just be repeated.

Watching a Directory Tree

To get started, we'll develop an application that extends the preceding example to watch the entire C:\rafaelnadal directory tree. Moreover, if a CREATE event creates a new directory somewhere in this tree, it will get registered immediately as if it were there from the beginning.

First, create a watch service:

```
private WatchService watchService = FileSystems.getDefault().newWatchService();
```

Next, we need to register the directory tree for create, delete, and modify events. This is trickier than it was in the original application because we need to register each subdirectory of C:\rafaelnadal, not only this directory. Therefore, we need a walk (see Chapter 5) to traverse each subdirectory and register it individually in the watch service. This case is perfect for implementing a walk by extending the SimpleFileVisitor class, since we only need to get involved when a directory is previsited (additionally, you may want to override the visitFileFailed() method for explicitly treating an unexpected traversal error). To accomplish this, we will create a method, named registerTree(), as follows:

```
private void registerTree(Path start) throws IOException {

  Files.walkFileTree(start, new SimpleFileVisitor<Path>() {

    @Override
    public FileVisitResult preVisitDirectory(Path dir, BasicFileAttributes attrs)
                                                              throws IOException {
      System.out.println("Registering:" + dir);
      registerPath(dir);
      return FileVisitResult.CONTINUE;
      }
  });
}
```

As you can see, no registration happens here. For each traversed directory, this code calls another method, named `registerPath()`, which will register the received path with the watch service as follows:

```
private void registerPath(Path path) throws IOException {

  //register the received path
  WatchKey key = path.register(watchService, StandardWatchEventKinds.ENTRY_CREATE,
               StandardWatchEventKinds.ENTRY_MODIFY, StandardWatchEventKinds.ENTRY_DELETE);
  }
```

At this point, the initial `C:\rafaelnadal` directory and all subdirectories are registered for create, delete, and modify events.

Next, we will focus on the infinite loop that will "capture" these events. When an event occurs, we are especially interested whether it is a `CREATE` event, since it may signal that a new subdirectory has been created, in which case it is our responsibility to add this subdirectory into the watch service process by calling the `registerTree()` method with the corresponding path. The issue we need to resolve here is that we do not know which key has been queued, so we do not know which path should be passed for registration. The solution may be to keep the keys and corresponding paths in a `HashMap` that is updated at every registration in the `registerPath()` method, as follows, after which, when an event occurs, we can just extract the associated key from the hash map:

```
private final Map<WatchKey, Path> directories = new HashMap<>();

...
private void registerPath(Path path) throws IOException {
  //register the received path
  WatchKey key = path.register(watchService, StandardWatchEventKinds.ENTRY_CREATE,
               StandardWatchEventKinds.ENTRY_MODIFY, StandardWatchEventKinds.ENTRY_DELETE);

  //store the key and path
  directories.put(key, path);
}
```

Now, in the infinite loop, we can register any new subdirectory as follows:

```
...
while (true) {
  ...
  if (kind == StandardWatchEventKinds.ENTRY_CREATE) {
      final Path directory_path = directories.get(key);
      final Path child = directory_path.resolve(filename);

      if (Files.isDirectory(child, LinkOption.NOFOLLOW_LINKS)) {
        registerTree(child);
      }
  }
  ...
}
...
```

The HashMap can also be used to stop the infinite loop when no more valid keys are available. To accomplish this, when a key is invalid, it is removed from the HashMap, and when the HashMap is empty, the loop is broken:

```
...
while (true) {
  ...
  //reset the key
  boolean valid = key.reset();

  //remove the key if it is not valid
  if (!valid) {
      directories.remove(key);

      if (directories.isEmpty()) {
         break;
      }
  }
}
}
...
```

That's it! At this point, let's put everything together into a single shot:

```java
import java.io.IOException;
import java.nio.file.FileSystems;
import java.nio.file.FileVisitResult;
import java.nio.file.Files;
import java.nio.file.LinkOption;
import java.nio.file.Path;
import java.nio.file.Paths;
import java.nio.file.SimpleFileVisitor;
import java.nio.file.StandardWatchEventKinds;
import java.nio.file.WatchEvent;
import java.nio.file.WatchEvent.Kind;
import java.nio.file.WatchKey;
import java.nio.file.WatchService;
import java.nio.file.attribute.BasicFileAttributes;
import java.util.HashMap;
import java.util.Map;

class WatchRecursiveRafaelNadal {

    private WatchService watchService;
    private final Map<WatchKey, Path> directories = new HashMap<>();

    private void registerPath(Path path) throws IOException {
        //register the received path
        WatchKey key = path.register(watchService, StandardWatchEventKinds.ENTRY_CREATE,
                StandardWatchEventKinds.ENTRY_MODIFY, StandardWatchEventKinds.ENTRY_DELETE);

        //store the key and path
        directories.put(key, path);
    }
```

```java
private void registerTree(Path start) throws IOException {

    Files.walkFileTree(start, new SimpleFileVisitor<Path>() {

        @Override
        public FileVisitResult preVisitDirectory(Path dir, BasicFileAttributes attrs)
                throws IOException {
            System.out.println("Registering:" + dir);
            registerPath(dir);
            return FileVisitResult.CONTINUE;
        }
    });

}

public void watchRNDir(Path start) throws IOException, InterruptedException {

    watchService = FileSystems.getDefault().newWatchService();

    registerTree(start);

    //start an infinite loop
    while (true) {

        //retrieve and remove the next watch key
        final WatchKey key = watchService.take();

        //get list of events for the watch key
        for (WatchEvent<?> watchEvent : key.pollEvents()) {

            //get the kind of event (create, modify, delete)
            final Kind<?> kind = watchEvent.kind();

            //get the filename for the event
            final WatchEvent<Path> watchEventPath = (WatchEvent<Path>) watchEvent;
            final Path filename = watchEventPath.context();

            //handle OVERFLOW event
            if (kind == StandardWatchEventKinds.OVERFLOW) {
                continue;
            }

            //handle CREATE event
            if (kind == StandardWatchEventKinds.ENTRY_CREATE) {
                final Path directory_path = directories.get(key);
                final Path child = directory_path.resolve(filename);

                if (Files.isDirectory(child, LinkOption.NOFOLLOW_LINKS)) {
                    registerTree(child);
                }
            }
```

```
                //print it out
                System.out.println(kind + " -> " + filename);
            }

            //reset the key
            boolean valid = key.reset();

            //remove the key if it is not valid
            if (!valid) {
                directories.remove(key);

                //there are no more keys registered
                if (directories.isEmpty()) {
                    break;
                }
            }
        }
    }
    watchService.close();
    }
}

public class Main {

    public static void main(String[] args) {

        final Path path = Paths.get("C:/rafaelnadal");
        WatchRecursiveRafaelNadal watch = new WatchRecursiveRafaelNadal();

        try {
            watch.watchRNDir(path);
        } catch (IOException | InterruptedException ex) {
            System.err.println(ex);
        }

    }
}
```

For testing purposes, try to create new subdirectories and files, modify them, and then delete them. At the same time, keep an eye on the console output to see how events are reported. The following is example output from adding a new picture named rafa_champ.jpg to the C:\rafaelnadal\photos directory and deleting it after a few seconds:

```
Registering:C:\rafaelnadal

Registering:C:\rafaelnadal\equipment

Registering:C:\rafaelnadal\grandslam

Registering:C:\rafaelnadal\grandslam\AustralianOpen
```

```
Registering:C:\rafaelnadal\grandslam\RolandGarros

Registering:C:\rafaelnadal\grandslam\USOpen

...

Registering:C:\rafaelnadal\wiki


ENTRY_CREATE -> rafa_champ.jpg

ENTRY_MODIFY -> rafa_champ.jpg

ENTRY_MODIFY -> photos

ENTRY_MODIFY -> rafa_champ.jpg

ENTRY_DELETE -> rafa_champ.jpg

ENTRY_MODIFY -> photos
```

Watching a Video Camera

For this scenario, suppose that we have a surveillance video camera that captures at least one image every 10 seconds and sends it in JPG format to a computer directory. Behind the scenes, a controller is responsible for checking if the camera sends the image captures on time and in the correct, JPG format. It displays an alert message if the camera does not work properly.

This scenario can be easily reproduced in code lines thanks to the Watch Service API. We are especially interested in writing the controller that watches the video camera. Since the video camera sends the captures to a directory, our controller can watch that directory for the CREATE event. The directory in this example is C:\security (which you should manually create) and it is mapped as a Path by the path variable:

```
...
final Path path = Paths.get("C:/security");
...
WatchService watchService = FileSystems.getDefault().newWatchService();
path.register(watchService, StandardWatchEventKinds.ENTRY_CREATE);
...
```

Next, we know that the video camera sends images every 10 seconds, which means that the poll(long, TimeUnit) method should be perfect for monitoring this (remember that if an event occurs during the specified time period, this method exits, returning the relevant WatchKey). We set it to wait exactly 11 seconds, and if in this time no new capture is created, then we report this through a message and stop the system:

```
...
```

```
while (true) {
    final WatchKey key = watchService.poll(11, TimeUnit.SECONDS);
    if (key == null) {
    System.out.println("The video camera is jammed - security watch system is canceled!");
    break;
    } else {
    ...
    }
}
...
```

Finally, if we have a new capture available, then all we need to do is check whether it is in the JPG image format. For this, we can use a helper method from the Files class, named probeContentType(), which probes the content type of a file. We pass the file, and it returns null or the content type as a MIME. For JPG images, this method should return image/jpeg.

```
...
OUTERMOST:
while (true) {

    ...
    if (kind == StandardWatchEventKinds.ENTRY_CREATE) {

        //get the filename for the event
        final WatchEvent<Path> watchEventPath = (WatchEvent<Path>) watchEvent;
        final Path filename = watchEventPath.context();
        final Path child = path.resolve(filename);

        if (Files.probeContentType(child).equals("image/jpeg")) {

            //print out the video capture time
            SimpleDateFormat dateFormat = new SimpleDateFormat("yyyy-MMM-dd HH:mm:ss");
            System.out.println("Video capture successfully at: " + dateFormat.format(new Date()));
        } else {
            System.out.println("The video camera capture format failed! This could be a virus!");
            break OUTERMOST;
        }
    }
}
...
```

We have accomplished the main tasks in writing the controller, so now all we need to do is fill in the missing code (imports, declarations, main function, etc.) to give us the complete application, as follows:

```
import java.io.IOException;
import java.nio.file.FileSystems;
import java.nio.file.Files;
import java.nio.file.Path;
import java.nio.file.Paths;
import java.nio.file.StandardWatchEventKinds;
import java.nio.file.WatchEvent;
import java.nio.file.WatchEvent.Kind;
import java.nio.file.WatchKey;
import java.nio.file.WatchService;
```

```java
import java.text.SimpleDateFormat;
import java.util.Date;
import java.util.concurrent.TimeUnit;

class SecurityWatch {

    WatchService watchService;

    private void register(Path path, Kind<Path> kind) throws IOException {
        //register the directory with the watchService for Kind<Path> event
        path.register(watchService, kind);
    }

    public void watchVideoCamera(Path path) throws IOException, InterruptedException {

        watchService = FileSystems.getDefault().newWatchService();
        register(path, StandardWatchEventKinds.ENTRY_CREATE);

        //start an infinite loop
        OUTERMOST:
        while (true) {

            //retrieve and remove the next watch key
            final WatchKey key = watchService.poll(11, TimeUnit.SECONDS);

            if (key == null) {
                System.out.println("The video camera is jammed - security watch system is
                                                                        canceled!");

                break;
            } else {

                //get list of events for the watch key
                for (WatchEvent<?> watchEvent : key.pollEvents()) {

                    //get the kind of event (create, modify, delete)
                    final Kind<?> kind = watchEvent.kind();

                    //handle OVERFLOW event
                    if (kind == StandardWatchEventKinds.OVERFLOW) {
                        continue;
                    }

                    if (kind == StandardWatchEventKinds.ENTRY_CREATE) {

                        //get the filename for the event
                        final WatchEvent<Path> watchEventPath = (WatchEvent<Path>) watchEvent;
                        final Path filename = watchEventPath.context();
                        final Path child = path.resolve(filename);

                        if (Files.probeContentType(child).equals("image/jpeg")) {

                            //print out the video capture time
```

```
                            SimpleDateFormat dateFormat = new
                                       SimpleDateFormat("yyyy-MMM-dd HH:mm:ss");
                            System.out.println("Video capture successfully at: " +
                                       dateFormat.format(new Date()));
                    } else {
                        System.out.println("The video camera capture format failed!
                                                    This could be a virus!");
                        break OUTERMOST;
                    }
                }
            }

            //reset the key
            boolean valid = key.reset();

            //exit loop if the key is not valid
            if (!valid) {
                break;
            }
        }
    }

    watchService.close();
    }
}

public class Main {

    public static void main(String[] args) {

        final Path path = Paths.get("C:/security");
        SecurityWatch watch = new SecurityWatch();

        try {
            watch.watchVideoCamera(path);
        } catch (IOException | InterruptedException ex) {
            System.err.println(ex);
        }

    }
}
```

For testing purposes, you may need to write a tester class or, much easier, play the role of the video camera. Just start the application and copy and paste JPG images in C:\security before the critical time passes. Try different cases, such as using a wrong file format, waiting more than 11 seconds before copying another image, and so on.

Watching a Printer Tray System

In this section, we will develop an application that monitors a large-scale printer tray. Suppose that we have a multithreading base class that receives documents to be printed and dispatches them to a suite of network printers based on an algorithm that is intended to optimize use of the printers—a printing thread terminates after the corresponding document has been printed. The class is implemented as follows:

```java
import java.nio.file.Path;
import java.util.Random;

class Print implements Runnable {

    private Path doc;

    Print(Path doc) {
        this.doc = doc;
    }

    @Override
    public void run() {
        try {
            //sleep a random number of seconds for simulating dispatching and printing
            Thread.sleep(20000 + new Random().nextInt(30000));
            System.out.println("Printing: " + doc);
        } catch (InterruptedException ex) {
            System.err.println(ex);
        }
    }
}
```

■ **Note** Java 7 recommends using the new `ThreadLocalRandom` class for generating random numbers in multithreading cases. But I prefer the old `Random` class because the new class seems to have a bug; it generates the same numbers over multiple threads. If the bug has been resolved by the time you read this book, then you may want to use this line instead: `ThreadLocalRandom.current().nextInt(20000, 50000);`.

Now the printers are "fed" from a common public tray represented by a directory (`C:\printertray`, which you need to create manually). Our job is to implement a watch service to manage this tray. When a new document arrives into the tray, we have to pass it to the `Print` class, and after a document has been printed, we have to delete it from the tray.

We start by obtaining a watch service via the classical approach and registering the `C:\printertray` directory for `CREATE` and `DELETE` events:

```java
...
final Path path = Paths.get("C:/printertray");
...
WatchService watchService = FileSystems.getDefault().newWatchService();
path.register(watchService, StandardWatchEventKinds.ENTRY_CREATE,
                                    StandardWatchEventKinds.ENTRY_DELETE);
...
```

Next, when a new document arrives into the tray, we have to create a new `Print` thread and store the thread and the document path for further tracking the thread state. This will help us to know when a document has been printed and thus should be deleted from the tray and removed for storage (we use a `HashMap` for this task). The following code snippet contains the block of code executed when a new document arrives into the tray (a `CREATE` event was queued):

```java
private final Map<Thread, Path> threads = new HashMap<>();
...
if (kind == StandardWatchEventKinds.ENTRY_CREATE) {

    System.out.println("Sending the document to print -> " + filename);

    Runnable task = new Print(path.resolve(filename));
    Thread worker = new Thread(task);

    //we can set the name of the thread
    worker.setName(path.resolve(filename).toString());

    //store the thread and the path
    threads.put(worker, path.resolve(filename));

    //start the thread, never call method run() direct
    worker.start();
}
...
```

After a document is deleted from the tray (a `DELETE` event is queued), we just print a message:

```java
...
if (kind == StandardWatchEventKinds.ENTRY_DELETE) {
    System.out.println("Document " + filename + " was successfully printed!");
}
...
```

But when is the document deleted? To solve this task, we use a little trick. Instead of using the `take()` method for waiting keys to be queued, we use the `poll(long, TimeUnit)` method, which will give us control in the infinite loop at the specified time interval—when we have control (no matter whether or not any key was queued), we can loop the `HashMap` of threads to see if any printing job has terminated (the associated thread state is `TERMINATED`). Every `TERMINATED` state will be followed by deletion of the associated path and removal of the `HashMap` entry. When the path is deleted, a `DELETE` event will be queued. The following code shows you how to accomplish this:

```java
...
if (!threads.isEmpty()) {
    for (Iterator<Map.Entry<Thread, Path>> it = threads.entrySet().iterator(); it.hasNext();)
        Map.Entry<Thread, Path> entry = it.next();
        if (entry.getKey().getState() == Thread.State.TERMINATED) {
            Files.deleteIfExists(entry.getValue());
            it.remove();
        }
    }
}
...
```

Now, put everything together to obtain the complete application:

```java
import java.io.IOException;
import java.nio.file.FileSystems;
import java.nio.file.Files;
import java.nio.file.Path;
import java.nio.file.Paths;
import java.nio.file.StandardWatchEventKinds;
import java.nio.file.WatchEvent;
import java.nio.file.WatchEvent.Kind;
import java.nio.file.WatchKey;
import java.nio.file.WatchService;
import java.util.HashMap;
import java.util.Iterator;
import java.util.Map;
import java.util.Random;
import java.util.concurrent.TimeUnit;

class Print implements Runnable {

    private Path doc;

    Print(Path doc) {
        this.doc = doc;
    }

    @Override
    public void run() {
        try {
            //sleep a random number of seconds for simulating dispatching and printing
            Thread.sleep(20000 + new Random().nextInt(30000));
            System.out.println("Printing: " + doc);
        } catch (InterruptedException ex) {
            System.err.println(ex);
        }
    }
}

class WatchPrinterTray {

    private final Map<Thread, Path> threads = new HashMap<>();

    public void watchTray(Path path) throws IOException, InterruptedException {
        try (WatchService watchService = FileSystems.getDefault().newWatchService()) {
            path.register(watchService, StandardWatchEventKinds.ENTRY_CREATE,
                                        StandardWatchEventKinds.ENTRY_DELETE);

            //start an infinite loop
            while (true) {

                //retrieve and remove the next watch key
                final WatchKey key = watchService.poll(10, TimeUnit.SECONDS);
```

```java
            //get list of events for the watch key
            if (key != null) {
                for (WatchEvent<?> watchEvent : key.pollEvents()) {

                    //get the filename for the event
                    final WatchEvent<Path> watchEventPath = (WatchEvent<Path>) watchEvent;
                    final Path filename = watchEventPath.context();

                    //get the kind of event (create, modify, delete)
                    final Kind<?> kind = watchEvent.kind();

                    //handle OVERFLOW event
                    if (kind == StandardWatchEventKinds.OVERFLOW) {
                        continue;
                    }

                    if (kind == StandardWatchEventKinds.ENTRY_CREATE) {
                        System.out.println("Sending the document to print ->" + filename);

                        Runnable task = new Print(path.resolve(filename));
                        Thread worker = new Thread(task);

                        //we can set the name of the thread
                        worker.setName(path.resolve(filename).toString());

                        //store the thread and the path
                        threads.put(worker, path.resolve(filename));

                        //start the thread, never call method run() direct
                        worker.start();
                    }

                    if (kind == StandardWatchEventKinds.ENTRY_DELETE) {
                        System.out.println(filename + " was successfully printed!");
                    }
                }

                //reset the key
                boolean valid = key.reset();

                //exit loop if the key is not valid
                if (!valid) {
                    threads.clear();
                    break;
                }
            }

            if (!threads.isEmpty()) {
                for (Iterator<Map.Entry<Thread, Path>> it = threads.entrySet().iterator();
                                                            it.hasNext();) {
                    Map.Entry<Thread, Path> entry = it.next();
```

```
                        if (entry.getKey().getState() == Thread.State.TERMINATED) {
                            Files.deleteIfExists(entry.getValue());
                            it.remove();
                        }
                    }
                }
            }
        }
    }
}

public class Main {

    public static void main(String[] args) {

        final Path path = Paths.get("C:/printertray");
        WatchPrinterTray watch = new WatchPrinterTray();

        try {
            watch.watchTray(path);
        } catch (IOException | InterruptedException ex) {
            System.err.println(ex);
        }

    }
}
```

For testing purposes, start the application and copy a set of files into the C:\printertray directory. For example, the following is output from testing with a set of files:

```
Sending the document to print -> rafa_1.jpg

Sending the document to print -> AEGON.txt

Sending the document to print -> BNP.txt

Printing: C:\printertray\rafa_1.jpg

Printing: C:\printertray\AEGON.txt

rafa_1.jpg was successfully printed!

AEGON.txt was successfully printed!

Printing: C:\printertray\BNP.txt

Sending the document to print -> rafa_winner.jpg

BNP.txt was successfully printed!
```

```
Printing: C:\printertray\rafa_winner.jpg

rafa_winner.jpg was successfully printed
```

Summary

In this chapter you have explored a great facility of NIO.2, the Watch Service API. You learned how to watch a directory or directory tree for events such as create, delete, and modify. After an overview of this API and an introductory application, you saw how to combine this API with NIO.2 walks, how to simulate video camera surveillance, and how to watch a large-scale printer tray. These examples were simply meant to stimulate your curiosity to explore further the exciting world of this API. Since it is very versatile, it can be applied in many other scenarios. For example, you might use it to update a file listing in a GUI display or to detect the modification of configuration files that could then be reloaded.

■ ■ ■

CHAPTER 7

Random Access Files

In previous chapters we have explored files sequentially. Files that can be explored sequentially are known as *sequential files*. In this chapter you will see the advantages of using nonsequential (random) access to a file's contents. Files that permit random access to their contents are known as *random access files (RAFs)*. Sequential files are used more often because they are easy to create, but RAFs are more flexible and their data can be located faster.

With a RAF, you can open the file, seek a particular location, and read from or write to that file. After you open a RAF, you can read from it or write to it in a random manner just by using a record number, or you can add to the beginning or end of the file since you know how many records are in the file. A RAF allows you to read a single character, read a chunk of bytes or a line, replace a portion of the file, append lines, delete lines, and so forth, and allows you to perform all of these actions in a random manner.

Java 7 (NIO.2) introduces a brand-new interface for working with RAFs. Its name is `SeekableByteChannel` and it is available in the `java.nio.channels` package. It extends the older `ByteChannel` interface and represents a byte channel that maintains a current position and allows that position to be modified. Moreover, Java 7 improves the well-known `FileChannel` class by implementing this interface and providing RAF and `FileChannel` power in a single shot. With a simple cast we can transform a `SeekableByteChannel` into a `FileChannel`.

This chapter uses the `java.nio.ByteBuffer` class extensively, so we will start with a short overview of it. We will continue by detailing the `SeekableByteChannel` interface with applications that will read and write files randomly to accomplish different types of common tasks. You will then see how to get a `FileChannel` with RAF capabilities and explore the main facilities provided by `FileChannel`, such as mapping a region of the file directly into memory for faster access, locking a region of the file, and reading and writing bytes from an absolute location without affecting the channel's current position. The chapter ends with a benchmarking application that will help you to determine the fastest way to copy a file using `FileChannel` capabilities versus other common approaches, like `Files.copy()`, buffered streams, and so on.

Brief Overview of ByteBuffer

A buffer is essentially an array (usually of bytes, but other kinds of arrays can be used—the `Buffer` interface offers `ByteBuffer`, `CharBuffer`, `IntBuffer`, `ShortBuffer`, `LongBuffer`, `FloatBuffer`, and `DoubleBuffer`) that holds some data to be written or that was just read.

The two most important components of buffers in NIO are properties and ancestor methods, as discussed next in turn.

ByteBuffer Properties

The following are the essential properties of a buffer:

- *Limit*: When writing from a buffer, the limit specifies how much data remains to get. When you are reading into a buffer, the limit specifies how much room remains to put data into.

- *Position*: The position keeps track of how much data you have read or written. It specifies into which or from which array element the next byte will go or come. A buffer's position is never negative and is never greater than its limit.

- *Capacity*: The capacity specifies the maximum amount of data that can be stored in a buffer. The limit can never be larger than the capacity.

■ **Note** As an invariant, these three properties respect the following relationship: $0 \leq$ position $\leq$ limit $\leq$ capacity.

As an example, suppose a buffer has a 6-byte capacity, as represented in Figure 7-1.

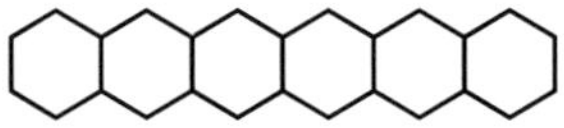

Figure 7-1. Java buffer representation (a)

At the starting point, the limit and capacity are equal (the limit cannot be larger than the capacity, but the converse is perfectly normal) and are set to a virtual slot (in our case, slot number 7), as shown in Figure 7-2.

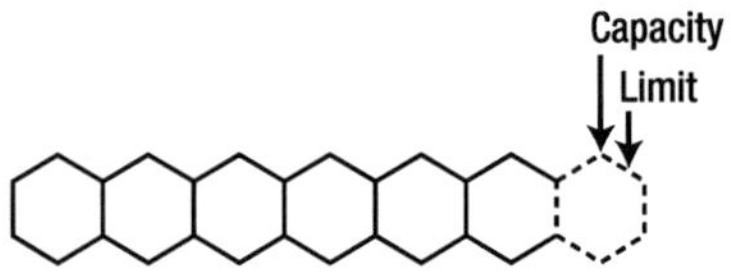

Figure 7-2. Java buffer representation (b)

■ **Note** In some cases, the initial limit may be 0, or it may be some other value, depending on the type of the buffer and the manner in which it is constructed.

Also, at the starting point the position is set to 0 (slot 1, as shown in Figure 7-3)—a read or write byte will access position 0.

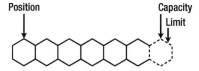

Figure 7-3. *Java buffer representation (c)*

Next, suppose that we read 2 bytes of data into our buffer. The 2 bytes of data go into the buffer starting at position 0. Therefore, the first 2 bytes are filled and the position goes to the third byte, as shown in Figure 7-4.

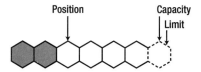

Figure 7-4. *Java buffer representation (d)*

Continuing with a second read, another 3 bytes go into the buffer. The position is increased to 5 (slot 6), as you can see in Figure 7-5.

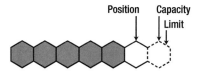

Figure 7-5. *Java buffer representation (e)*

At this point, suppose that we are not reading into the buffer anymore and want to write from the buffer. To do this, we first need to call the `flip()` method before we write any bytes. This will set the limit to the current position, and set the position to 0. After the flip, the buffer appears as shown in Figure 7-6.

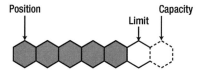

Figure 7-6. *Java buffer representation (f)*

Suppose we write 3 bytes from the buffer. Since the position is 0, the first 3 bytes are written and the position moves to 3 (slot 4), as shown in Figure 7-7. The limit and capacity remain unchanged.

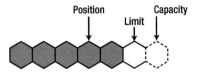

Figure 7-7. Java buffer representation (g)

Next, we write 2 more bytes, and the position moves forward to slot 6, as shown in Figure 7-8; the limit and capacity remain unchanged.

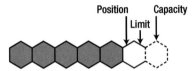

Figure 7-8. Java buffer representation (h)

There are two additional operations we may want to accomplish. Continuing with Figure 7-8 as a reference, we may want to rewind the buffer or clear the buffer. Rewinding the buffer (calling the `rewind()` method) will prepare the buffer for re-reading the data that it already contains—the limit remains unchanged and the position is set to 0. Clearing the buffer (calling the `clear()` method) will reset the buffer for receiving more bytes (the data is not deleted)—the limit is set to the capacity and the position is set to 0. Figure 7-9 shows the effect of the `clear()`method, and Figure 7-10 shows the effect of the `rewind()` method.

Figure 7-9. Java buffer representation (i)

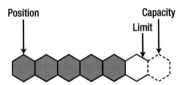

Figure 7-10. Java buffer representation (j)

In addition, a buffer holds a *mark*. This is the index to which its position will be reset when the `reset()` method is invoked. The mark is not always defined, but it is never negative and is never greater than the position. If the mark is defined, then it is discarded when the position or the limit is adjusted to a value smaller than the mark. If the mark is not defined, then invoking the `reset()` method causes an `InvalidMarkException` to be thrown.

■ **Note** Inserting the mark into the relationship results in the following: 0 ≤ mark ≤ position ≤ limit ≤ capacity.

ByteBuffer Ancestor Methods

ByteBuffer provides a set of get() and put() methods for accessing data. Since they are pretty intuitive, I will simply list them here. For more details, consult the official documentation at http://download.oracle.com/javase/7/docs/api/index.html and http://download.oracle.com/javase/7/docs/index.html.

```
public abstract byte get()
public ByteBuffer get(byte[] dst)
public ByteBuffer get(byte[] dst, int offset, int length)
public abstract byte get(int index)

public abstract ByteBuffer put(byte b)
public final ByteBuffer put(byte[] src)
public ByteBuffer put(byte[] src, int offset, int length)
public ByteBuffer put(ByteBuffer src)
public abstract ByteBuffer put(int index, byte b)
```

In addition to the get() and put() methods, ByteBuffer also has extra methods for reading and writing values of different types, as follows:

```
public abstract char getChar()
public abstract char getChar(int index)
public abstract double getDouble()
public abstract double getDouble(int index)
public abstract float getFloat()
public abstract float getFloat(int index)
public abstract int getInt()
public abstract int getInt(int index)
public abstract long getLong()
public abstract long getLong(int index)
public abstract short getShort()
public abstract short getShort(int index)

public abstract ByteBuffer putChar(char value)
public abstract ByteBuffer putChar(int index, char value)
public abstract ByteBuffer putDouble(double value)
public abstract ByteBuffer putDouble(int index, double value)
public abstract ByteBuffer putFloat(float value)
public abstract ByteBuffer putFloat(int index, float value)
public abstract ByteBuffer putInt(int value)
public abstract ByteBuffer putInt(int index, int value)
public abstract ByteBuffer putLong(int index, long value)
public abstract ByteBuffer putLong(long value)
public abstract ByteBuffer putShort(int index, short value)
public abstract ByteBuffer putShort(short value)
```

A byte buffer can be direct or non-direct. The JVM will perform native I/O operations on direct buffers. Direct buffers are created by using the `allocateDirect()` method, while non-direct buffers are created by using the `allocate()` method.

At this point you have sufficient information about `ByteBuffer` to understand the following applications. (To get deeper into the bowels of `ByteBuffer`, access dedicated tutorials on the Web.) Therefore, we leave behind `ByteBuffer` for the moment and proceed to the main topic of this chapter, the `SeekableByteChannel` interface. The next section will introduce you to channels and relate them with buffers.

Brief Overview of Channels

In a *stream-oriented I/O* system, an input stream produces 1 byte of data and an output stream consumes 1 byte of data—such a system is often rather slow. By contrast, in a *block-oriented I/O* system, the input/output stream produces or consumes a block of data in one step.

Channels are analogous to streams, but with a few differences:

- While streams are typically one-way (read or write), channels support read and write.

- Channels can be read and written asynchronously.

- Channels always read to, or write from, a buffer. All data that is sent to a channel must first be placed in a buffer. Any data that is read from a channel is read into a buffer.

Using the SeekableByteChannel Interface for Random Access to Files

The new `SeekableByteChannel` interface provides support for RAF by implementing the notion of position over channels. We can read or write a `ByteBuffer` from or to a channel, get or set the current position, and truncate an entity connected to a channel to a specified dimension. The following methods are associated with these features (more details are available in the official documentation at `http://download.oracle.com/javase/7/docs/api/index.html`):

- `position()`: Returns the channel's current position (non-negative).

- `position(long)`: Sets the channel's position to the specified `long` (non-negative). Setting the position to a value that is greater than the current size is legal but does not change the size of the entity.

- `truncate(long)`: Truncates the entity connected to the channel to the specified `long`.

- `read(ByteBuffer)`: Reads bytes into the buffer from the channel.

- `write(ByteBuffer)`: Writes bytes from the buffer to the channel.

- `size()`: Returns the current size of entity to which this channel is connected.

Getting an instance of `SeekableByteChannel` can be accomplished through two methods of the `Files` class, named `newByteChannel()`. The first (simplest) `newByteChannel()` method receives the path to the file to open or create and a set of options specifying how the file is opened. The `StandardOpenOption` enum constants were described in the Chapter 4 section "Using Standard Open Options," but they are repeated here for easy reference:

READ	Opens file for read access
WRITE	Opens file for write access
CREATE	Creates a new file if it does not exist
CREATE_NEW	Creates a new file, failing with an exception if the file already exists
APPPEND	Appends data to the end of the file (used with WRITE and CREATE)
DELETE_ON_CLOSE	Deletes the file when the stream is closed (used for deleting temporary files)
TRUNCATE_EXISTING	Truncates the file to 0 bytes (used with the WRITE option)
SPARSE	Causes the newly created file to be sparse
SYNC	Keeps the file content and metadata synchronized with the underlying storage device
DSYNC	Keeps the file content synchronized with the underlying storage device

The second `newByteChannel()` method receives the path to the file to open or create, a set of options specifying how the file is opened, and, optionally, a list of file attributes to set atomically when the file is created.

Both of these methods open or create a file, returning a `SeekableByteChannel` to access the file.

Reading a File with SeekableByteChannel

Focusing on the first `newByteChannel()` method, we get a `SeekableByteChannel` for reading the path `C:\rafaelnadal\grandslam\RolandGarros\story.txt` (the file must exist):

```
...
Path path = Paths.get("C:/rafaelnadal/grandslam/RolandGarros", "story.txt");
...
try (SeekableByteChannel seekableByteChannel = Files.newByteChannel(path,
                                          EnumSet.of(StandardOpenOption.READ)))
{
```

```
...
} catch (IOException ex) {
   System.err.println(ex);
}
```

As an example, the following application will read and display the content of story.txt using a ByteBuffer (the file must exist). I chose a buffer of 12 bytes, but feel free to use any other size.

```java
import java.io.IOException;
import java.nio.ByteBuffer;
import java.nio.channels.SeekableByteChannel;
import java.nio.charset.Charset;
import java.nio.file.Files;
import java.nio.file.Path;
import java.nio.file.Paths;
import java.util.EnumSet;
import java.nio.file.StandardOpenOption;

public class Main {

 public static void main(String[] args) {

  Path path = Paths.get("C:/rafaelnadal/grandslam/RolandGarros", "story.txt");

  //read a file using SeekableByteChannel
  try (SeekableByteChannel seekableByteChannel = Files.newByteChannel(path,
                                      EnumSet.of(StandardOpenOption.READ))) {

   ByteBuffer buffer = ByteBuffer.allocate(12);
   String encoding = System.getProperty("file.encoding");
   buffer.clear();

   while (seekableByteChannel.read(buffer) > 0) {
        buffer.flip();
        System.out.print(Charset.forName(encoding).decode(buffer));
        buffer.clear();
   }
  } catch (IOException ex) {
    System.err.println(ex);
  }
 }
}
```

The output should be similar to the following:

Rafa Nadal produced another masterclass of clay-court tennis to win his fifth French Open title ...

Writing a File with SeekableByteChannel

Writing a file with SeekableByteChannel involves using the WRITE option. In addition, if we want to clean up the existing content before writing, we can add the TRUNCATE_EXISTING option as follows. Here we truncate story.txt and prepare it for writing (the story.txt file must exist).

```
...
Path path = Paths.get("C:/rafaelnadal/grandslam/RolandGarros", "story.txt");
...
try (SeekableByteChannel seekableByteChannel = Files.newByteChannel(path,
                EnumSet.of(StandardOpenOption.WRITE, StandardOpenOption.TRUNCATE_EXISTING))) {
...
} catch (IOException ex) {
    System.err.println(ex);
}
```

As an example, the following application will truncate and write some text in story.txt using a ByteBuffer (in this case the file already exists; if it did not exist, then we would add CREATE or CREATE_NEW and WRITE options and take out the TRUNCATE_EXISTING option since the file is empty anyway):

```
import java.io.IOException;
import java.nio.ByteBuffer;
import java.nio.channels.SeekableByteChannel;
import java.nio.file.Files;
import java.nio.file.Path;
import java.nio.file.Paths;
import java.nio.file.StandardOpenOption;
import java.util.EnumSet;

public class Main {

 public static void main(String[] args) {

    Path path = Paths.get("C:/rafaelnadal/grandslam/RolandGarros", "story.txt");

    //write a file using SeekableByteChannel
    try (SeekableByteChannel seekableByteChannel = Files.newByteChannel(path,
                EnumSet.of(StandardOpenOption.WRITE, StandardOpenOption.TRUNCATE_EXISTING))) {

    ByteBuffer buffer = ByteBuffer.wrap("Rafa Nadal produced another masterclass of clay-court
                              tennis to win his fifth French Open title ...".getBytes());

    int write = seekableByteChannel.write(buffer);
    System.out.println("Number of written bytes: " + write);

    buffer.clear();
    } catch (IOException ex) {
     System.err.println(ex);
    }
 }
}
```

When you write a file, there a few common cases that involve combining the open options:

- To write into a file that exists, at the beginning, use `WRITE`

- To write into a file that exists, at the end, use `WRITE` and `APPEND`

- To write into a file that exists and clean up its content before writing, use `WRITE` and `TRUNCATE_EXISTING`

- To write into a file that does not exist, use `CREATE` (or `CREATE_NEW`) and `WRITE`

SeekableByteChannel and File Attributes

The following code snippet (written for Unix and other POSIX file systems) creates a file with a specific set of file permissions. This code creates the file email.txt in the home\rafaelnadal\email directory or appends to it if it already exists. The email.txt file is created with read and write permissions for the owner and read-only permissions for the group.

```java
import java.io.IOException;
import java.nio.ByteBuffer;
import java.nio.channels.SeekableByteChannel;
import java.nio.file.Files;
import java.nio.file.Path;
import java.nio.file.Paths;
import java.nio.file.StandardOpenOption;
import java.nio.file.attribute.FileAttribute;
import java.nio.file.attribute.PosixFilePermission;
import java.nio.file.attribute.PosixFilePermissions;
import java.util.EnumSet;
import java.util.Set;

public class Main {

  public static void main(String[] args) {

    Path path = Paths.get("home/rafaelnadal/email", "email.txt");
    ByteBuffer buffer = ByteBuffer.wrap("Hi Rafa, I want to congratulate you for the amazing
                                        match that you played ... ".getBytes());

    //create the custom permissions attribute for the email.txt file
    Set<PosixFilePermission> perms = PosixFilePermissions.fromString("rw-r------");
    FileAttribute<Set<PosixFilePermission>> attr = PosixFilePermissions.asFileAttribute(perms);

    //write a file using SeekableByteChannel
    try (SeekableByteChannel seekableByteChannel = Files.newByteChannel(path,
                EnumSet.of(StandardOpenOption.CREATE, StandardOpenOption.APPEND), attr)) {

      int write = seekableByteChannel.write(buffer);
      System.out.println("Number of written bytes: " + write);

    } catch (IOException ex) {
      System.err.println(ex);
```

```
    }
  buffer.clear();
  }
}
```

Reading a File with the Old ReadableByteChannel Interface

The new SeekableByteChannel interface is based on the old interfaces ReadableByteChannel (represents a channel that reads bytes; only one thread can read at a time) and WritableByteChannel (represents a channel that writes bytes; only one thread can write at a time) that have been available in NIO since JDK 1.4. These two interfaces are super interfaces for SeekableByteChannel. Thanks to this relationship between them, we can use the old ReadableByteChannel interface with the new Files.newByteChannel() method as follows, in which we read the content of the existing story.txt file:

```java
import java.io.IOException;
import java.nio.ByteBuffer;
import java.nio.channels.ReadableByteChannel;
import java.nio.charset.Charset;
import java.nio.file.Files;
import java.nio.file.Path;
import java.nio.file.Paths;

public class Main {

  public static void main(String[] args) {

    Path path = Paths.get("C:/rafaelnadal/grandslam/RolandGarros", "story.txt");

    //read a file using ReadableByteChannel
    try (ReadableByteChannel readableByteChannel = Files.newByteChannel(path)) {

      ByteBuffer buffer = ByteBuffer.allocate(12);
      buffer.clear();

      String encoding = System.getProperty("file.encoding");

      while (readableByteChannel.read(buffer) > 0) {
            buffer.flip();
            System.out.print(Charset.forName(encoding).decode(buffer));
            buffer.clear();
      }
    } catch (IOException ex) {
       System.err.println(ex);
    }
  }
}
```

As you can see, there is no need to specify the READ option.

Writing a File with the Old WritableByteChannel Interface

We can also combine the old `WritableByteChannel` interface with the new `Files.newByteChannel()` method as follows, in which we append some text into `story.txt`:

```java
import java.io.IOException;
import java.nio.ByteBuffer;
import java.nio.channels.WritableByteChannel;
import java.nio.file.Files;
import java.nio.file.Path;
import java.nio.file.Paths;
import java.nio.file.StandardOpenOption;
import java.util.EnumSet;
public class Main {

public static void main(String[] args) {

 Path path = Paths.get("C:/rafaelnadal/grandslam/RolandGarros", "story.txt");

 //write a file using WritableByteChannel
 try (WritableByteChannel writableByteChannel = Files.newByteChannel(path,
                       EnumSet.of(StandardOpenOption.WRITE, StandardOpenOption.APPEND))) {

  ByteBuffer buffer = ByteBuffer.wrap("Vamos Rafa!".getBytes());

  int write = writableByteChannel.write(buffer);
  System.out.println("Number of written bytes: " + write);

  buffer.clear();

 } catch (IOException ex) {
   System.err.println(ex);
 }
}
}
```

Even if we use a `WritableByteChannel`, we still need to explicitly specify the `WRITE` option. The `APPEND` option is optional, and is specific to the preceding example.

Playing with SeekableByteChannel Position

Now that you know how to read and write an entire file with `SeekableByteChannel`, you are ready to discover how you can do the same operations but at a specified channel (entity) position. For this, we will exploit the `position()` and `position(long)` methods in a suite of four examples meant to familiarize you with the RAF concept. Keep in mind that the `position()` method without arguments returns the current channel (entity) position, while the `position(long)` method sets the current position in the channel (entity) by counting the number of bytes from the beginning of it. The first position is 0 and the last valid position is the channel (entity) size.

Example 1: Read One Character from Different Positions

We start with a simple example that reads exactly one character from a text file from the first, middle, and last positions. The file is MovistarOpen.txt and it is located in the C:\rafaelnadal\tournaments\2009 directory.

```java
import java.io.IOException;
import java.nio.ByteBuffer;
import java.nio.channels.SeekableByteChannel;
import java.nio.charset.Charset;
import java.nio.file.Files;
import java.nio.file.Path;
import java.nio.file.Paths;
import java.nio.file.StandardOpenOption;
import java.util.EnumSet;

public class Main {

 public static void main(String[] args) {

  Path path = Paths.get("C:/rafaelnadal/tournaments/2009", "MovistarOpen.txt");
  ByteBuffer buffer = ByteBuffer.allocate(1);
  String encoding = System.getProperty("file.encoding");

  try (SeekableByteChannel seekableByteChannel = (Files.newByteChannel(path,
                                          EnumSet.of(StandardOpenOption.READ)))) {

   //the initial position should be 0 anyway
   seekableByteChannel.position(0);

   System.out.println("Reading one character from position: " +
                                             seekableByteChannel.position());
   seekableByteChannel.read(buffer);
   buffer.flip();
   System.out.print(Charset.forName(encoding).decode(buffer));
   buffer.rewind();

   //get into the middle
   seekableByteChannel.position(seekableByteChannel.size()/2);

   System.out.println("\nReading one character from position: " +
                                             seekableByteChannel.position());
   seekableByteChannel.read(buffer);
   buffer.flip();
   System.out.print(Charset.forName(encoding).decode(buffer));
   buffer.rewind();

   //get to the end
   seekableByteChannel.position(seekableByteChannel.size()-1);

   System.out.println("\nReading one character from position: " +
                                             seekableByteChannel.position());
```

```
    seekableByteChannel.read(buffer);
    buffer.flip();
    System.out.print(Charset.forName(encoding).decode(buffer));
    buffer.clear();

  } catch (IOException ex) {
   System.err.println(ex);
  }
 }
}
```

The preceding application will produce the following output:

```
Reading one character from position: 0

T

Reading one character from position: 181

n

Reading one character from position: 361


.
```

Example 2: Write Characters at Different Positions

Next, we will try to write to a specific position. Suppose that the MovistarOpen.txt file has the following default content:

The Movistar Open moved to Santiago from Viña del Mar in 2010. It is the first clay-court tournament of the ATP World Tour season and also the opening leg of the four-tournament swing through Latin America, aptly coined the "Golden Swing" in honour of top Chileans and Olympic Gold medalists Fernando Gonsales and Nicolas Massu. Gonzalez is a four-time champion.

We want to accomplish two tasks: first, add some text at the end of the preceding text, and second, replace "Gonsales" with "Gonzalez" because Fernando's last name was misspelled in the first instance. Here is the application:

```
import java.io.IOException;
import java.nio.ByteBuffer;
import java.nio.channels.SeekableByteChannel;
import java.nio.file.Files;
import java.nio.file.Path;
import java.nio.file.Paths;
import java.nio.file.StandardOpenOption;
import java.util.EnumSet;

public class Main {
```

```
public static void main(String[] args) {

  Path path = Paths.get("C:/rafaelnadal/tournaments/2009", "MovistarOpen.txt");
  ByteBuffer buffer_1 = ByteBuffer.wrap("Great players participate in our tournament, like:
              Tommy Robredo, Fernando Gonzalez, Jose Acasuso or Thomaz Bellucci.".getBytes());
  ByteBuffer buffer_2 = ByteBuffer.wrap("Gonzalez".getBytes());

  try (SeekableByteChannel seekableByteChannel = (Files.newByteChannel(path,
                                      EnumSet.of(StandardOpenOption.WRITE)))) {

    //append some text at the end
    seekableByteChannel.position(seekableByteChannel.size());

    while (buffer_1.hasRemaining()) {
          seekableByteChannel.write(buffer_1);
    }

    //replace "Gonsales" with "Gonzalez"
    seekableByteChannel.position(301);

    while (buffer_2.hasRemaining()) {
          seekableByteChannel.write(buffer_2);
    }

    buffer_1.clear();
    buffer_2.clear();

  } catch (IOException ex) {
    System.err.println(ex);
  }
 }
}
```

If everything worked fine, the new `MovistarOpen.txt` content should be as follows:

```
The Movistar Open moved to Santiago from Viña del Mar in 2010. It is the first clay-court
tournament of the ATP World Tour season and also the opening leg of the four-tournament swing
through Latin America, aptly coined the "Golden Swing" in honour of top Chileans and Olympic
Gold medalists Fernando Gonzalez and Nicolas Massu. Gonzalez is a four-time champion. Great
players participate in our tournament, like: Tommy Robredo, Fernando Gonzalez, Jose Acasuso or
Thomaz Bellucci.
```

Example 3: Copy a Portion of a File from the Beginning to the End

Moving on to a new application, we next want to copy a portion of text from the beginning of a file to the end of the same file. As an example, we'll use the `HeinekenOpen.txt` file (located in the `C:\rafaelnadal\tournaments\2009` directory), which has the following content:

```
The Pride Of New Zealand
The Heineken Open is the biggest men's professional sporting event in New Zealand, held in...
```

We want to copy the text "The Pride of New Zealand" at the end, like this:

```
The Pride Of New Zealand
The Heineken Open is the biggest men's professional sporting event in New Zealand, held in...
The Pride Of New Zealand
```

The following application accomplishes this task:

```java
import java.io.IOException;
import java.nio.ByteBuffer;
import java.nio.channels.SeekableByteChannel;
import java.nio.file.Files;
import java.nio.file.Path;
import java.nio.file.Paths;
import java.nio.file.StandardOpenOption;
import java.util.EnumSet;

public class Main {

 public static void main(String[] args) {

  Path path = Paths.get("C:/rafaelnadal/tournaments/2009", "HeinekenOpen.txt");

  ByteBuffer copy = ByteBuffer.allocate(25);
  copy.put("\n".getBytes());

  try (SeekableByteChannel seekableByteChannel = (Files.newByteChannel(path,
                          EnumSet.of(StandardOpenOption.READ, StandardOpenOption.WRITE)))) {

   int nbytes;
   do {
      nbytes = seekableByteChannel.read(copy);
   } while (nbytes != -1 && copy.hasRemaining());

   copy.flip();

   seekableByteChannel.position(seekableByteChannel.size());
   while (copy.hasRemaining()) {
        seekableByteChannel.write(copy);
   }

   copy.clear();

  } catch (IOException ex) {
    System.err.println(ex);
  }
 }
}
```

Example 4: Replace a File Portion with Truncate Capability

In this example we will truncate a file and append new text in place of the truncated text. We will use the BrasilOpen.txt file (found in the C:\rafaelnadal\tournaments\2009 directory), which has the following content:

Brasil Open At Forefront Of Green Movement
The Brasil Open, the second stop of the four-tournament Latin American swing, is held in an area renowned for its lush natural beauty and stunning beaches. From this point forward ...

We want to truncate the file content to remove the text "From this point forward ..." and append new text in its place. Here is the solution:

```java
import java.io.IOException;
import java.nio.ByteBuffer;
import java.nio.channels.SeekableByteChannel;
import java.nio.file.Files;
import java.nio.file.Path;
import java.nio.file.Paths;
import java.nio.file.StandardOpenOption;
import java.util.EnumSet;

public class Main {

 public static void main(String[] args) {

  Path path = Paths.get("C:/rafaelnadal/tournaments/2009", "BrasilOpen.txt");

  ByteBuffer buffer = ByteBuffer.wrap("The tournament has taken a lead in environmental
conservation efforts, with highlights including the planting of 500 trees to neutralise carbon
emissions and providing recyclable materials to local children for use in craft
work.".getBytes());

  try (SeekableByteChannel seekableByteChannel = (Files.newByteChannel(path,
                            EnumSet.of(StandardOpenOption.READ, StandardOpenOption.WRITE)))) {

   seekableByteChannel.truncate(200);

   seekableByteChannel.position(seekableByteChannel.size()-1);
   while (buffer.hasRemaining()) {
        seekableByteChannel.write(buffer);
   }

   buffer.clear();

  } catch (IOException ex) {
    System.err.println(ex);
  }
 }
}
```

The effect of this application is the following modification of the BrasilOpen.txt file:

Brasil Open At Forefront Of Green Movement
The Brasil Open, the second stop of the four-tournament Latin American swing, is held in an
area renowned for its lush natural beauty and stunning beaches. The tournament has taken a
lead in environmental conservation efforts, with highlights including the planting of 500
trees to neutralise carbon emissions and providing recyclable materials to local children for
use in craft work.

This suite of examples should help you to understand how to randomly access file content. Next, we are going to cast the SeekableByteChannel interface to FileChannel to give us access to more advanced features.

Working with FileChannel

FileChannel was introduced in Java 4, but recently it was updated to implement the new SeekableByteChannel interface, combining their forces to achieve more power. SeekableByteChannel provides the random access file feature, while FileChannel offers great advanced features such as mapping a region of the file directly into memory for faster access and locking a region of the file.

Getting a FileChannel for a Path can be accomplished with the two new FileChannel.open() methods. Both methods are able to open or create a file for the given Path and return a new channel. The first (simplest) method receives the path of the file to open or create and a set of options specifying how the file is opened. The second method receives the path of the file to open or create, a set of options specifying how the file is opened, and, optionally, a list of file attributes to set atomically when the file is created.

For example, the following code gets for the specified path a file channel with read/write capabilities:

```
Path path = Paths.get("…");
…
try (FileChannel fileChannel = (FileChannel.open(path, EnumSet.of(
                                StandardOpenOption.READ, StandardOpenOption.WRITE)))) {
…
} catch (IOException ex) {
  System.err.println(ex);
}
```

Explicitly casting a SeekableByteChannel to a FileChannel can be an alternative to the preceding code:

```
Path path = Paths.get("…");
…
try (FileChannel fileChannel = (FileChannel)(Files.newByteChannel(path,
                        EnumSet.of(StandardOpenOption.READ, StandardOpenOption.WRITE))))
{
…
} catch (IOException ex) {
  System.err.println(ex);
}
```

Now, the fileChannel instance has access to the methods provided by SeekableByteChannel and FileChannel.

Mapping a Channel's File Region Directly into Memory

One of the great FileChannel facilities is the capability to map a region of a channel's file directly into memory. This is possible thanks to the FileChannel.map() method, which gets the following three arguments:

- **mode**: Mapping a region into memory can be accomplished in one of three modes: MapMode.READ_ONLY (*read-only* mapping; writing attempts will throw ReadOnlyBufferException), MapMode.READ_WRITE (*read/write* mapping; changes in the resulting buffer can be propagated to the file and can be visible from other programs that map the same file), or MapMode.PRIVATE (*copy-on-write* mapping; changes in the resulting buffer can't be propagated to the file and aren't visible from other programs).

- **position**: The mapped region starts at the indicated position within the file (non-negative).

- **size**: Indicates the size of the mapped region (0 ≤ size ≤ Integer.MAX_VALUE).

▦ **Note** Only channels opened for reading can be mapped as read-only, and only channels opened for reading and writing can be mapped as read/write or private.

The map() method will return a MappedByteBuffer that actually represents the extracted region. This extends the ByteBuffer with the following three methods, more details of which you can find in the official documentation at http://download.oracle.com/javase/7/docs/api/index.html:

- **force()**: Forces the changed over buffer to be propagated to the originating file

- **load()**: Loads the buffer content into physical memory

- **isLoaded()**: Verifies whether the buffer content is in physical memory

The next application gets a new channel for the file BrasilOpen.txt (located in C:\rafaelnadal\tournaments\2009) and maps its entire content into a byte buffer in READ_ONLY mode. To test if the operation completes successfully, the following is a printout of the byte buffer content:

```
import java.io.IOException;
import java.nio.CharBuffer;
import java.nio.MappedByteBuffer;
import java.nio.channels.FileChannel;
import java.nio.charset.CharacterCodingException;
import java.nio.charset.Charset;
import java.nio.charset.CharsetDecoder;
import java.nio.file.Path;
import java.nio.file.Paths;
import java.nio.file.StandardOpenOption;
import java.util.EnumSet;

public class Main {
```

```java
public static void main(String[] args) {

    Path path = Paths.get("C:/rafaelnadal/tournaments/2009", "BrasilOpen.txt");
    MappedByteBuffer buffer = null;

    try (FileChannel fileChannel = (FileChannel.open(path,
                                            EnumSet.of(StandardOpenOption.READ)))) {

        buffer = fileChannel.map(FileChannel.MapMode.READ_ONLY, 0, fileChannel.size());

    } catch (IOException ex) {
        System.err.println(ex);
    }

    if (buffer != null) {
        try {
            Charset charset = Charset.defaultCharset();
            CharsetDecoder decoder = charset.newDecoder();
            CharBuffer charBuffer = decoder.decode(buffer);
            String content = charBuffer.toString();
            System.out.println(content);

            buffer.clear();
        } catch (CharacterCodingException ex) {
            System.err.println(ex);
        }
    }
}
```

If everything worked fine, you should see the `BrasilOpen.txt` content output to the console.

Locking a Channel's File

File locking is a mechanism that restricts access to a file or other piece of data to ensure that two or more users can't modify the same file simultaneously. This prevent the classic *interceding update* scenario. Usually the file is locked when the first user accesses it and stays locked (can be read, but not modified) until that user is finished with the file.

The exact behavior of file locking is platform dependent. On some platforms, file locking is advisory (any application can access the file if the application does not check for a file lock), while on others it is mandatory (file locking prevents any application from accessing a file).

We can take advantage of file locking in Java applications through the NIO API. However, there is no guarantee that the file locking mechanism will always work as you expect. Underlying OS support or, sometimes, a faulty implementation may affect the expected behavior. Keep in mind the following:

- "File locks are held on behalf of the entire Java virtual machine. They are not suitable for controlling access to a file by multiple threads within the same virtual machine." (Java Platform SE 7 official documentation, http://download.oracle.com/javase/7/docs/api/java/nio/channels/FileLock.html .)

- Windows takes care of locking directories and other structures for you, so a delete, rename, or write operation will fail if another process has the file open. Therefore, creating a Java lock over a system lock will fail.

- The Linux kernel manages a set of functions known as *advisory locking mechanisms*. In addition, you can enforce locking at the kernel level with mandatory locks. Therefore, when using Java locks, keep in mind this aspect.

The FileChannel class provides four methods for file locking: two lock() methods and two tryLock() methods. The lock() methods block the application until the desired lock can be retrieved, while the tryLock() methods do not block the application and return null or throw an exception if the file is already locked. There is one lock()/tryLock() method for retrieving an exclusive lock on this channel's file and one for retrieving a lock over a region of the channel's file—this method also allows a lock to be shared.

To demonstrate file locking, we'll look at two applications. The first one locks a file named vamos.txt (under C:\rafaelnadal\email) for 2 minutes while writing some text into it. The second application will attempt to write to the same file during this time. If the file was successfully locked for 2 minutes, then the second application will throw a java.io.IO.Exception and output a message like the following:

```
The process cannot access the file because another process has locked a portion of the file.
```

Here is the first application:

```
import java.io.IOException;
import java.nio.ByteBuffer;
import java.nio.channels.FileChannel;
import java.nio.channels.FileLock;
import java.nio.file.Path;
import java.nio.file.Paths;
import java.nio.file.StandardOpenOption;
import java.util.EnumSet;

public class Main {

 public static void main(String[] args) {

    Path path = Paths.get("C:/rafaelnadal/email", "vamos.txt");
    ByteBuffer buffer = ByteBuffer.wrap("Vamos Rafa!".getBytes());

    try (FileChannel fileChannel = (FileChannel.open(path, EnumSet.of(StandardOpenOption.READ,
                                                    StandardOpenOption.WRITE)))) {

      // Use the file channel to create a lock on the file.
      // This method blocks until it can retrieve the lock.
      FileLock lock = fileChannel.lock();

      // Try acquiring the lock without blocking. This method returns
      // null or throws an exception if the file is already locked.
      //try {
      //     lock = fileChannel.tryLock();
```

```
//} catch (OverlappingFileLockException e) {
    // File is already locked in this thread or virtual machine
//}

if (lock.isValid()) {

    System.out.println("Writing to a locked file ...");
    try {
        Thread.sleep(60000);
        } catch (InterruptedException ex) {
          System.err.println(ex);
        }
    fileChannel.position(0);
    fileChannel.write(buffer);
    try {
        Thread.sleep(60000);
    } catch (InterruptedException ex) {
      System.err.println(ex);
    }
}

// Release the lock
lock.release();

System.out.println("\nLock released!");

} catch (IOException ex) {
  System.err.println(ex);
}
}
}
```

Run the preceding application and, within a maximum of 2 minutes, start the following application in parallel:

```
import java.io.IOException;
import java.nio.ByteBuffer;
import java.nio.channels.FileChannel;
import java.nio.file.Path;
import java.nio.file.Paths;
import java.nio.file.StandardOpenOption;
import java.util.EnumSet;

public class Main {

 public static void main(String[] args) {

    Path path = Paths.get("C:/rafaelnadal/email", "vamos.txt");
    ByteBuffer buffer = ByteBuffer.wrap("Hai Hanescu !".getBytes());

    try (FileChannel fileChannel = (FileChannel.open(path, EnumSet.of(StandardOpenOption.READ,
                                            StandardOpenOption.WRITE)))) {
```

```
        fileChannel.position(0);
        fileChannel.write(buffer);

    } catch (IOException ex) {
        System.err.println(ex);
    }
  }
}
```

You should find that the second application can write into vamos.txt only after the lock is released, after 2 minutes.

Copying Files with FileChannel

FileChannel provides a few ways to copy a file. You can use FileChannel with a direct or non-direct ByteBuffer, use FileChannel.transferTo() or FileChannel.transferFrom(), or use FileChannel.map().

Copying Files with FileChannel and a Direct or Non-direct ByteBuffer

To copy files with FileChannel and a direct or non-direct ByteBuffer, we need one channel for the source file, one channel for the target file, and a direct or non-direct ByteBuffer. For example, the following snippet of code will copy the file Rafa Best Shots.mp4 (located in the C:\rafaelnadal\tournaments\2009\videos directory) to the C:\ root using a direct ByteBuffer of 4KB:

```
...
final Path copy_from = Paths.get("C:/rafaelnadal/tournaments/2009/
                                            videos/Rafa Best Shots.mp4");
final Path copy_to = Paths.get("C:/Rafa Best Shots.mp4");
int bufferSizeKB = 4;
int bufferSize = bufferSizeKB * 1024;
...
System.out.println("Using FileChannel and direct buffer ...");
try (FileChannel fileChannel_from = (FileChannel.open(copy_from,
                    EnumSet.of(StandardOpenOption.READ)));
    FileChannel fileChannel_to = (FileChannel.open(copy_to,
                    EnumSet.of(StandardOpenOption.CREATE_NEW, StandardOpenOption.WRITE)))) {

    // Allocate a direct ByteBuffer
    ByteBuffer bytebuffer = ByteBuffer.allocateDirect(bufferSize);

    // Read data from file into ByteBuffer
    int bytesCount;
    while ((bytesCount = fileChannel_from.read(bytebuffer)) > 0) {
            //flip the buffer which set the limit to current position, and position to 0
            bytebuffer.flip();
            //write data from ByteBuffer to file
            fileChannel_to.write(bytebuffer);
            //for the next read
            bytebuffer.clear();
```

```
    }
} catch (IOException ex) {
  System.err.println(ex);
}
…
```

To use a non-direct `ByteBuffer`, just replace the line

```
ByteBuffer bytebuffer = ByteBuffer.allocateDirect(bufferSize);
```

with the following line:

```
ByteBuffer bytebuffer = ByteBuffer.allocate(bufferSize);
```

Copying Files with FileChannel.transferTo() or FileChannel.transferFrom()

`FileChannel.transferTo()` transfers bytes from one channel's file to the given writable byte channel. You choose the position, the maximum number of bytes to be transferred, and the target channel, and `FileChannel.transferTo()` returns the number of transferred bytes. The following example transfers the entire content of `Rafa Best Shots.mp4`:

```
…
System.out.println("Using FileChannel.transferTo method ...");
try (FileChannel fileChannel_from = (FileChannel.open(copy_from,
                    EnumSet.of(StandardOpenOption.READ)));
    FileChannel fileChannel_to = (FileChannel.open(copy_to,
                    EnumSet.of(StandardOpenOption.CREATE_NEW, StandardOpenOption.WRITE)))) {

        fileChannel_from.transferTo(0L, fileChannel_from.size(), fileChannel_to);

} catch (IOException ex) {
  System.err.println(ex);
}
…
```

Alternatively, you can use `FileChannel.transferFrom()` to transfer bytes into this channel's file from the given readable byte channel. To do so, modify the preceding code by replacing the line

```
fileChannel_from.transferTo(0L, fileChannel_from.size(), fileChannel_to);
```

with the following line:

```
fileChannel_to.transferFrom(fileChannel_from, 0L, (int) fileChannel_from.size());
```

Copying Files with FileChannel.map()

Earlier in the chapter you saw how to map a region of the channel's files into memory using a `MappedByteBuffer`. In this section, we extrapolate that example to copy the `Rafa Best Shots.mp4` content:

```
…
System.out.println("Using FileChannel.map method ...");
try (FileChannel fileChannel_from = (FileChannel.open(copy_from,
```

```
                        EnumSet.of(StandardOpenOption.READ)));
        FileChannel fileChannel_to = (FileChannel.open(copy_to,
                        EnumSet.of(StandardOpenOption.CREATE_NEW, StandardOpenOption.WRITE)))) {

        MappedByteBuffer buffer = fileChannel_from.map(FileChannel.MapMode.READ_ONLY, 0,
                                                        fileChannel_from.size());

        fileChannel_to.write(buffer);
        buffer.clear();

} catch (IOException ex) {
  System.err.println(ex);
}
...
```

Benchmarking FileChannel Copy Capabilities

In the previous three sections you saw different ways to copy a file using FileChannel capabilities. Java also comes with another set of solutions for copying a file, including using the Files.copy() method or buffered/unbuffered streams and a byte array. Which one should you choose? This is a hard question, and its answer depends on many factors. This section focuses on one factor, speed, because completing a copy task quickly increases productivity and, in some situations, is critical to success. Thus, this section implements an application that compares how much time each of the following solutions takes for each copy:

- FileChannel and a non-direct ByteBuffer

- FileChannel and a direct ByteBuffer

- FileChannel.transferTo()

- FileChannel.transferFrom()

- FileChannel.map()

- Using buffered streams and a byte array

- Using unbuffered streams and a byte array

- Files.copy() (Path to Path, InputStream to Path, and Path to OutputStream)

The test was made under the following conditions:

- Copied file type: MP4 video (the file is named Rafa Best Shots.mp4 and is initially located in C:\rafaelnadal\tournaments\2009\videos)

- Copied file size: 58.3MB

- Buffer size tested: 4KB, 16KB, 32KB, 64KB, 128KB, 256KB, and 1024KB

- Machine: Mobile AMD Sempron Processor 3400 + 1.80 GHz, 1.00GB RAM, 32-bit OS, Windows 7 Ultimate

- Measurement type: Using the System.nanoTime() method

- Time was captured only after three ignored consecutive runs; the first three runs are ignored to achieve a trend. The first-time run is always slower than the subsequent runs.

The application is listed next and is available in the Source Code Download section of this book's page on Apress.com:

```java
import java.nio.MappedByteBuffer;
import java.io.OutputStream;
import java.io.InputStream;
import java.io.BufferedInputStream;
import java.io.BufferedOutputStream;
import java.io.File;
import java.io.FileInputStream;
import java.io.FileOutputStream;
import java.io.IOException;
import java.nio.ByteBuffer;
import java.nio.channels.FileChannel;
import java.nio.file.Files;
import java.nio.file.Path;
import java.nio.file.Paths;
import java.nio.file.StandardOpenOption;
import java.util.EnumSet;
import static java.nio.file.LinkOption.NOFOLLOW_LINKS;

public class Main {

 public static void deleteCopied(Path path){

  try {
      Files.deleteIfExists(path);
  } catch (IOException ex) {
    System.err.println(ex);
  }

 }

 public static void main(String[] args) {

 final Path copy_from = Paths.get("C:/rafaelnadal/tournaments/2009/videos/
                                              Rafa Best Shots.mp4");
 final Path copy_to = Paths.get("C:/Rafa Best Shots.mp4");
 long startTime, elapsedTime;
 int bufferSizeKB = 4; //also tested for 16, 32, 64, 128, 256 and 1024
 int bufferSize = bufferSizeKB * 1024;

 deleteCopied(copy_to);

 //FileChannel and non-direct buffer
 System.out.println("Using FileChannel and non-direct buffer ...");
 try (FileChannel fileChannel_from = (FileChannel.open(copy_from,
                     EnumSet.of(StandardOpenOption.READ)));
```

```java
        FileChannel fileChannel_to = (FileChannel.open(copy_to,
                        EnumSet.of(StandardOpenOption.CREATE_NEW, StandardOpenOption.WRITE)))) {

        startTime = System.nanoTime();

        // Allocate a non-direct ByteBuffer
        ByteBuffer bytebuffer = ByteBuffer.allocate(bufferSize);

        // Read data from file into ByteBuffer
        int bytesCount;
        while ((bytesCount = fileChannel_from.read(bytebuffer)) > 0) {
         //flip the buffer which set the limit to current position, and position to 0
         bytebuffer.flip();
         //write data from ByteBuffer to file
         fileChannel_to.write(bytebuffer);
         //for the next read
         bytebuffer.clear();
        }

        elapsedTime = System.nanoTime() - startTime;
        System.out.println("Elapsed Time is " + (elapsedTime / 1000000000.0) + " seconds");
} catch (IOException ex) {
  System.err.println(ex);
}

deleteCopied(copy_to);

//FileChannel and direct buffer
System.out.println("Using FileChannel and direct buffer ...");
try (FileChannel fileChannel_from = (FileChannel.open(copy_from,
                    EnumSet.of(StandardOpenOption.READ)));
     FileChannel fileChannel_to = (FileChannel.open(copy_to,
                    EnumSet.of(StandardOpenOption.CREATE_NEW, StandardOpenOption.WRITE)))) {

        startTime = System.nanoTime();

        // Allocate a direct ByteBuffer
        ByteBuffer bytebuffer = ByteBuffer.allocateDirect(bufferSize);

        // Read data from file into ByteBuffer
        int bytesCount;
        while ((bytesCount = fileChannel_from.read(bytebuffer)) > 0) {
         //flip the buffer which set the limit to current position, and position to 0
         bytebuffer.flip();
         //write data from ByteBuffer to file
         fileChannel_to.write(bytebuffer);
         //for the next read
         bytebuffer.clear();
        }

        elapsedTime = System.nanoTime() - startTime;
        System.out.println("Elapsed Time is " + (elapsedTime / 1000000000.0) + " seconds");
```

```java
    } catch (IOException ex) {
      System.err.println(ex);
    }

    deleteCopied(copy_to);

    //FileChannel.transferTo()
    System.out.println("Using FileChannel.transferTo method ...");
    try (FileChannel fileChannel_from = (FileChannel.open(copy_from,
                        EnumSet.of(StandardOpenOption.READ)));
        FileChannel fileChannel_to = (FileChannel.open(copy_to,
                        EnumSet.of(StandardOpenOption.CREATE_NEW, StandardOpenOption.WRITE)))) {

        startTime = System.nanoTime();

        fileChannel_from.transferTo(OL, fileChannel_from.size(), fileChannel_to);

        elapsedTime = System.nanoTime() - startTime;
        System.out.println("Elapsed Time is " + (elapsedTime / 1000000000.0) + " seconds");
    } catch (IOException ex) {
      System.err.println(ex);
    }

    deleteCopied(copy_to);

    //FileChannel.transferFrom()
    System.out.println("Using FileChannel.transferFrom method ...");
    try (FileChannel fileChannel_from = (FileChannel.open(copy_from,
                        EnumSet.of(StandardOpenOption.READ)));
        FileChannel fileChannel_to = (FileChannel.open(copy_to,
                        EnumSet.of(StandardOpenOption.CREATE_NEW, StandardOpenOption.WRITE)))) {

        startTime = System.nanoTime();

        fileChannel_to.transferFrom(fileChannel_from, OL, (int) fileChannel_from.size());

        elapsedTime = System.nanoTime() - startTime;
        System.out.println("Elapsed Time is " + (elapsedTime / 1000000000.0) + " seconds");
    } catch (IOException ex) {
      System.err.println(ex);
    }

    deleteCopied(copy_to);

    //FileChannel.map
    System.out.println("Using FileChannel.map method ...");
    try (FileChannel fileChannel_from = (FileChannel.open(copy_from,
                        EnumSet.of(StandardOpenOption.READ)));
        FileChannel fileChannel_to = (FileChannel.open(copy_to,
                        EnumSet.of(StandardOpenOption.CREATE_NEW, StandardOpenOption.WRITE)))) {

        startTime = System.nanoTime();
```

```java
        MappedByteBuffer buffer = fileChannel_from.map(FileChannel.MapMode.READ_ONLY,
                                                        0, fileChannel_from.size());

        fileChannel_to.write(buffer);
        buffer.clear();

        elapsedTime = System.nanoTime() - startTime;
        System.out.println("Elapsed Time is " + (elapsedTime / 1000000000.0) + " seconds");
} catch (IOException ex) {
    System.err.println(ex);
}

deleteCopied(copy_to);

//Buffered Stream I/O
System.out.println("Using buffered streams and byte array ...");
File inFileStr = copy_from.toFile();
File outFileStr = copy_to.toFile();
try (BufferedInputStream in = new BufferedInputStream(new FileInputStream(inFileStr));
     BufferedOutputStream out = new BufferedOutputStream(new FileOutputStream(outFileStr))) {

        startTime = System.nanoTime();

        byte[] byteArray = new byte[bufferSize];
        int bytesCount;
        while ((bytesCount = in.read(byteArray)) != -1) {
                out.write(byteArray, 0, bytesCount);
        }

        elapsedTime = System.nanoTime() - startTime;
        System.out.println("Elapsed Time is " + (elapsedTime / 1000000000.0) + " seconds");
} catch (IOException ex) {
    System.err.println(ex);
}

deleteCopied(copy_to);

System.out.println("Using un-buffered streams and byte array ...");
try (FileInputStream in = new FileInputStream(inFileStr);
     FileOutputStream out = new FileOutputStream(outFileStr)) {

        startTime = System.nanoTime();

        byte[] byteArray = new byte[bufferSize];
        int bytesCount;
        while ((bytesCount = in.read(byteArray)) != -1) {
                out.write(byteArray, 0, bytesCount);
        }

        elapsedTime = System.nanoTime() - startTime;
        System.out.println("Elapsed Time is " + (elapsedTime / 1000000000.0) + " seconds");
```

```
        } catch (IOException ex) {
          System.err.println(ex);
        }

        deleteCopied(copy_to);

        System.out.println("Using Files.copy (Path to Path) method ...");
        try {
            startTime = System.nanoTime();

            Files.copy(copy_from, copy_to, NOFOLLOW_LINKS);

            elapsedTime = System.nanoTime() - startTime;
            System.out.println("Elapsed Time is " + (elapsedTime / 1000000000.0) + " seconds");
        } catch (IOException e) {
          System.err.println(e);
        }

        deleteCopied(copy_to);

        System.out.println("Using Files.copy (InputStream to Path) ...");
        try (InputStream is = new FileInputStream(copy_from.toFile())) {

            startTime = System.nanoTime();

            Files.copy(is, copy_to);

            elapsedTime = System.nanoTime() - startTime;
            System.out.println("Elapsed Time is " + (elapsedTime / 1000000000.0) + " seconds");
        } catch (IOException e) {
          System.err.println(e);
        }

        deleteCopied(copy_to);

        System.out.println("Using Files.copy (Path to OutputStream) ...");
        try (OutputStream os = new FileOutputStream(copy_to.toFile())) {

            startTime = System.nanoTime();

            Files.copy(copy_from, os);

            elapsedTime = System.nanoTime() - startTime;
            System.out.println("Elapsed Time is " + (elapsedTime / 1000000000.0) + " seconds");
        } catch (IOException e) {
          System.err.println(e);
        }
      }
    }
```

The output of this application is pretty hard to sort through since there are so many numbers involved, so I've plotted some of the data instead to give you a clearer image of the results of several comparisons, as shown in the figures in the following sections. The Y axis in these figures is the estimated time expressed in seconds, and the X axis is the size of the used buffer (or run number, after skipping the first three runs).

FileChannel and Non-direct Buffer vs. FileChannel and Direct Buffer

As shown in Figure 7-11, it seems that for buffers smaller than 256KB, the non-direct buffer is much faster, while for buffers larger than 256KB, the direct buffer is slightly faster (see Figure 7-11).

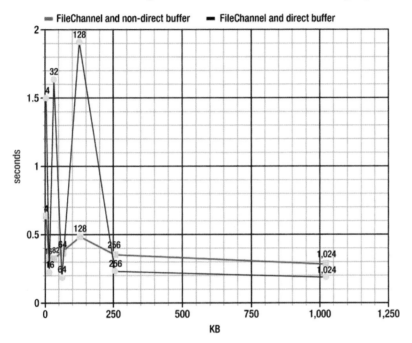

Figure 7-11. FileChannel and non-direct buffer vs. FileChannel and direct buffer

FileChannel.transferTo() vs. FileChannel.transferFrom() vs. FileChannel.map()

As shown in Figure 7-12, it looks like `transferTo()` and `transferFrom()` are almost the same over seven consecutive runs, while `FileChannel.map()` is the slowest solution.

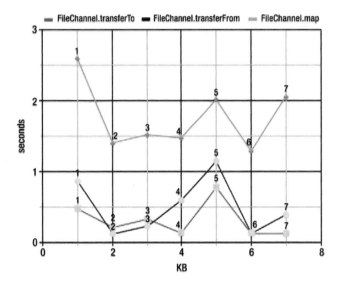

Figure 7-12. FileChannel.transferTo() vs. FileChannel.transferFrom() vs. FileChannel.map()

The three different Files.copy()approaches

As shown in Figure 7-13, the fastest `Files.copy()` method is `Path` to `Path`, followed by `Path` to `OutputStream`, and finally `InputStream` to `Path`.

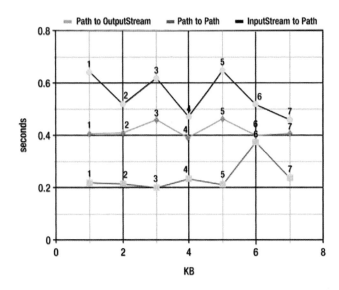

Figure 7-13. Files.copy() approches

FileChannel and Non-direct Buffer vs. FileChannel.transferTo() vs. Path to Path

As final test we took the fastest results from the above three diagrams and put them together in figure 7-14. Since we did not specify a buffer size for `FileChannel.transferTo()` and `Path` to `Path` we take as the reference the average time over the seven runs. As you can see, `Files.copy()` with `Path` to `Path` seams to be the fastest solution for copying a file.

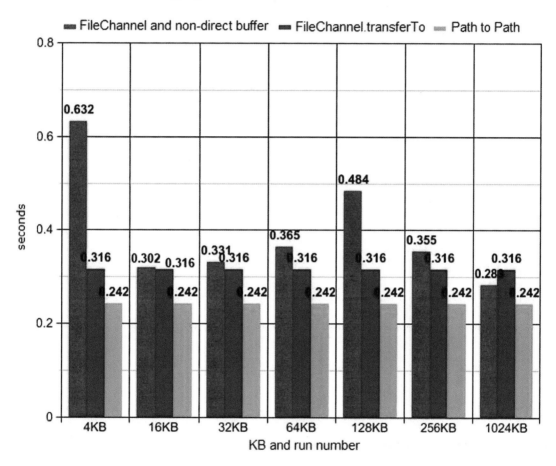

Figure 7-14. FileChannel with non-direct buffer vs. FileChannel.transferTo() vs. Path to Path

167

Summary

This chapter started with a short overview of the `ByteBuffer` class, which is commonly used with `SeekableByteChannel` and `FileChannel`. It continued by detailing the `SeekableByteChannel` interface with applications that will read and write files randomly to accomplish different types of common tasks. You then saw how to get a `FileChannel` with RAF capabilities and discovered the main facilities provided by `FileChannel`, including mapping a region of the file directly into memory for faster access, locking a region of the file, and reading and writing bytes from an absolute location without affecting the channel's current position. The chapter ended with a benchmarking application that tries to determine the fastest way to copy a file by comparing `FileChannel` capabilities against other common approaches, such as `Files.copy()`, using buffered streams and a byte array, and using unbuffered streams and a byte array.

CHAPTER 8

■ ■ ■

The Sockets APIs

The Internet was born around the 1950s and '60s. Some years later, around the '80s, the notion of the *socket* was introduced on BSD (Berkeley Software Distribution—a Unix variant) for communication between processes using Internet Protocol (IP). A few years later, in 1996, JDK 1.0 brought the notion of the socket to the programming world as a model for network communications that it is easy to use and cross-platform. Finally, programmers can now create network applications without years of study about network communications. Java developers can write a simple network application just by scratching the surface of a few subjects, such as IP, IP addresses, ports, and Java networks.

IP breaks all communications into *packets* (chunks of data) that are treated individually from source to destination—there is no delivery guarantee. On top of IP, we have other common protocols, such as TCP (Transmission Control Protocol) and UDP (User Datagram Protocol) (this chapter's applications exploit these protocols), and on top of these we have even more, including HTTP, TELNET, DNS, and so on. Sockets make use of IP for communication between machines, so Java network applications can "talk" to existing servers using their predefined protocol.

On the Internet, each machine can be identified by a numerical label, known as an *IP address*. Every Java developer should knows that we deal with two types of IP addresses: IPv4 (represented on 32-bits— e.g., 124.32.45.23) and IPv6 (represented on 128-bits —e.g., 2607:f0d0:1002:0051:0000:0000:0000:0004). Moreover, it is important to know that IP addresses are organized into classes A, B, C, D, and E. Since we have a special interest in class D of IP addresses, let's say that IPv4s addresses vary between 224.0.0.1 and 239.255.255.255, and denote multicast groups. In addition, remember that the address 127.0.0.1 is reserved for the *localhost* address.

Focusing on ports, TCP/UDP ports range between 0 and 65535 and they are represented in Java as integers. Certain types of servers are typically found on certain ports: for example if you connect to port 80 of a host, you can expect to find an HTTP server. On port 21 you can expect an FTP server, on 23 a Telnet server, on 119 an NNTP server, and so on. Therefore, be careful when choosing ports; make sure you don't interfere with other processes and that you keep in range.

Each of these notions has entire books dedicated to it, but this is enough information for the purposes of creating Java client/server applications. In a client/server model, a server runs on a host and listens to a port for connection requests from clients across the network, or even from the same machine. Clients use the IP address (hostname) and port to locate the server, while the server serves each client according to its request. On the connection process, the client identifies itself to the server through a local port number that can be explicitly set or assigned by the kernel—a socket is bound to this local port number to be used during this connection (we say that the client *binds* to a local port number). Upon acceptance, the server gets a new socket bound to a new local port number and also has its remote endpoint set to the address and port of the client—it needs a new port number so that it can continue to listen for connection requests on the original port. Once the communication is settled, data can go back and forth between the sockets until the communication is purposely shut down or accidentally broken.

We can conclude that, for Java, a socket is a bidirectional software *endpoint* between a server program and its client programs, or more generally, between two programs running on the network that are involved in a two-way communication. An *endpoint* is a combination of an IP address and a port number.

Java introduced support for sockets in JDK 1.0, but things have of course changed over time from version to version. Jumping to Java 7, NIO.2 has improved this support by updating existing classes with new methods and adding new interfaces/classes for writing TCP/UDP-based applications. First of all, NIO.2 introduces an interface named `NetworkChannel` that provides methods commons to all network channel classes—any channel that implements this interface is a channel to a network socket. The main classes dedicated to synchronous socket channels, `ServerSocketChannel`, `SocketChannel`, and `DatagramChannel`, implement this interface, which comes with methods for binding to and returning local addresses, and methods for setting and getting socket options through the new `SocketOption<T>` interface and `StandardSocketOptions` class. This interface's methods and the ones added directly into classes (for checking connection state, getting remote addresses, and shutdown) will prevent you from having to call the `socket()` method.

NIO.2 also introduces the `MulticastChannel` interface as a subinterface of `NetworkChannel`. As its name suggests, the `MulticastChannel` interface maps a network channel that supports IP multicasting. Keep in mind that `MulticastChannel` is implemented *only* by the datagram channel (the `DatagramChannel` class). When joining a multicast group you get a *membership key*, which is a token that represents the membership of a multicast group. Through the membership key, you can block/unblock datagrams from different addresses, drop membership, get the channel and/or multicast group for which this membership key was created, and more.

■ **Note** For a short overview of Java channels, please take a look at the "Short Overview of Channels" section of Chapter 7. In addition, the "Short Overview of ByteBuffer" section may be taken in consideration to understand how Java buffers work.

NetworkChannel Overview

In this section we will have a short overview of the `NetworkChannel` methods. This interface represents a channel to a network socket and comes with a set of five common methods for all sockets. We present them here since they will be very useful in the next sections.

We'll start with the `bind()` method, which binds the channel's socket to a local address. More precisely, this method will establish an association between the socket and a local address, which is usually explicitly specified as an `InetSocketAddress` instance (this class represents a socket address with IP (or hostname) and port, and extends the abstract `SocketAddress` class). The local address can also be automatically assigned if we pass `null` to the `bind()` method. This method is used to bind server socket channels, socket channels, and datagram socket channels with the local machine. It will return the current channel:

```
NetworkChannel bind(SocketAddress local) throws IOException
```

NetworkChannel can extract the bound address by calling the getLocalAddress() method. If the channel's socket is not bound, then it returns null:

```
SocketAddress getLocalAddress() throws IOException
```

Socket Options

The remaining three methods of NetworkChannel deal with socket options supported by the current channel. A socket option associated with a socket is represented by the SocketOption<T> interface. Currently, NIO.2 implements this interface with a set of standard options in the StandardSocketOptions class. Here they are:

- IP_MULTICAST_IF: This option is used to specify the network interface (NetworkInterface) used for multicast datagrams sent by the datagram-oriented socket; if it is null, then the OS will choose the outgoing interface (if one is available). By default, it is null, but the option's value can be set after the socket is bound. When we talk about sending datagrams, you will see how to find out what multicast interfaces are available on your machine.

- IP_MULTICAST_LOOP: This option's value is a boolean that controls the *loopback* of multicast datagrams (this is OS dependent). You have to decide, as the application writer, whether you want the data you send to be looped back to your host or not. By default, this is TRUE, but the option's value can be set after the socket is bound.

- IP_MULTICAST_TTL: This option's value is an integer between 0 and 255, and it represents the *time-to-live* for multicast packets sent out by the datagram-oriented socket. If not otherwise specified, multicast datagrams are sent with a default value of 1, to prevent them to be forwarded beyond the local network. With this option we can control the scope of the multicast datagrams. By default this is set to 1, but the option's value can be set after the socket is bound.

- IP_TOS: This option's value is an integer representing the value of the Type of Service (ToS) octet in IP packets sent by sockets—the interpretation of this value is specific to the network. Currently this is available only for IPv4, and by default its value is typically 0. The option's value can be set any time after the socket is bound.

- SO_BROADCAST: This option's value it is a boolean that indicates if transmission of broadcast datagrams is allowed or not (specific to datagram-oriented sockets sending to IPv4 broadcast addresses). By default, it is FALSE, but the option's value can be set any time.

- SO_KEEPALIVE: This option's value it is a boolean indicating if the connection should be kept alive or not. By default, it is set to FALSE, but the option's value can be set any time.

- SO_LINGER: This option's value is an integer that represents a timeout in seconds (the *linger interval*). When attempting to close a blocking-mode socket via the close() method, it will wait for the duration of the linger interval before transmitting the unsent data (not defined for non-blocking mode). By default, it is a negative value, which means that this option is disabled. The option's value can be set any time and the maximum value is OS dependent.

- **SO_RCVBUF:** This option's value is an integer that represents the size in bytes of the socket *receive buffer*—the input buffer used by the networking implementation. By default, the value is OS dependent, but it can be set before the socket is bound or connected. Depending on the OS, the value can be changed after the socket is bound. Negative values are not allowed.

- **SO_SNDBUF:** This option's value is an integer that represents the size in bytes of the socket *send buffer*—the output buffer used by the networking implementation. By default, the value is OS dependent, but it can be set before the socket is bound or connected. Depending on the OS, the value can be changed after the socket is bound. Negative values are not allowed.

- **SO_REUSEADDR:** This option's value is an integer that represents if an address can be reused or not. This is very useful in datagram multicasting when we want multiple programs to be bound to the same address. In the case of stream-oriented sockets, the socket can be bound to an address when a previous connection is in the TIME_WAIT state – TIME_WAIT means the OS has received a request to close the socket, but waits for possible late communications from the client side. By default, the option's value is OS dependent, but it can be set before the socket is bound or connected.

- **TCP_NODELAY:** This option's value is an integer that enables/disables Nagle's algorithm (for more information on Nagle's algorithm, see http://en.wikipedia.org/wiki/Nagle%27s_algorithm). By default it is FALSE, but it can be set at any time.

Now, setting and getting an option can be accomplished by the NetworkChannel.getOption() and NetworkChannel.setOption() methods:

```
<T> T getOption(SocketOption<T> name) throws IOException
<T> NetworkChannel setOption(SocketOption<T> name, T value) throws IOException
```

Retrieving the supported options for a specific channel (for a network socket) can be accomplished by calling the NetworkChannel.supportedOptions() method over that channel:

```
Set<SocketOption<?>> supportedOptions()
```

Writing TCP Server/Client Applications

It is far from our aim to write a TCP tutorial, since this is a very well-documented and large subject, and involves many technical notions and aspects, but we'll give a quick overview. TCP is like a telephone connection—it establishes a connection between two endpoints through a socket, and the socket remains open throughout the duration of the communications. The primary function of TCP is to provide a point-to-point communication mechanism. One process on one machine communicates with another process on another machine or within the same machine. A unique TCP connection is identified by five elements: the IP address and port of the server, the IP address and port of the client, and the protocol (TCP/IP, UDP, etc.). The server listens to one single port and can talk to many clients at the same time. TCP provides many advantages (e.g., over UDP) that involve data packets. TCP is responsible for many important tasks, including breaking data into packets, buffering data, tracking lost packets (for resending lost or out-of-order packets), and controlling the speed of transmitting data with respect to application-processing capabilities. Moreover, TCP supports sending data as byte arrays or using streams, which are very popular in Java.

Blocking vs. Non-Blocking Mechanisms

When you decide to write a Java TCP server/client application, you must consider whether you need to write a blocking or non-blocking application. This decision is important because the implementations are different and the complexity may also be critical.

The main characteristic of a blocking mechanism presumes that a given thread cannot do anything more until the I/O is fully received, which may take a while in some cases—the application's flow is blocked because the methods do not return right away. Non-blocking mechanisms, on the other hand, immediately queue an I/O request and return the control to application flow (methods return right away). The request will be processed later by the kernel.

From a Java developer perspective, you also must take into account the degree of complexity involved by these mechanisms. Non-blocking mechanisms are much more complex to implement than blocking mechanisms, but they allow you more performance and scalability.

■ **Note** Non-blocking mechanisms are *not* the same as asynchronous mechanisms (although this is often debated depending on who you ask). For example, in a non-blocking environment, if an answer can't be returned rapidly, the API returns immediately with an error and does nothing else, while in an asynchronous environment, the API always returns immediately, having started a behind-the-scenes effort to serve your request. In other words, with a non-blocking mechanism, a function won't wait while on the stack, and with an asynchronous mechanism, work may continue on behalf of the function call after that call has left the stack. Asynchronous is more familiar with parallel (as threading), while non-blocking often refers to polling.

Both blocking and non-blocking modes have been implemented since NIO, but we will try to spice up the code with the new NIO.2 features.

In the next sections, we will develop both types of application. Let's start with the easy one that uses the blocking mechanism.

Writing a Blocking TCP Server

The easiest approach for a better understanding of how to accomplish this task is to follow a straightforward set of steps accompanied by chunks of codes that will be glued together at the end of the discussion. We want to develop a single-thread blocking TCP server that will echo to the client everything that it gets from it. Many of the steps to accomplish this are transferable to other blocking TCP servers as well.

Creating a New Server Socket Channel

The first step involves creating a selectable channel for stream-oriented listening socket, which is possible thanks to the `java.nio.channels.ServerSocketChannel` class, which is safe for use by multiple concurrent threads. More precisely, this task is accomplished by the `ServerSocketChannel.open()` method, as show here:

```
ServerSocketChannel serverSocketChannel = ServerSocketChannel.open();
```

Keep in mind that a newly created server socket channel is not bound or connected. Binding and connecting will be accomplished in the next steps.

You can check if a server socket is already open or has been successfully opened by calling the `ServerSocketChannel.isOpen()` method, which returns the corresponding `Boolean` value:

```
if (serverSocketChannel.isOpen()) {
    ...
}
```

Configuring Blocking Mechanisms

If the server socket channel has been successfully opened, it is time to specify the blocking mechanism. For this we call the `ServerSocketChannel.configureBlocking()` method which receives a `boolean` value. If we pass `true`, then the blocking mechanism will be used; if we pass `false`, then the non-blocking mechanism will be used:

```
serverSocketChannel.configureBlocking(true);
```

Notice that this method returns a `SelectableChannel` object, which represents a channel that can be multiplexed via a `Selector`. This is useful when we are in non-blocking mode; therefore we will ignore it for the moment.

Setting Server Socket Channel Options

This is an optional step. There is no required option (you can use the default values), but we'll explicitly set a few options to show you how this can be done. More precisely, a server socket channel supports two options: `SO_RCVBUF` and `SO_REUSEADDR`. We'll set them both, as shown here:

```
serverSocketChannel.setOption(StandardSocketOptions.SO_RCVBUF, 4 * 1024);
serverSocketChannel.setOption(StandardSocketOptions.SO_REUSEADDR, true);
```

You can find out the supported options for a server socket channel by calling the inherited method `supportedOptions()`:

```
Set<SocketOption<?>> options = serverSocketChannel.supportedOptions();
for(SocketOption<?> option : options) System.out.println(option);
```

Binding the Server Socket Channel

At this point we can bind the channel's socket to a local address and configure the socket to listen for connections. For this we call the new `ServerSocketChannel.bind()` method (this method was introduced earlier in the "NetworkChannel Overview" section). Our server will wait for an incoming connection on localhost (127.0.0.1), port 5555 (arbitrarily chosen):

```
final int DEFAULT_PORT = 5555;
final String IP = "127.0.0.1";
serverSocketChannel.bind(new InetSocketAddress(IP, DEFAULT_PORT));
```

Another common approach consists of creating an `InetSocketAddress` object without specifying the IP address, only the port (there is a constructor for that). In this case, the IP address is the *wildcard* address, and the port number is a specified value. The wildcard address is a special local IP address that can be used *only* for bind operations, and usually means "any":

```
serverSocketChannel.bind(new InetSocketAddress(DEFAULT_PORT));
```

■ **Caution** When you are using an IP wildcard address, take care to avoid any undesirable complications that may occur if you have multiple network interfaces with separate IP addresses. In this case, if you are not sure how to accomplish this without issues, is it recommended to bind the socket to a specific network address, rather than use a wildcard.

In addition, there is one more `bind()` method that receives the address to bind the socket and the maximum number of pending connections:

```
public abstract ServerSocketChannel bind(SocketAddress local,int pc) throws IOException
```

The local address can also be automatically assigned if we pass `null` to the `bind()` method. You can also find out the bound local address by calling the `ServerSocketChannel.getLocalAddress()` method, which is inherited from the `NetworkChannel` interface. This returns `null` if the server socket channel has not been bound yet.

```
System.out.println(serverSocketChannel.getLocalAddress());
```

Accepting Connections

After opening and binding, we finally reach the accepting milestone. Since we are in blocking mode, accepting a connection will block the application until a new connection is available or an I/O error occurs. We signal our impatience to accept new connections by calling the `ServerSocketChannel.accept()` method. When a new connection is available, this method returns the client socket channel (or simply, socket channel) for the new connection. This is an instance of the `SocketChannel` class, which represents a selectable channel for stream-oriented connecting sockets.

```
SocketChannel socketChannel = serverSocketChannel.accept();
```

■ **Note** Trying to invoke the `accept()` method for an unbound server socket channel will throw a `NotYetBoundException` exception.

Once we have accepted a new connection, we can find out the remote address by calling the `SocketChannel.getRemoteAddress()` method. This method is new in Java 7 (NIO.2), and it returns the remote address to which this channel's socket is connected:

```
System.out.println("Incoming connection from: " + socketChannel.getRemoteAddress());
```

Transmitting Data over a Connection

At this point the server and client can transmit data over a connection. They can send and receive different kinds of data packets mapped as byte arrays or using streams along with the standard Java file I/O mechanism. Implementing the transmission (send/receive) is a flexible and implementation-specific process since it involves many aspects. For example, for our server we chose to use `ByteBuffer`s and we kept in mind that this is an echo server—what it reads from the client is what it writes back. Here it is the transmission code snippet:

```
ByteBuffer buffer = ByteBuffer.allocateDirect(1024);
...
while (socketChannel.read(buffer) != -1) {

        buffer.flip();

        socketChannel.write(buffer);

        if (buffer.hasRemaining()) {
            buffer.compact();
            } else {
                    buffer.clear();
            }
}
```

The `SocketChannel` class provides a set of `read()`/`write()` methods for `ByteBuffer`s. Since they are pretty intuitive, we'll just list them:

- Read a sequence of bytes from this channel into the given buffer. These methods return the number of bytes read (it can be zero) or –1 if the channel has reached end-of-stream:

```
public abstract int read(ByteBuffer dst) throws IOException
public final long read(ByteBuffer[] dsts) throws IOException
public abstract long read(ByteBuffer[] dsts, int offset, int length) throws IOException
```

- Write a sequence of bytes to this channel from the given buffer. These methods return the number of bytes written; it can be zero:

```
public abstract int write(ByteBuffer src) throws IOException
public final long write(ByteBuffer[] srcs) throws IOException
public abstract long write(ByteBuffer[] srcs, int offset, int length) throws IOException
```

Using Streams Instead of Buffers

As you know, channels are very good friends with buffers, but if you decide to use streams instead (`InputStream` and `OutputStream`), then you need to use the following code; once you have obtained an I/O stream you can further explore the standard Java file I/O mechanism.

```
InputStream in = socketChannel.socket().getInputStream();
OutputStream out = socketChannel.socket().getOutputStream();
```

Shutting Down a Connection for I/O

You can shut down a connection for I/O without closing the channel by calling the new NIO.2 `SocketChannel.shutdownInput()` or `SocketChannel.shutdownOutput()` method. Shutting down the connection for input (or reading) will reject any further read attempts by returning the end-of-stream indicator, –1. Shutting down the connection for output (or writing) will reject any writing attempts by throwing a `ClosedChannelException` exception.

```
//shut down connection for reading
socketChannel.shutdownInput();

//shut down connection for writing
socketChannel.shutdownOutput();
```

These methods are very useful if you want to reject read/write attempts without closing the channel. Checking if a connection is currently shut down for I/O can be accomplished with the following code:

```
boolean inputdown = socketChannel.socket().isInputShutdown();
boolean outputdown = socketChannel.socket().isOutputShutdown();
```

Closing the Channel

When a channel becomes useless, it must be closed. For this, you can call the `SocketChannel.close()` method (this will not close the server for listening for incoming connections, it will just close a channel for a client) and/or the `ServerSocketChannel.close()` method (this will close the server for listening for incoming connections; further clients won't be able to locate the server anymore).

```
serverSocketChannel.close();
socketChannel.close();
```

Alternatively, we can close these resources by placing the code into the Java 7 *try-with-resources* feature —this is possible because the `ServerSocketChannel` and `SocketChannel` classes implement the `AutoCloseable` interface. Using this feature will ensure that the resources are closed automatically. If you are not familiar with *try-with-resources* feature, check out `http://download.oracle.com/javase/tutorial/essential/exceptions/tryResourceClose.html`.

Putting it All Together into the Echo Server

Now we have everything we need for creating our echo server. Putting together the preceding chunks, adding the necessary imports and spaghetti code, and so on will provide us the following echo sever:

```
import java.io.IOException;
import java.net.InetSocketAddress;
import java.net.StandardSocketOptions;
import java.nio.ByteBuffer;
import java.nio.channels.ServerSocketChannel;
import java.nio.channels.SocketChannel;

public class Main {

 public static void main(String[] args) {
```

```java
        final int DEFAULT_PORT = 5555;
        final String IP = "127.0.0.1";

        ByteBuffer buffer = ByteBuffer.allocateDirect(1024);

        //create a new server socket channel
        try (ServerSocketChannel serverSocketChannel = ServerSocketChannel.open()) {

            //continue if it was successfully created
            if (serverSocketChannel.isOpen()) {

                //set the blocking mode
                serverSocketChannel.configureBlocking(true);
                //set some options
                serverSocketChannel.setOption(StandardSocketOptions.SO_RCVBUF, 4 * 1024);
                serverSocketChannel.setOption(StandardSocketOptions.SO_REUSEADDR, true);
                //bind the server socket channel to local address
                serverSocketChannel.bind(new InetSocketAddress(IP, DEFAULT_PORT));

                //display a waiting message while ... waiting clients
                System.out.println("Waiting for connections ...");
                //wait for incoming connections
                while(true){
                  try (SocketChannel socketChannel = serverSocketChannel.accept()) {
                      System.out.println("Incoming connection from: " +
                                                    socketChannel.getRemoteAddress());

                      //transmitting data
                      while (socketChannel.read(buffer) != -1) {

                            buffer.flip();

                            socketChannel.write(buffer);

                            if (buffer.hasRemaining()) {
                                buffer.compact();
                            } else {
                                buffer.clear();
                            }
                      }
                  } catch (IOException ex) {
                  }
                }

            } else {
                System.out.println("The server socket channel cannot be opened!");
            }
        } catch (IOException ex) {
            System.err.println(ex);
        }
      }
    }
}
```

Writing a Blocking TCP Client

What good is a server without a client? We do not want to find out the answer to this question, so let's develop a client for our echo server. Suppose the following scenario: the client connects to our server, sends a "Hello!" message, and then keeps sending random numbers between 0 and 100 until the number 50 is generated. When the number 50 is generated, the client stops sending and closes the channel. The server will echo (write back) everything it reads from the client. Now that we have a scenario, let's see the steps for implementing it.

Creating a New Socket Channel

The first step is to create a selectable channel for a stream-oriented connecting socket. This is accomplished with the `java.nio.channels.SocketChannel` class, which is safe for use by multiple concurrent threads. More precisely, this task is accomplished by the `SocketChannel.open()` method, as follows:

```
SocketChannel socketChannel = SocketChannel.open();
```

Keep in mind that a newly created socket channel is not connected. Creating and connecting a socket channel in a single shot involves calling the `SocketChannel.open(SocketAddress)` method. It is also possible to do this in two steps, as we will discuss.

You can check if a server socket is already open or has been successfully opened by calling the `SocketChannel.isOpen()` method, which returns the corresponding `Boolean` value:

```
if (socketChannel.isOpen()) {
    ...
}
```

Configuring Blocking Mechanisms

If the socket channel has been successfully opened, it is time to specify the blocking mechanism. We will pass the `true` value, since we want to activate the blocking mechanism:

```
socketChannel.configureBlocking(true);
```

Setting Socket Channel Options

A socket channel supports the following options: `SO_RCVBUF`, `SO_LINGER`, `IP_TOS`, `SO_OOBINLINE`, `SO_REUSEADDR`, `TCP_NODELAY`, `SO_KEEPALIVE`, and `SO_SNDBUF`. Some of them are shown following:

```
socketChannel.setOption(StandardSocketOptions.SO_RCVBUF, 128 * 1024);
socketChannel.setOption(StandardSocketOptions.SO_SNDBUF, 128 * 1024);
socketChannel.setOption(StandardSocketOptions.SO_KEEPALIVE, true);
socketChannel.setOption(StandardSocketOptions.SO_LINGER, 5);
```

You can find the supported options for a server socket channel by calling the inherited method `supportedOptions()`:

```
Set<SocketOption<?>> options = socketChannel.supportedOptions();
for(SocketOption<?> option : options) System.out.println(option);
```

Connecting the Channel's Socket

After opening a socket channel (and optionally binding it), you should connect to the remote address (the server-side address). Since we are in blocking mode, connecting to a remote address will block the application until a new connection is available or an I/O error occurs. The intention to connect is signaled by calling the SocketChannel.connect() method and passing to it the remote address as an instance of InetSocketAddress, as follows (remember that our echo servers runs on 127.0.0.1, port 5555):

```
final int DEFAULT_PORT = 5555;
final String IP = "127.0.0.1";
socketChannel.connect(new InetSocketAddress(IP, DEFAULT_PORT));
```

The method returns a boolean value representing a successful connection attempt. You can use this boolean value to check the connection availability, until sending/receiving packets through this connection. In addition, the same check can be accomplished by calling the SocketChannel.isConnected() method, like so:

```
if (socketChannel.isConnected()) {
    ...
}
```

■ **Note** Obviously, in real-world cases it's considered bad practice to hard-code IP addresses within the application. In this case the client will only be able to run on the same machine with the server, which sort of defeats the purpose of remote communication. In your case, the client may likely use the hostname of the server instead of the IP address (likely configured through DNS). IP addresses often change, and are sometimes even dynamically assigned via DHCP.

Transmitting Data over a Connection

The connection has been established, so we can start transmitting data packets. The following code sends the "Hello!" message, and then sends random numbers until the number 50 is generated. We used ByteBuffer, CharBuffer, and the read()/write() methods of SocketChannel class (we listed these methods previously when we developed the server-side code, so you should be familiar with them already):

```
ByteBuffer buffer = ByteBuffer.allocateDirect(1024);
ByteBuffer helloBuffer = ByteBuffer.wrap("Hello !".getBytes());
ByteBuffer randomBuffer;
CharBuffer charBuffer;
Charset charset = Charset.defaultCharset();
CharsetDecoder decoder = charset.newDecoder();
...
socketChannel.write(helloBuffer);

while (socketChannel.read(buffer) != -1) {

        buffer.flip();
```

```
        charBuffer = decoder.decode(buffer);
        System.out.println(charBuffer.toString());

        if (buffer.hasRemaining()) {
            buffer.compact();
        } else {
            buffer.clear();
        }

        int r = new Random().nextInt(100);
        if (r == 50) {
            System.out.println("50 was generated! Close the socket channel!");
            break;
        } else {
            randomBuffer = ByteBuffer.wrap("Random number:"
                                    .concat(String.valueOf(r)).getBytes());
            socketChannel.write(randomBuffer);
        }
    }
}
```

Closing the Channel

When a channel becomes useless, it must be closed. For this, you can call SocketChannel.close(), and the client will be disconnected from the server:

```
socketChannel.close();
```

Again, the Java 7 try-with-resources feature may be used for automatic closing.

Putting It All Together into the Client

Now we have everything we need for creating our client. Putting together all the required elements will provide us the following client:

```
import java.io.IOException;
import java.net.InetSocketAddress;
import java.net.StandardSocketOptions;
import java.nio.ByteBuffer;
import java.nio.CharBuffer;
import java.nio.channels.SocketChannel;
import java.nio.charset.Charset;
import java.nio.charset.CharsetDecoder;
import java.util.Random;

public class Main {

 public static void main(String[] args) {

  final int DEFAULT_PORT = 5555;
  final String IP = "127.0.0.1";
```

```
ByteBuffer buffer = ByteBuffer.allocateDirect(1024);
ByteBuffer helloBuffer = ByteBuffer.wrap("Hello !".getBytes());
ByteBuffer randomBuffer;
CharBuffer charBuffer;
Charset charset = Charset.defaultCharset();
CharsetDecoder decoder = charset.newDecoder();

//create a new socket channel
try (SocketChannel socketChannel = SocketChannel.open()) {

    //continue if it was successfully created
    if (socketChannel.isOpen()) {

        //set the blocking mode
        socketChannel.configureBlocking(true);
        //set some options
        socketChannel.setOption(StandardSocketOptions.SO_RCVBUF, 128 * 1024);
        socketChannel.setOption(StandardSocketOptions.SO_SNDBUF, 128 * 1024);
        socketChannel.setOption(StandardSocketOptions.SO_KEEPALIVE, true);
        socketChannel.setOption(StandardSocketOptions.SO_LINGER, 5);
        //connect this channel's socket
        socketChannel.connect(new InetSocketAddress(IP, DEFAULT_PORT));

        //check if the connection was successfully accomplished
        if (socketChannel.isConnected()) {

            //transmitting data
            socketChannel.write(helloBuffer);

            while (socketChannel.read(buffer) != -1) {

                buffer.flip();

                charBuffer = decoder.decode(buffer);
                System.out.println(charBuffer.toString());

                if (buffer.hasRemaining()) {
                    buffer.compact();
                } else {
                    buffer.clear();
                }

                int r = new Random().nextInt(100);
                if (r == 50) {
                    System.out.println("50 was generated! Close the socket channel!");
                    break;
                } else {
                    randomBuffer = ByteBuffer.wrap("Random number:".
                                            concat(String.valueOf(r)).getBytes());
                    socketChannel.write(randomBuffer);
                }
            }
        }
```

```
            } else {
                System.out.println("The connection cannot be established!");
            }
        } else {
            System.out.println("The socket channel cannot be opened!");
        }
    } catch (IOException ex) {
        System.err.println(ex);
    }
  }
 }
}
```

Testing the Blocking Echo Application

Testing the application is a simple task. First, start the server and wait until you see the message "Waiting for connections ...". Continue by starting the client and check out the output. Following is some possible server output:

```
Waiting for connections ...

Incoming connection from: /127.0.0.1:49911
```

And here is some possible client output:

```
Hello !

Random number:71

Random number:60

Random number:22

Random number:4

Random number:60

Random number:13

...

50 was generated! Close the socket channel!
```

Writing a Non-Blocking TCP Client/Server Application

Before we start developing, let's have a short overview of the non-blocking API, which has been available since NIO, so it shouldn't look totally new to you. Keeping this in mind, we won't go into too much detail about the things you likely already know.

Non-blocking socket mode is all about allowing I/O operation on a channel without blocking the processes using it. The story begins exactly as in a blocking application: the server side is opened, is bound to a local address, and receives requests from the client side, which, obviously, is open, connected to the remote address, and sending requests to the server.

Things start to go wild when the main entity of all non-blocking technology—the `java.nio.channels.Selector` class—comes onto the scene. A `Selector` is created through a no-argument `open()` method (`Selector` was not modified in Java 7). Basically, this class has the ability to recognize when one or more channels are available for data transfer and serializes the requests for helping the server to satisfy its clients (it monitors each recorded socket channel).

Moreover, the `Selector` processes multiple sockets' I/O read/write operations in a single thread, thanks to a concept known as *multiplexing*—this solves the problem of dedicating one thread to each socket connection. In API terms, the `Selector` is a *multiplexor* for `java.nio.channels.SelectableChannels`, which can be registered through the `register()` method (available in the `ServerSocketChannel` and `SocketChannel` classes, which are indirect subclasses of `SelectableChannel`) and deregistered by deallocating the resources that were allocated to the channel by the `Selector`.

Using the SelectionKey Class

If you are still on track, then let's go deeper! Each time a channel is registered with a `Selector`, it is represented through an instance of the `java.nio.channels.SelectionKey` class, and those instances are known as *selection keys*—Java 7 does not modify this class. Think of keys as the helpers used by the selector to sort the client requests—each helper (key) represents a single client subrequest and contains information for identifying the client and the type of the request (connect, read,write, etc.).When registering, we indicate the selector and, usually, the interest set for the resulting key (the interest set identifies the operations for which the key's channel is monitored by the `Selector`). There are four possible types for a key:

- `SelectionKey.OP_ACCEPT` *(acceptable)*: The associated client requests a connection (usually created on the server side for indicating that a client requires a connection).

- `SelectionKey.OP_CONNECT` *(connectable)*: The server accepts the connection (usually created on the client side).

- `SelectionKey.OP_READ` *(readable)*: This indicates a read operation.

- `SelectionKey.OP_WRITE` *(writable)*: This indicates a write operation.

A selector is responsible for maintaining three sets of selection keys:

- `key-set`: Contains the keys representing the current channel registrations of this selector

- `selected-key`: Contains the set of keys such that each key's channel was detected to be ready for at least one of the operations identified in the key's interest set during a prior selection operation

- `cancelled-key`: Contains the set of keys that have been cancelled but whose channels have not yet been deregistered

---

■ **Note** All three sets are empty in a newly created selector. Selectors are themselves safe for use by multiple concurrent threads, but their key sets however are not.

When something happens on the battlefield, the selector wakes up and creates the corresponding keys (instances of the `SelectionKey` class). Each key holds information about the application making the request and the type of the request (attempting/accepting connection and read/write operations).

The selector waits for incoming connections into an infinite loop (waits for events recorded on the selector). Usually the `Selector.select()` method is the first line in the loop, and it blocks the application until at least one channel is selected, the selector's `Selector.wakeup()` method is invoked, or the current thread is interrupted—whichever comes first. (In addition, a "`select()` with timeout" method is available, as is a non-blocking method called `selectNow()`.)

The `Selector` waits for a client to attempt a connection, and when that happens, the server application gets the keys created by the selector. For each key, it checks the type (each processed key is removed from the set by explicitly calling the `remove()` method of an `Iterator` over keys—this will prevent the same key from coming up again). The acceptable key is hunted here, and when the `SelectionKey.isAcceptable()` method returns `true`, the server locates the client socket channel by invoking the `accept()` methods, sets it to be non-blocking, and registers it to the selector using the `OP_READ` and/or `OP_WRITE` options.

At this point, the client socket channel is registered to the selector for reading/writing operations. In keeping with this trend, when the client writes data on the socket channel, the selector will tell the server that there is some data to read—for this, the `SelectionKey.isReadable()` method returns `true`. If the client attempts to read data from server, the process is similar, but the server instead writes data and the `SelectionKey.isWritable()` method returns `true`.

Figure 8-1 shows a diagram of a non-blocking flow.

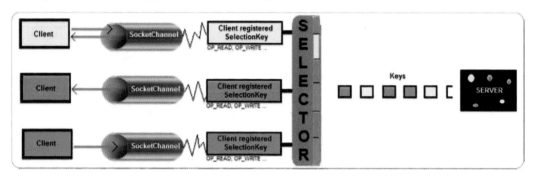

Figure 8-1. Selector base non-blocking flow.

So, the server is ready to rock!

■ **Note** In non-blocking mode, an I/O operation may transfer fewer bytes than were requested (partial read or write), or possibly no bytes at all.

Using the Selector's Methods

Next, we'll go over the methods invoked in this section, as well as a few more, are overviewed next (most of the following descriptions were taken from the official Java 7 Javadoc).

- `Selector.open()`: Creates a new selector.

- `Selector.select()`: Selects a set of keys by performing a blocking selection operation.

- `Selector.select(t)`: Same as `select`, but the blocking is performed only for the specified milliseconds. If time expires and there is nothing to select, it returns 0.

- `Selector.selectNow()`: Same as `select`, but with non-blocking selection operation. It returns 0 if there is nothing to select.

- `Selector.selectedKeys()`: Returns this selector's selected key set as `Set<SelectionKey>`.

- `Selector.keys()`: Returns this selector's key set as `Set<SelectionKey>`.

- `Selector.wakeup()`: Causes the first selection operation that has not yet returned to return immediately.

- `SelectionKey.isValid()`: Checks if the key is valid. A key is invalid if it is cancelled, its channel is closed, or its selector is closed.

- `SelectionKey.isReadable()`: Tests whether this key's channel is ready for reading.

- `SelectionKey.isWritable()`: Tests whether this key's channel is ready for writing.

- `SelectionKey.isAcceptable()`: Tests whether this key's channel is ready to accept a new socket connection.

- `SelectionKey.isConnectable()`: Tests whether this key's channel has either finished or failed to finish its socket connection operation.

- `SelectionKey.cancel()`: Requests that the registration of this key's channel with its selector be cancelled.

- `SelectionKey.interestOps()`: Retrieves this key's interest set.

- `SelectionKey.interestOps(t)`: Sets this key's interest set to the given value.

- `SelectionKey.readyOps()`: Retrieves this key's ready-operation set.

Moreover, `ServerSocketChannel` and `SocketChannel` contain the `register()` method, which is used for registering the current channel with the given selector and returning a selection key. It gets the selector, the interest set for the resulting key, and the attachment for the resulting key (may be `null`).

```
public final SelectionKey register(Selector s,int p,Object a) throws ClosedChannelException
```

Writing the Server

Based on these methods and the preceding discussion, we have written the following non-blocking echo server (every step is commented to help give you a good understanding):

```java
import java.io.IOException;
import java.net.InetSocketAddress;
import java.net.StandardSocketOptions;
import java.nio.ByteBuffer;
import java.nio.channels.SelectionKey;
import java.nio.channels.Selector;
import java.nio.channels.ServerSocketChannel;
import java.nio.channels.SocketChannel;
import java.util.ArrayList;
import java.util.HashMap;
import java.util.Iterator;
import java.util.List;
import java.util.Map;

public class Main {

 private Map<SocketChannel, List<byte[]>> keepDataTrack = new HashMap<>();
 private ByteBuffer buffer = ByteBuffer.allocate(2 * 1024);

 private void startEchoServer() {

  final int DEFAULT_PORT = 5555;
```

```
//open Selector and ServerSocketChannel by calling the open() method
try (Selector selector = Selector.open();
    ServerSocketChannel serverSocketChannel = ServerSocketChannel.open()) {

    //check that both of them were successfully opened
    if ((serverSocketChannel.isOpen()) && (selector.isOpen())) {

        //configure non-blocking mode
        serverSocketChannel.configureBlocking(false);

        //set some options
        serverSocketChannel.setOption(StandardSocketOptions.SO_RCVBUF, 256 * 1024);
        serverSocketChannel.setOption(StandardSocketOptions.SO_REUSEADDR, true);

        //bind the server socket channel to port
        serverSocketChannel.bind(new InetSocketAddress(DEFAULT_PORT));

        //register the current channel with the given selector
        serverSocketChannel.register(selector, SelectionKey.OP_ACCEPT);

        //display a waiting message while ... waiting!
        System.out.println("Waiting for connections ...");

        while (true) {
            //wait for incomming events
            selector.select();

            //there is something to process on selected keys
            Iterator keys = selector.selectedKeys().iterator();

            while (keys.hasNext()) {
                SelectionKey key = (SelectionKey) keys.next();

                //prevent the same key from coming up again
                keys.remove();

                if (!key.isValid()) {
                    continue;
                }

                if (key.isAcceptable()) {
                    acceptOP(key, selector);
                } else if (key.isReadable()) {
                    this.readOP(key);
                } else if (key.isWritable()) {
                    this.writeOP(key);
                }
            }
        }
    } else {
        System.out.println("The server socket channel or selector cannot be opened!");
    }
```

```java
  } catch (IOException ex) {
    System.err.println(ex);
  }
}

//isAcceptable returned true
private void acceptOP(SelectionKey key, Selector selector) throws IOException {

  ServerSocketChannel serverChannel = (ServerSocketChannel) key.channel();
  SocketChannel socketChannel = serverChannel.accept();
  socketChannel.configureBlocking(false);

  System.out.println("Incoming connection from: " + socketChannel.getRemoteAddress());

  //write a welcome message
  socketChannel.write(ByteBuffer.wrap("Hello!\n".getBytes("UTF-8")));

  //register channel with selector for further I/O
  keepDataTrack.put(socketChannel, new ArrayList<byte[]>());
  socketChannel.register(selector, SelectionKey.OP_READ);
}

//isReadable returned true
private void readOP(SelectionKey key) {

  try {
      SocketChannel socketChannel = (SocketChannel) key.channel();

      buffer.clear();

      int numRead = -1;
      try {
          numRead = socketChannel.read(buffer);
      } catch (IOException e) {
        System.err.println("Cannot read error!");
      }

      if (numRead == -1) {
          this.keepDataTrack.remove(socketChannel);
          System.out.println("Connection closed by: " + socketChannel.getRemoteAddress());
          socketChannel.close();
          key.cancel();
          return;
      }

      byte[] data = new byte[numRead];
      System.arraycopy(buffer.array(), 0, data, 0, numRead);
      System.out.println(new String(data, "UTF-8") + " from " +
                                                socketChannel.getRemoteAddress());

      // write back to client
      doEchoJob(key, data);
```

```
    } catch (IOException ex) {
      System.err.println(ex);
    }
  }

  //isWritable returned true
  private void writeOP(SelectionKey key) throws IOException {

    SocketChannel socketChannel = (SocketChannel) key.channel();

    List<byte[]> channelData = keepDataTrack.get(socketChannel);
    Iterator<byte[]> its = channelData.iterator();

    while (its.hasNext()) {
        byte[] it = its.next();
        its.remove();
        socketChannel.write(ByteBuffer.wrap(it));
    }

    key.interestOps(SelectionKey.OP_READ);
  }

  private void doEchoJob(SelectionKey key, byte[] data) {

    SocketChannel socketChannel = (SocketChannel) key.channel();
    List<byte[]> channelData = keepDataTrack.get(socketChannel);
    channelData.add(data);

    key.interestOps(SelectionKey.OP_WRITE);
  }

  public static void main(String[] args) {
   Main main = new Main();
   main.startEchoServer();
  }
}
```

Writing the Client

Focusing on the client side, the structure is almost the same, with a few differences:

- First, the client socket channel is registered with the SelectionKey.OP_CONNECT option, since the client wants to be informed by the selector when the server accepts the connection.

- Second, the client does not attempt a connection infinitely, since the server may not be active; therefore, the Selector.select() method with timeout is proper for it (a timeout of 500 to 1,000 milliseconds will do the job).

- Third, the client must check if the key is connectable (i.e., if the
  `SelectionKey.isConnectable()` method returns `true`). If the key is connectable, it
  mixes the socket channel `isConnectionPending()` and `finishConnect()` methods in
  a conditional statement for closing the pending connections. When you need to
  tell whether or not a connection operation is in progress on this channel, call the
  `SocketChannel.isConnectionPending()` method, which returns a `Boolean` value.
  Also, finishing the process of connecting a socket channel can be accomplished by
  the `SocketChannel.finishConnect()` method.

Finally, the client is ready for I/O operations. We reproduced the same scenario as in the blocking
client/server application: the client connects to our server and sends a "Hello!" message, and then keeps
sending random numbers between 0 and 100 until the number 50 is generated. When 50 is generated,
the client stops sending and closes the channel. The server will echo (write back) everything it reads
from the client.

```java
import java.io.IOException;
import java.net.StandardSocketOptions;
import java.nio.ByteBuffer;
import java.nio.CharBuffer;
import java.nio.channels.SelectionKey;
import java.nio.channels.Selector;
import java.nio.channels.SocketChannel;
import java.nio.charset.Charset;
import java.nio.charset.CharsetDecoder;
import java.util.Iterator;
import java.util.Random;
import java.util.Set;

public class Main {

 public static void main(String[] args) {

  final int DEFAULT_PORT = 5555;
  final String IP = "127.0.0.1";

  ByteBuffer buffer = ByteBuffer.allocateDirect(2 * 1024);
  ByteBuffer randomBuffer;
  CharBuffer charBuffer;

  Charset charset = Charset.defaultCharset();
  CharsetDecoder decoder = charset.newDecoder();

  //open Selector and ServerSocketChannel by calling the open() method
  try (Selector selector = Selector.open();
       SocketChannel socketChannel = SocketChannel.open()) {

      //check that both of them were successfully opened
      if ((socketChannel.isOpen()) && (selector.isOpen())) {

          //configure non-blocking mode
          socketChannel.configureBlocking(false);
          //set some options
```

```
socketChannel.setOption(StandardSocketOptions.SO_RCVBUF, 128 * 1024);
socketChannel.setOption(StandardSocketOptions.SO_SNDBUF, 128 * 1024);
socketChannel.setOption(StandardSocketOptions.SO_KEEPALIVE, true);

//register the current channel with the given selector
socketChannel.register(selector, SelectionKey.OP_CONNECT);

//connect to remote host
socketChannel.connect(new java.net.InetSocketAddress(IP, DEFAULT_PORT));

System.out.println("Localhost: " + socketChannel.getLocalAddress());

//waiting for the connection
while (selector.select(1000) > 0) {

    //get keys
    Set keys = selector.selectedKeys();
    Iterator its = keys.iterator();

    //process each key
    while (its.hasNext()) {
        SelectionKey key = (SelectionKey) its.next();

        //remove the current key
        its.remove();

        //get the socket channel for this key
        try (SocketChannel keySocketChannel=(SocketChannel) key.channel()) {

            //attempt a connection
            if (key.isConnectable()) {

                //signal connection success
                System.out.println("I am connected!");

                //close pending connections
                if (keySocketChannel.isConnectionPending()) {
                    keySocketChannel.finishConnect();
                }

                //read/write from/to server
                while (keySocketChannel.read(buffer) != -1) {

                    buffer.flip();

                    charBuffer = decoder.decode(buffer);
                    System.out.println(charBuffer.toString());

                    if (buffer.hasRemaining()) {
                        buffer.compact();
                    } else {
                        buffer.clear();
```

```
                }

                int r = new Random().nextInt(100);
                if (r == 50) {
                    System.out.println("50 was generated! Close
                                        the socket channel!");
                    break;
                } else {
                  randomBuffer = ByteBuffer.wrap("Random number:"
                   .concat(String.valueOf(r)).getBytes("UTF-8"));
                  keySocketChannel.write(randomBuffer);
                  try {
                      Thread.sleep(1500);
                  } catch (InterruptedException ex) {
                  }
                }
              }
            }
        } catch (IOException ex) {
          System.err.println(ex);
        }
      }
    }
  } else {
    System.out.println("The socket channel or selector cannot be opened!");
  }
} catch (IOException ex) {
  System.err.println(ex);
}


  }
}
```

Testing the Non-Blocking Echo Application

Testing the application is a simple task. First, start the server and wait until you see the message "Waiting for connections ...." Continue by starting a set of clients and check out the output. Figure 8-2 shows an example of running the server and three client instances.

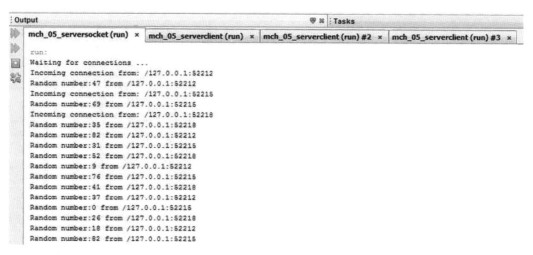

Figure 8-2. Non-blocking server echo application output.

Figure 8-3 shows the output of client 2.

Figure 8-3. Non-blocking client echo application output

Keep in mind that even if it looks like a multithreading application, this is a single-thread application based on the multiplexing technique.

Writing UDP Server/Client Applications

Since TCP has had its moment of glory, it is time for UDP to get our attention. UDP is built on top of IP, and has a couple of important characteristics. For one, the packet sizes are limited to the amount that can be contained in a single IP packet—at most 65507 bytes; this is the 65535-byte IP packet size minus the minimum IP header of 20 bytes, and minus the 8-byte UDP header. Additionally, each packet is an individual, and is handled separately (no packet is aware of other packets). Moreover, the packets can arrive in any order, and some of them can be lost without the sender being informed, or they can arrive faster or slower than they can be processed—there's no guarantee of delivering/receiving data in a particular sequence and no guarantee that the delivered data will be received.

Since the sender can't track the packets' routes, each packet encapsulates the remote IP address and the port. If TCP is like a telephone, UDP is like a letter. The sender writes the receiver address (remote IP and port) and sender address (local IP and port) on the envelope (UDP packet), puts the letter (data to be sent) into the envelope, and sends the letter. He doesn't know if the letter will arrive to the receiver or not. Moreover, a more recent letter can arrive faster than and old one, and a letter might never arrive at all—the letters are not aware of one another. Keep in mind that TCP is for high-reliability data transmissions while UDP is for low-overhead transmissions. Typically, use UDP in applications in which reliability is not critical but speed is. UDP is good for sending messages from one system to another when the order isn't important and you don't need all of the messages to get to the other machine.

In the next sections, we will write a single-thread blocking client/server application based on UDP. We'll start with the server side.

Writing a UDP Server

To aid your understanding, we will split the developing process into discrete steps and bring to the front the features of NIO.2 meant to increase performance and ease of development. Again, we will write an echo server and a client that sends some text to it and receives it back.

Creating a Server Datagram–Oriented Socket Channel

The entire process of writing a client/server UDP application involves the java.nio.channels.DatagramChannel class, which represents a thread-safe selectable channel for datagram-oriented sockets. Therefore, we'll start our server by creating a new DatagramChannel, which can be accomplished by calling the NIO.2 DatagramChannel.open() method. This method gets a parameter known as a *protocol family* parameter, which is actually a java.net.ProtocolFamily object. This interface is new in NIO.2, and it represents a family of communication protocols—currently it has an implementation as java.net.StandardProtocolFamily and defines two enum constants:

- StandardProtocolFamily.INET: IP version 4 (IPv4)

- StandardProtocolFamily.INET6: IP version 6 (IPv6)

So, we can create a server datagram–oriented socket for IPv4 like this:

```
DatagramChannel datagramChannel = DatagramChannel.open(StandardProtocolFamily.INET);
```

The old NIO no-argument DatagramChannel.open() method is still available and can be used since it is not deprecated. But in this case, the ProtocolFamily of the channel's socket is platform (configuration) dependent and therefore unspecified.

You can check if a datagram-oriented socket channel is already open or has been successfully opened by calling the DatagramChannel.isOpen() method, which returns the corresponding Boolean value:

```
if (datagramChannel.isOpen()) {
    ...
}
```

A client datagram–oriented socket channel can be created and checked in the same manner.

Setting Datagram-Oriented Socket Channel Options

Datagram-oriented socket channels support the following options (although you can use the default values in most cases): SO_REUSEADDR, SO_BROADCAST, IP_MULTICAST_LOOP, SO_SNDBUF, IP_MULTICAST_TTL, IP_TOS, IP_MULTICAST_IF, and SO_RCVBUF. As an example, we can set the input and output buffers used by the networking implementation as follows:

```
datagramChannel.setOption(StandardSocketOptions.SO_RCVBUF, 4 * 1024);
datagramChannel.setOption(StandardSocketOptions.SO_SNDBUF, 4 * 1024);
```

Notice that you can find out the supported options for a datagram-oriented socket channel by calling the inherited method supportedOptions():

```
Set<SocketOption<?>> options = datagramChannel.supportedOptions();
for(SocketOption<?> option : options) System.out.println(option);
```

Binding the Datagram-Oriented Socket Channel

At this point we can bind the channel's socket to a local address and configure the socket to listen for connections. For this we call the new DatagramChannel.bind() method (this method was introduced earlier in the "NetworkChannel Overview" section). Our server will wait for an incoming connection on localhost (127.0.0.1), port 5555 (arbitrarily chosen):

```
final int LOCAL_PORT = 5555;
final String LOCAL_IP = "127.0.0.1";
datagramChannel.bind(new InetSocketAddress(LOCAL_IP, LOCAL_PORT));
```

The wildcard address can also be used:

```
datagramChannel.bind(new InetSocketAddress(LOCAL_PORT));
```

The local address can also be automatically assigned if we pass null to the bind() method. You can also discover the bound local address by calling the ServerSocketChannel.getLocalAddress() method, which is inherited from the NetworkChannel interface. This returns null if the datagram-oriented socket channel has not been bound yet.

```
System.out.println(datagramChannel.getLocalAddress());
```

Transmitting Data Packets

At this point our server is ready to receive and send packets. Since UDP is a connectionless network protocol, you cannot just by default read and write to a DatagramChannel like you do from other channels—later, you will see how to set up a connection over UDP. Instead, you send and receive packets of data using the DatagramChannel.send() and DatagramChannel.receive() methods.

When you send a packet, you pass to the send() method a ByteBuffer that contains the precious data and the remote address (of the server or client, depending who is sending). Here's how this works according to the official documentation (see http://download.oracle.com/javase/7/docs/api/):

If this channel is in non-blocking mode and there is sufficient room in the underlying output buffer, or if this channel is in blocking mode and sufficient room becomes available, then the remaining bytes in the given buffer are transmitted as a single datagram to the given target address. This method may be invoked at any time. If another thread has already initiated a write operation upon this channel, however, then an invocation of this method will block until the first operation is complete. If this channel's socket is not bound then this method will first cause the socket to be bound to an address that is assigned automatically, as if by invoking the bind() method with a parameter of null.

The method will return the number of bytes sent.

When you receive a packet, you pass to the `receive()` method the buffer (`ByteBuffer`) into which the datagram is to be transferred. Again, here's how it works according to the documentation (see `http://download.oracle.com/javase/7/docs/api/`):

If a datagram is immediately available, or if this channel is in blocking mode and one eventually becomes available, then the datagram is copied into the given byte buffer and its source address is returned. If this channel is in non-blocking mode and a datagram is not immediately available then this method immediately returns null. This method may be invoked at any time. If another thread has already initiated a read operation upon this channel, however, then an invocation of this method will block until the first operation is complete. If this channel's socket is not bound then this method will first cause the socket to be bound to an address that is assigned automatically, as if by invoking the bind() method with a parameter of null.

The method will return the datagram's source address, or `null` if this channel is in non-blocking mode and no datagram is immediately available. The remote address can be used to find out where to send an answer packet.

In addition, you can find out the remote address by calling the `DatagramChannel.getRemoteAddress()` method. This method is new in Java 7 (NIO.2), and it returns the remote address to which this channel's socket is connected—keep in mind that for a UDP connectionless case, this method returns `null`:

```
System.out.println("Connected to: " + datagramChannel.getRemoteAddress());
```

Our datagram echo server will listen for incoming packets in an infinite loop, in blocking mode (by default), and when a packet arrives, it will extract from it the remote address and data. The data is sent back based on the remote address:

```
final int MAX_PACKET_SIZE = 65507;
ByteBuffer echoText = ByteBuffer.allocateDirect(MAX_PACKET_SIZE);
...
while (true) {

    SocketAddress clientAddress = datagramChannel.receive(echoText);

    echoText.flip();
    System.out.println("I have received " + echoText.limit() + " bytes from " +
                                    clientAddress.toString() + "! Sending them back ...");
    datagramChannel.send(echoText, clientAddress);
    echoText.clear();
}
```

Closing the Datagram Channel

When a datagram channel becomes useless, it must be closed. For this, you can call the
DatagramChannel.close() method:

datagramChannel.close();

Again, the Java 7 try-with-resources features can be used for automatic closing.

Putting All Together into the Server

Now we have everything we need for creating our server. Putting all of the previous information together
will provide us the following server:

```java
import java.io.IOException;
import java.net.InetSocketAddress;
import java.net.SocketAddress;
import java.net.StandardProtocolFamily;
import java.nio.channels.DatagramChannel;
import java.net.StandardSocketOptions;
import java.nio.ByteBuffer;
import java.nio.channels.ClosedChannelException;

public class Main {

 public static void main(String[] args) {
  final int LOCAL_PORT = 5555;
  final String LOCAL_IP = "127.0.0.1";  //modify this to your local IP
  final int MAX_PACKET_SIZE = 65507;

  ByteBuffer echoText = ByteBuffer.allocateDirect(MAX_PACKET_SIZE);

  //create a new datagram channel
  try (DatagramChannel datagramChannel = DatagramChannel.open(StandardProtocolFamily.INET)) {

      //check if the channel was successfully opened
      if (datagramChannel.isOpen()) {

          System.out.println("Echo server was successfully opened!");
          //set some options
          datagramChannel.setOption(StandardSocketOptions.SO_RCVBUF, 4 * 1024);
          datagramChannel.setOption(StandardSocketOptions.SO_SNDBUF, 4 * 1024);
          //bind the channel to local address
          datagramChannel.bind(new InetSocketAddress(LOCAL_IP, LOCAL_PORT));
          System.out.println("Echo server was binded on:"+datagramChannel.getLocalAddress());
          System.out.println("Echo server is ready to echo ...");

          //transmitting data packets
          while (true) {

                  SocketAddress clientAddress = datagramChannel.receive(echoText);
```

```
                    echoText.flip();
                    System.out.println("I have received " + echoText.limit() + " bytes from " +
                                        clientAddress.toString() + "! Sending them back ...");
                    datagramChannel.send(echoText, clientAddress);
                    echoText.clear();
                }
        } else {
            System.out.println("The channel cannot be opened!");
        }
    } catch (Exception ex) {
            if (ex instanceof ClosedChannelException) {
                System.err.println("The channel was unexpected closed ...");
            }
            if (ex instanceof SecurityException) {
                System.err.println("A security exception occured ...");
            }
            if (ex instanceof IOException) {
                System.err.println("An I/O error occured ...");
            }

            System.err.println("\n" + ex);
    }
  }
 }
}
```

Writing a Connectionless UDP Client

Writing a connectionless UDP client is similar to writing a UDP server. After creating a new DatagramChannel in the same manner as shown previously, and setting whatever options you need, you can start sending and receiving data packets. A client datagram–oriented socket channel doesn't have to be bound to a local address, since the server will extract the IP address and port from each received data packet—in other words, it knows where the client lives. Moreover, if this channel's socket is not bound, then the send() and receive() methods will first cause the socket (client or server) to be bound to an address that is assigned automatically, as if by invoking the bind() method with a parameter of null. But keep in mind that if the server side is automatically bound (not explicitly), then the client should be aware of the chosen address (or more precisely, of the chosen IP address and port). The opposite is also true if the server sends the first data packet.

Our client knows that the server lives at the address 127.0.0.1, port 5555; therefore, it sends the first data packet and receives the answer from it. Here it is the code:

```java
import java.io.IOException;
import java.net.InetSocketAddress;
import java.net.StandardProtocolFamily;
import java.nio.channels.DatagramChannel;
import java.net.StandardSocketOptions;
import java.nio.ByteBuffer;
import java.nio.CharBuffer;
import java.nio.channels.ClosedChannelException;
import java.nio.charset.Charset;
import java.nio.charset.CharsetDecoder;

public class Main {

 public static void main(String[] args) throws IOException {

  final int REMOTE_PORT = 5555;
  final String REMOTE_IP = "127.0.0.1"; //modify this accordingly if you want to test remote
  final int MAX_PACKET_SIZE = 65507;

  CharBuffer charBuffer = null;
  Charset charset = Charset.defaultCharset();
  CharsetDecoder decoder = charset.newDecoder();
  ByteBuffer textToEcho = ByteBuffer.wrap("Echo this: I'm a big and ugly server!".getBytes());
  ByteBuffer echoedText = ByteBuffer.allocateDirect(MAX_PACKET_SIZE);

  //create a new datagram channel
  try (DatagramChannel datagramChannel = DatagramChannel.open(StandardProtocolFamily.INET)) {

      //check if the channel was successfully opened
      if (datagramChannel.isOpen()) {

          //set some options
          datagramChannel.setOption(StandardSocketOptions.SO_RCVBUF, 4 * 1024);
          datagramChannel.setOption(StandardSocketOptions.SO_SNDBUF, 4 * 1024);

          //transmitting data packets
          int sent = datagramChannel.send(textToEcho,
                                      new InetSocketAddress(REMOTE_IP, REMOTE_PORT));
          System.out.println("I have successfully sent "+sent+ " bytes to the Echo Server!");

          datagramChannel.receive(echoedText);

          echoedText.flip();
          charBuffer = decoder.decode(echoedText);
          System.out.println(charBuffer.toString());
          echoedText.clear();

      } else {
        System.out.println("The channel cannot be opened!");
```

```
    }
  } catch (Exception ex) {
    if (ex instanceof ClosedChannelException) {
        System.err.println("The channel was unexpected closed ...");
    }
    if (ex instanceof SecurityException) {
        System.err.println("A security exception occured ...");
    }
    if (ex instanceof IOException) {
        System.err.println("An I/O error occured ...");
    }

    System.err.println("\n" + ex);
  }
 }
}
```

Testing the UDP Connectionless Echo Application

Testing the application is a simple task. First, start the server and wait until you see the following message:

```
Echo server was successfully opened!
Echo server was binded on: /127.0.0.1:5555
Echo server is ready to echo ...
```

Then start the client and check out the output. Here is some possible output from the UDP server:

```
Echo server was successfully opened!

Echo server was binded on: /127.0.0.1:5555

Echo server is ready to echo ...

I have received 37 bytes from /127.0.0.1:49155! Sending them back ...
```

And here is some possible UDP client output:

```
I have successfully sent 37 bytes to the Echo Server!

Echo this: I'm a big and ugly server!
```

■ **Caution** Don't forget to manually stop the UDP server after finishing tests!

Writing a Connected UDP Client

If you want to use the `DatagramChannel.read()` and `DatagramChannel.write()` methods (based on `ByteBuffer`s), rather then `send()` and `receive()`, you need to write a connected UDP client. In a connected-client scenario, the channel's socket is configured so that it only receives/sends datagrams from/to the given remote *peer* address. After the connection is established, data packets may not be received/sent from/to any other address. A datagram-oriented socket remains connected until it is explicitly disconnected or until it is closed.

This type of client must explicitly call the `DatagramChannel.connect()` method and pass to it the server-side remote address, as follows:

```
final int REMOTE_PORT = 5555;
final String REMOTE_IP = "127.0.0.1";
datagramChannel.connect(new InetSocketAddress(REMOTE_IP, REMOTE_PORT));
```

Notice that, unlike the `SocketChannel.connect()` method, this method does not actually send/receive any packets across the network, since UDP is a connectionless protocol—this method returns pretty quickly, and does not block the application in a concrete sense. There is no need here for a `finishConnect()` or `isConnectionPending()` method. This method may be invoked at any time, because it will not affect read/write operations that are already in progress at the moment that it is invoked. If this channel's socket is not bound, then this method will first cause the socket to be bound to an address that is assigned automatically, as if invoking the `bind()` method with a parameter of `null`.

You can check out a connection status by calling the `DatagramChannel.isConnected()` method. A corresponding `boolean` value will be returned (`true` if this channel's socket is open and connected):

```
if (datagramChannel.isConnected()) {
    ...
}
```

The following application is a UDP connected client for our UDP echo server. It connects to the remote address and uses `read()`/`write()` methods for transmitting data:

```
import java.io.IOException;
import java.net.InetSocketAddress;
import java.net.StandardProtocolFamily;
import java.nio.channels.DatagramChannel;
import java.net.StandardSocketOptions;
import java.nio.ByteBuffer;
import java.nio.CharBuffer;
import java.nio.channels.ClosedChannelException;
import java.nio.charset.Charset;
import java.nio.charset.CharsetDecoder;

public class Main {

 public static void main(String[] args) throws IOException {

    final int REMOTE_PORT = 5555;
    final String REMOTE_IP = "127.0.0.1"; //modify this accordingly if you want to test remote
    final int MAX_PACKET_SIZE = 65507;

    CharBuffer charBuffer = null;
    Charset charset = Charset.defaultCharset();
```

```java
CharsetDecoder decoder = charset.newDecoder();
ByteBuffer textToEcho = ByteBuffer.wrap("Echo this: I'm a big and ugly server!".getBytes());
ByteBuffer echoedText = ByteBuffer.allocateDirect(MAX_PACKET_SIZE);

//create a new datagram channel
try (DatagramChannel datagramChannel = DatagramChannel.open(StandardProtocolFamily.INET)) {

    //set some options
    datagramChannel.setOption(StandardSocketOptions.SO_RCVBUF, 4 * 1024);
    datagramChannel.setOption(StandardSocketOptions.SO_SNDBUF, 4 * 1024);

    //check if the channel was successfully opened
    if (datagramChannel.isOpen()) {

        //connect to remote address
        datagramChannel.connect(new InetSocketAddress(REMOTE_IP, REMOTE_PORT));

        //check if the channel was successfully connected
        if (datagramChannel.isConnected()) {

            //transmitting data packets
            int sent = datagramChannel.write(textToEcho);
            System.out.println("I have successfully sent "+sent
                                                +" bytes to the Echo Server!");

            datagramChannel.read(echoedText);

            echoedText.flip();
            charBuffer = decoder.decode(echoedText);
            System.out.println(charBuffer.toString());
            echoedText.clear();

        } else {
            System.out.println("The channel cannot be connected!");
        }
    } else {
        System.out.println("The channel cannot be opened!");
    }
} catch (Exception ex) {
    if (ex instanceof ClosedChannelException) {
        System.err.println("The channel was unexpected closed ...");
    }
    if (ex instanceof SecurityException) {
        System.err.println("A security exception occured ...");
    }
    if (ex instanceof IOException) {
        System.err.println("An I/O error occured ...");
    }

    System.err.println("\n" + ex);
}
}
```

```
}
```
The well-known read()/write() methods are available in DatagramChannel:

- Reading sequence of bytes from this channel into the given buffer. These methods return the number of bytes read (it can be zero) or –1 if the channel has reached the end of the stream:

```
public abstract int read(ByteBuffer dst) throws IOException
public final long read(ByteBuffer[] dsts) throws IOException
public abstract long read(ByteBuffer[] dsts, int offset, int length) throws IOException
```

- Writing a sequence of bytes to this channel from the given buffer. These methods return the number of bytes written; it can be zero:

```
public abstract int write(ByteBuffer src) throws IOException
public final long write(ByteBuffer[] srcs) throws IOException
public abstract long write(ByteBuffer[] srcs, int offset, int length) throws IOException
```

Testing the UDP Connected Echo Application

Testing the application is a simple task. First, start the server and wait until you see this message:

```
Echo server was successfully opened!

Echo server was binded on: /127.0.0.1:5555

Echo server is ready to echo ...
```

Then start the client and check out the output. The UDP server output is shown here:

```
Echo server was successfully opened!

Echo server was binded on: /127.0.0.1:5555

Echo server is ready to echo ...

I have received 37 bytes from /127.0.0.1:57374! Sending them back ...
```

Here's the UDP client output:

```
I have successfully sent 37 bytes to the Echo Server!

Echo this: I'm a big and ugly server!
```

Multicasting

You are probably already familiar with the term *multicasting*. But, if you are not, let's have a short overview of this concept. Without academic descriptions and definitions, think of multicasting as the Internet's version of broadcasting. For example, a television station broadcasts its signal from one source, but the signal can reach everyone that lives in the signal area—only the ones that do not have the right equipment or refuse to catch the signal will fail to receive the transmission.

In the computer world, the TV station can be translated to a main node, or machine, that spreads datagrams to a group of destination hosts. This is possible thanks to the *multicast transport service*, which sends datagrams from a source to multiple receivers in a single call—this opposed to the *unicast transport service*, which is specific to high-level network protocols that are based on point-to-point connections and requires a replicated unicast for sending the same data to multiple points (actually, it sends a copy of the data to each point).

Multicasting introduces the notion of a group for representing the receivers of the datagrams. A group is identified by a class D IP address (a multicast group IPv4 address is between 224.0.0.1 and 239.255.255.255). When a new receiver (client) wants to join a multicast group, it needs to connect to the group through the corresponding IP address and listen for the incoming datagrams.

Many real-life cases can be programmed based on multicasting, such as online conferencing, news distribution, advertising, e-mail groups, and data-sharing management.

Next, we'll discuss NIO.2's contribution to multicasting.

MulticastChannel Overview

NIO.2 comes with a new interface for mapping a network channel that supports IP multicasting. This is the java.nio.channels.MulticastChannel interface. At the API level, this is a subinterface of the NetworkChannel interface presented earlier in this chapter, and it is implemented by a single class: the DatagramChannel class.

Basically, it defines two join() methods and a close() method. Focusing on the join() methods, here it is a short overview:

- The first join() method is called by a client who wants to join a multicast group for receiving the incoming datagrams. We need to pass the IP address of the group and the network interface on which to join the group (you will see shortly how to check if your machine has a network interface capable of multicasting). If the indicated group is successfully joined, this method returns a MembershipKey instance. This is new in NIO.2, and it is a token representing the membership of an IP multicast group (see the next section).

```
MembershipKey join(InetAddress g, NetworkInterface i) throws IOException
```

- The second join() method is also used for joining a multicast group. In this case, however, we indicate a source address from which group members can begin receiving datagrams. Membership is *cumulative*, which means that this method may be invoked again with the same group and interface for receiving datagrams sent by other source addresses to the group.

```
MembershipKey join(InetAddress g, NetworkInterface i, InetAddress s) throws IOException
```

> ■ **Note** A multicast channel may join several multicast groups, including the same group on more than one interface.

The `close()` method is used to drop the membership (if any group was joined) and close the channel.

MembershipKey Overview

When you join a multicast group, you get a membership key that can be used to perform different kinds of actions inside that group. The most common are presented here:

- *Block/unblock*: You can block the sent datagrams from a specific source by calling the `block()` method and passing the source address. Moreover, you can unblock the blocked source by calling the `unblock()` method with the same address.

- *Get group*: You can get the source address of the multicast group for which this membership key was created by calling the no-argument `group()` method. This method returns an `InetAddress` object.

- *Get channel*: You can get the channel for which this membership key was created by calling the no-argument method `channel()`. This method returns a `MulticastChannel` object.

- *Get source address*: If the membership key is source specific (receives only datagrams from a specific source address), you can get the source address by calling the no-argument `sourceAddress()` method. This method returns an `InetAddress` object.

- *Get network interface*: You can get the network interface for which this membership key was created by calling the no-argument `networkInterface()` method. This method returns a `NetworkInterface` object.

- *Check validity*: You can check if a membership is valid by calling the `isValid()` method. This method returns a `boolean` value.

- *Drop*: You can drop membership (the channel will no longer receive any datagrams sent to the group) by calling the no-argument `drop()` method.

A membership key is valid when you create it and remains valid until the membership is dropped by using the `drop()` method or the channel is closed.

NetworkInterface Overview

The `NetworkInterface` class represents a *network interface*, which is made up of a name and a list of IP addresses assigned to this interface. It is used to identify the local interface to which a multicast group is joined. For example, the following code will return information about all the network interfaces found on your machine:

```java
import java.net.InetAddress;
import java.net.NetworkInterface;
import java.util.Enumeration;

public class Main {

 public static void main(String argv[]) throws Exception {

  Enumeration enumInterfaces = NetworkInterface.getNetworkInterfaces();
  while (enumInterfaces.hasMoreElements()) {
     NetworkInterface net = (NetworkInterface) enumInterfaces.nextElement();
     System.out.println("Network Interface Display Name: " + net.getDisplayName());
     System.out.println(net.getDisplayName() + " is up and running ?" + net.isUp());
     System.out.println(net.getDisplayName()+" Supports Multicast: "+net.supportsMulticast());
     System.out.println(net.getDisplayName() + " Name: " + net.getName());
     System.out.println(net.getDisplayName() + " Is Virtual:  " + net.isVirtual());
     System.out.println("IP addresses:");
     Enumeration enumIP = net.getInetAddresses();
     while (enumIP.hasMoreElements()) {
        InetAddress ip = (InetAddress) enumIP.nextElement();
        System.out.println("IP address:" + ip);
     }
  }
 }
}
```

This application will return all the network interfaces found on your machine, and for each one will render its *display name* (a human-readable `String` describing the network device) and *name* (the real name used to identify a network interface). Moreover, each network interface is checked to see if it supports multicast, if it is virtual (a subinterface), and if it is up and running.

Figure 8-4 shows a fragment of output on my machine. The framed interface is the one used for testing multicast applications—its name is eth3 and will be used later in the client/server multicast application for indicating this interface.

207

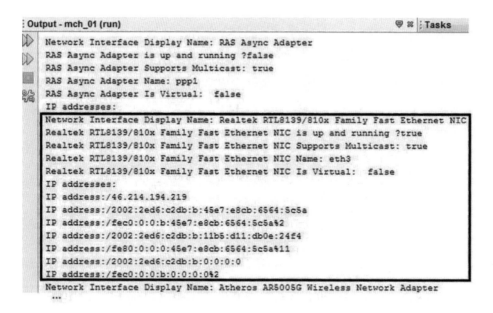

Figure 8-4. *Find out local interfaces.*

Writing a UDP Multicast Server

In this section, we will write a UDP multicast server that sends to the group datagrams containing the current date and time on the server. This will be repeated every 10 seconds. Now that we have some experience with writing UDP client/server applications, there is no need to repeat the entire process step by step. We'll just point out the main differences that transform a usual UDP client/server application into a UDP multicast client/server application.

We start the developing process by creating a new `DatagramChannel` object by calling the `open()` method. Next, we set two important options, `IP_MULTICAST_IF` and `SO_REUSEADDR`. The first one will indicate the network interface for IP multicast datagrams used in this case, and the second one should be enabled prior to binding the socket—this is required to allow multiple members of the group to bind to the same address:

```
NetworkInterface networkInterface = NetworkInterface.getByName("eth3");
...
datagramChannel.setOption(StandardSocketOptions.IP_MULTICAST_IF, networkInterface);
datagramChannel.setOption(StandardSocketOptions.SO_REUSEADDR, true);
```

Next, we bind the channel's socket to the local address by calling the `bind()` method:

```
final int DEFAULT_PORT = 5555;
datagramChannel.bind(new InetSocketAddress(DEFAULT_PORT));
```

Finally, we prepare the datagram-transmitting code. Since we send to the group the server date and time every 10 seconds, we need an infinite loop containing a sleep duration of 10 seconds and a call to the **send()** method. The multicast group IP address was arbitrarily chosen as 225.4.5.6, and it is mapped by an **InetAddress** object:

```
final int DEFAULT_PORT = 5555;
final String GROUP = "225.4.5.6";
ByteBuffer datetime;
...
while (true) {

    //sleep for 10 seconds
    try {
        Thread.sleep(10000);
    } catch (InterruptedException ex) {}

    System.out.println("Sending data ...");
    datetime = ByteBuffer.wrap(new Date().toString().getBytes());
    datagramChannel.send(datetime, new
                    InetSocketAddress(InetAddress.getByName(GROUP), DEFAULT_PORT));
    datetime.flip();
}
```

Putting everything together will result in the following application:

```
import java.io.IOException;
import java.net.InetAddress;
import java.net.InetSocketAddress;
import java.net.NetworkInterface;
import java.net.StandardProtocolFamily;
import java.nio.channels.DatagramChannel;
import java.net.StandardSocketOptions;
import java.nio.ByteBuffer;
import java.util.Date;

public class Main {

 public static void main(String[] args) {

  final int DEFAULT_PORT = 5555;
  final String GROUP = "225.4.5.6";
  ByteBuffer datetime;

  //create a new channel
  try (DatagramChannel datagramChannel = DatagramChannel.open(StandardProtocolFamily.INET)) {

      //check if the channel was successfully created
      if (datagramChannel.isOpen()) {

          //get the network interface used for multicast
          NetworkInterface networkInterface = NetworkInterface.getByName("eth3");

          //set some options
```

```
                datagramChannel.setOption(StandardSocketOptions.IP_MULTICAST_IF, networkInterface);
                datagramChannel.setOption(StandardSocketOptions.SO_REUSEADDR, true);

                //bind the channel to the local address
                datagramChannel.bind(new InetSocketAddress(DEFAULT_PORT));
                System.out.println("Date-time server is ready ... shortly I'll start sending ...");

                //transmitting datagrams
                while (true) {

                        //sleep for 10 seconds
                        try {
                            Thread.sleep(10000);
                        } catch (InterruptedException ex) {}

                        System.out.println("Sending data ...");
                        datetime = ByteBuffer.wrap(new Date().toString().getBytes());
                        datagramChannel.send(datetime, new
                                    InetSocketAddress(InetAddress.getByName(GROUP), DEFAULT_PORT));
                        datetime.flip();
                }
        } else {
            System.out.println("The channel cannot be opened!");
        }
    } catch (IOException ex) {
        System.err.println(ex);
    }
  }
 }
}
```

Writing a UDP Multicast Client

The code for a UDP multicast client is almost the same as for a server, with a few differences. First, you may want to check if the remote address is actually a multicast address—this is possible by calling the InetAddress.isMulticastAddress() method, which returns a boolean. And second, since this is a client, it must join the group by calling one of the two join() methods. The datagram-transmitting code is adapted only for receiving datagrams from the UDP multicast server. The following application is a possible client implementation:

```
import java.io.IOException;
import java.net.InetAddress;
import java.net.InetSocketAddress;
import java.net.NetworkInterface;
import java.net.StandardProtocolFamily;
import java.nio.channels.DatagramChannel;
import java.net.StandardSocketOptions;
import java.nio.ByteBuffer;
import java.nio.CharBuffer;
import java.nio.channels.MembershipKey;
import java.nio.charset.Charset;
import java.nio.charset.CharsetDecoder;
```

```
public class Main {

 public static void main(String[] args) {

  final int DEFAULT_PORT = 5555;
  final int MAX_PACKET_SIZE = 65507;
  final String GROUP = "225.4.5.6";

  CharBuffer charBuffer = null;
  Charset charset = Charset.defaultCharset();
  CharsetDecoder decoder = charset.newDecoder();
  ByteBuffer datetime = ByteBuffer.allocateDirect(MAX_PACKET_SIZE);

  //create a new channel
  try (DatagramChannel datagramChannel = DatagramChannel.open(StandardProtocolFamily.INET)) {

      InetAddress group = InetAddress.getByName(GROUP);
      //check if the group address is multicast
      if (group.isMulticastAddress()) {
          //check if the channel was successfully created
          if (datagramChannel.isOpen()) {
              //get the network interface used for multicast
              NetworkInterface networkInterface = NetworkInterface.getByName("eth3");

              //set some options
              datagramChannel.setOption(StandardSocketOptions.SO_REUSEADDR, true);
              //bind the channel to the local address
              datagramChannel.bind(new InetSocketAddress(DEFAULT_PORT));
              //join the multicast group and get ready to receive datagrams
              MembershipKey key = datagramChannel.join(group, networkInterface);

              //wait for datagrams
              while (true) {

                      if (key.isValid()) {

                          datagramChannel.receive(datetime);
                          datetime.flip();
                          charBuffer = decoder.decode(datetime);
                          System.out.println(charBuffer.toString());
                          datetime.clear();
                      } else {
                        break;
                      }
                  }

          } else {
            System.out.println("The channel cannot be opened!");
          }
      } else {
        System.out.println("This is not  multicast address!");
```

```
        }

    } catch (IOException ex) {
        System.err.println(ex);
    }
  }
}
```

Blocking and Unblocking Datagrams

Sometimes joining multicast groups can bring to you undesired datagrams (the reasons are not relevant here). You can block receiving a datagram from a sender by calling the `MembershipKey.block()` method and passing to it the `InetAddress` of that sender. In addition, you can unblock the same sender, and start receiving datagrams from it again, by calling the `MembershipKey.unblock()` method and passing it the same `InetAddress`. Usually, you'll be in one of the following two scenarios:

- You have a list of senders' addresses that you'd like to join. Supposing that the addresses are stored in a `List`, you can loop it and join each address separately, as shown here:

```
List<InetAddress> like = ...;
DatagramChannel datagramChannel =...;

if(!like.isEmpty()){
    for(InetAddress source: like){
        datagramChannel.join(group, network_interface, source);
    }
}
```

- You have a list of senders' addresses that you don't want to join. Supposing that the addresses are stored in a `List`, then you can loop it and block each address separately, as shown here:

```
List<InetAddress> dislike = ...;
DatagramChannel datagramChannel =...;

MembershipKey key = datagramChannel.join(group, network_interface);

if(!dislike.isEmpty()){
    for(InetAddress source: dislike){
        key.block(source);
    }
}
```

Testing the UDP Multicast Application

Testing the application is a simple task. First, start the multicast server and wait until you see this message:

```
Date-time server is ready ... shortly I'll start sending ..
```

Then start the client and check out the output. Here is some example output for the UDP multicast server:

```
Date-time server is ready ... shortly I'll start sending ...

Sending data ...

Sending data ...

Sending data ...

Sending data ...

Sending data ...
```

Here is the UDP client output (the client is started after a few minutes):

```
Sat Oct 08 09:40:09 GMT+02:00 2011

Sat Oct 08 09:40:19 GMT+02:00 2011
```

Performing some tests on this example will reveal some issues. When the server is started, it sends datagrams without being aware of whether any client is listening for those datagrams. Also, it is not aware of when clients join or leave the group. On the opposite side, the client starts receiving datagrams when it joins the group, but is not aware of whether the server stops sending because of any causes. If the server goes offline, the client is still waiting, and it will receive again when the server is online again and begins sending. It can be an interesting exercise to try solving these issues if your case requires more control. Also, you may want to experiment with threads, blocking /non-blocking modes, and connectionless/connected features to add more flexibly and performance to your multicasting applications.

Summary

This chapter covered the NIO.2 features for creating TCP/UDP client/server applications. As discussed, NIO.2 has improved this support by updating existing classes with new methods and adding new interfaces/classes for writing such applications.

The chapter began with the NetworkChannel interface, which provides methods commons to all network channel classes. It also covered the main classes dedicated to synchronous socket channels: ServerSocketChannel, SocketChannel, and DatagramChannel. It also discussed the MulticastChannel interface—a subinterface of NetworkChannel that maps a network channel that supports IP multicasting. Finally, you saw how to write a single-thread blocking/non-blocking TCP client/server application, a single-thread blocking UDP client/server application, and a single-thread multicast UDP client/server application.

CHAPTER 9

■ ■ ■

The Asynchronous Channel API

We've finally reached the most powerful feature introduced in NIO.2, the asynchronous channel API. As you'll see in this chapter, the asynchronous I/O (AIO) Java 7 journey starts in the `java.nio.channels.AsynchronousChannel` interface, which extends a channel with asynchronous I/O operations support. This interface is implemented by three classes: `AsynchronousFileChannel`, `AsynchronousSocketChannel`, and `AsynchronousServerSocketChannel`. There is a fourth class, `AsynchronousDatagramChannel`, which was added in the Java 7 beta release and then removed in the Java 7 final release; at this writing, this class is not available, but it may appear in future Java 7 releases, so this chapter covers it in sufficient depth to make you aware of its purpose. These classes are similar in style to the NIO.2 channel APIs. In addition, there is an asynchronous channel named `AsynchronousByteChannel` that can read and write bytes and stands up as a subinterface of `AsynchronousChannel` (this subinterface is implemented by the `AsynchronousSocketChannel` class). Moreover, the new API introduces a class named `AsynchronousChannelGroup`, which presents the concept of an *asynchronous channel group*, in which each asynchronous channel belongs to a channel group (the default one or a specified one) that shares a pool of Java threads. These threads receive instructions to perform I/O events and they dispatch the results to the completion handlers. All the effort is for the purpose of handling the completion of initiated asynchronous I/O operations.

In this chapter, you will see the asynchronous mechanism from the Java perspective. You will see the big picture of how Java implements asynchronous I/O, after which you will develop related applications for files and sockets. We will start with asynchronous I/O for files by exploring the `AsynchronousFileChannel` class and continue with asynchronous I/O for TCP sockets and UDP sockets.

But, before we jump into the features of the API, a short overview of the difference between synchronous I/O and asynchronous I/O is in order.

Synchronous I/O vs. Asynchronous I/O

The difference between synchronous and asynchronous execution may seem a bit confusing at first, so let's clear it up. Basically, there are two types of input/output (I/O) synchronization: *synchronous I/O* and *asynchronous I/O* (also referred to as *overlapped I/O*). In a synchronous I/O operation, a thread enters into action and waits until the I/O request is completed (the program is "stuck" waiting for the process to end, with no way out). When the same action occurs in an asynchronous environment, a thread performs the I/O operation with more kernel help. Actually, it immediately passes the request to the kernel and continues on to process another job. The kernel signals to the thread when the operation has completed, and the thread "respects" the signal by interrupting its current job and processing the data from the I/O operation as necessary. In the Java spirit of platform independence, asynchronous I/O can be tied to multiple threads—basically, allowing something to be processed on a separate thread.

Asynchronous I/O and synchronous I/O serve different purposes. You can use synchronous I/O if you simply want to make a request and receive a response. Synchronous I/O limits performance and scalability since it is *one thread per I/O connection*, and running thousands of threads significantly increases overhead on the operating system. Asynchronous I/O is a different programming model, because you don't necessarily wait for a response, but rather submit your work for execution and then come back for a response either almost immediately or sometime later. Therefore, asynchronous I/O seems to be better than synchronous I/O, since performance and scalability are keywords of the I/O system. Various important operating systems, such as Windows and Linux, support fast, scalable I/O based on the use of asynchronous notifications of I/O operations taking place in the OS layers.

In summary, I/O processing that is expected to take a large amount of time can be optimized by using asynchronous I/O. For relatively fast I/O operations, synchronous I/O would be better because the overhead of processing kernel I/O requests and kernel signals may make asynchronous I/O less beneficial.

Asynchronous I/O Big Picture

When talking about asynchronous I/O in Java, we are talking about the *asynchronous channels*. An asynchronous channel is a connection that supports multiple I/O operations in parallel through separate threads (connecting, reading, and writing, for example) and provides mechanisms for controlling the operations after they've been initiated.

This section discusses a few important aspects that are common to all asynchronous channels. Foremost, note that all asynchronous channels initiate I/O operations (does not block the application to perform other tasks) and provide notifications when I/O completes. This rule is the foundation of asynchronous channels, and from it derives the entire asynchronous channel API.

To begin our discussion of the asynchronous I/O big picture, we'll look at forms. All asynchronous I/O operations have one of two *forms*:

- Pending result

- Complete result

Pending Result and the Future Class

The first form returns a `java.util.concurrent.Future<V>` object and represents the *pending result* of an asynchronous I/O operation. Through `Future`'s methods we can check if the operation is complete, wait for its completion (if it's not already complete), and retrieve the result of the operation.

For example, you can perform boolean checks through the `Future.isXXX()` methods: you can find out if the operation is complete by calling the `Future.isDone()` method, or you can check if the operation was canceled by calling the `Future.isCancelled()` method. You can explicitly cancel an operation by calling the Future.`cancel()` method, which will return a boolean representing the success of the cancellation—if the thread executing this task should be interrupted, then pass `true` to this method; otherwise, in-progress tasks are allowed to complete. This attempt will fail if the task has already completed, has already been canceled, or could not be canceled for some other reason. If successful, and this task had not started when `cancel()` was called, the task should never run.

■ **Caution** When canceling an asynchronous I/O operation, all threads waiting on the result will throw `CancellationException`. There is no guarantee that the underlying I/O operation will be canceled right away, but it is guaranteed that further attempts to initiate I/O operations that are "the same" as the operation that was canceled will not be allowed (i.e., the channel is put into an implementation-specific *error state*). Also, keep in mind that if the `cancel()` method argument was set to `true`, then the I/O operation may be interrupted by closing the channel—all threads waiting on the result of the I/O operation will throw `CancellationException`, and any other I/O operations outstanding on the channel complete with the exception `AsynchronousCloseException`.

■ **Tip** Make sure that the I/O buffers involved in a canceled read/write operation are not further accessed while the channel remains open.

The result of the operation can only be retrieved using the methods `Future.get()` and `Future.get(long timeout, TimeUnit unit)` after the operation has completed, waiting if necessary until it is ready or the specified timeout has expired. In this case, a `TimeoutException` will be thrown. The `V` represents the result type returned by this `Future`'s `get()` method, which means that this is the result type of the operation.

Complete Result and the CompletionHandler Interface

The second form, complete result, is reminiscent of the well-known *callback* mechanism (such as AJAX callbacks). This is an alternative mechanism to the `Future` form. We register a callback to the asynchronous I/O operation (read or write, for example), and when the operation completes or fails, a handler (`CompletionHandler`) is invoked to consume the result of the operation.

A completion handler is of the form `CompletionHandler<V,A>`, where `V` is the type of the result value and `A` is the type of object attached to the I/O operation. A handler should override two methods: the `completed()` method, which is invoked when the I/O operation completes successfully, and the `failed()` method, which is invoked if the I/O operation fails. If the operation completes successfully, then the result is passed as a parameter to the `completed()` method, and if the operation fails, a `Throwable` is passed to the `failed()` method. Ignoring the operation status, both methods receive an attachment parameter representing an object that is passed in to the asynchronous operation. It can be used to track which operation finished first if the same `CompletionHandler` object is used for multiple operations, but, of course, you may find it useful in other situations. The syntax of these methods looks like this:

```
void completed(V result, A attachment)
void failed(Throwable exc, A attachment)
```

■ **Tip**   Per the official Java Platform SE 7 documentation for CompletionHandler, "The implementations of these methods should complete in a timely manner so as to avoid keeping the invoking thread from dispatching to other completion handlers." The following sections will explain the reason.

Types of Asynchronous Channels

As of this writing, Java 7 comes with the following three types of asynchronous channels. The following subsections briefly describe each one in turn.

- AsynchronousFileChannel

- AsynchronousServerSocketChannel

- AsynchronousSocketChannel

AsynchronousFileChannel

As its name suggests, the AsynchronousFileChannel class represents an asynchronous channel for reading, writing, and manipulating a file. This class provides methods for reading and writing a file based on ByteBuffers. In addition, it provides methods for locking files, truncating files, and getting file sizes, but keep in mind that, unlike a synchronous FileChannel channel, this type of channel does not maintain a global file position (*current position*) or offset. Even if no global position or offset is available, each read or write operation should specify the position in the file from which to read or write. This allows accessing of different parts of the file concurrently.

When you work with an AsynchronousFileChannel channel, you must be careful to take into account the following aspects:

- Closing an asynchronous file channel by explicitly calling the inherited close() method (from the AsynchronousChannel interface) causes all outstanding asynchronous operations on the channel to complete with an AsynchronousCloseException exception. After a channel is closed, further attempts to initiate asynchronous I/O operations complete immediately with cause ClosedChannelException.

- A reading attempt may cause a NonReadableChannelException exception if the channel has not been opened for reading. A writing attempt may cause a NonWritableChannelException exception if this channel has not been opened for writing.

- A locking attempt when a lock is already held by this Java virtual machine, or there is already a pending attempt to lock a region, will cause an OverlappingFileLockException exception.

AsynchronousServerSocketChannel

The AsynchronousServerSocketChannel class represents an asynchronous channel for stream-oriented listening sockets. Opening such a channel type allows us to bind it to a group that has an associated thread pool to which tasks are submitted to handle I/O operations (there is also a *default group* when none is specified). After opening, the channel has the capability to accept incoming connections in an asynchronous manner, which means that we can choose between a Future and a CompletionHandler for tracking the connection status. Important tasks such as binding and setting channel options are provided through the implemented NetworkChannel interface.

When you work with an AsynchronousServerSocketChannel channel, be careful to take into account the following:

- Closing an asynchronous server socket channel by explicitly calling the inherited close() method (from the AsynchronousChannel interface) causes all outstanding asynchronous operations on the channel to complete with an AsynchronousCloseException exception. After a channel is closed, further attempts to initiate asynchronous I/O operations complete immediately with cause ClosedChannelException.

- An opening attempt will cause a ShutdownChannelGroupException exception if the channel group is shut down.

- An attempt to invoke the accept() method on an unbound channel will cause a NotYetBoundException exception to be thrown.

- If a thread initiates an accept operation before a previous accept operation has completed, then an AcceptPendingException exception will be thrown.

AsynchronousSocketChannel

The AsynchronousSocketChannel class represents an asynchronous channel for stream-oriented connecting sockets. Opening such a channel type allows us to bind it to a group that has an associated thread pool to which tasks are submitted to handle I/O operations (there is also a *default group* when none is specified). After opening, the channel has the capability to connect to the remote addresses in an asynchronous manner, which means that we can choose between a Future and a CompletionHandler for tracking the connection status. For a successful connection, this channel can read and write buffers of bytes (sequences of bytes, ByteBuffers) through a sct of read() and write() asynchronous methods—again, we can choose between a Future and a CompletionHandler for tracking the reading or writing status. Important tasks such as binding and setting channel options are provided through the implemented NetworkChannel interface.

When you work with an AsynchronousSocketChannel channel, be careful to take into account the following:

- Closing an asynchronous socket channel by explicitly calling the inherited close() method (from the AsynchronousChannel interface) causes all outstanding asynchronous operations on the channel to end up with an AsynchronousCloseException exception. Further attempts to initiate asynchronous I/O operations over a closed channel will finish immediately with a ClosedChannelException exception.

- An attempt to invoke an I/O operation upon an unconnected channel will cause a `NotYetConnectedException` exception to be thrown.

- If a thread initiates a read operation before a previous read operation has completed, then a `ReadPendingException` exception will be thrown. If a thread initiates a write operation before a previous write operation has completed, then a `WritePendingException` exception will be thrown.

- An attempt to connect to a channel may cause an `AlreadyConnectedException` exception if this channel is already connected.

- An attempt to connect to a channel may cause a `ConnectionPendingException` exception if a connection operation is already in progress on this channel.

- The `read()` and `write()` methods defined by the `AsynchronousSocketChannel` class allow a timeout to be specified when initiating a read or write operation, respectively. If the timeout elapses before an operation completes, then an `InterruptedByTimeoutException` exception will complete the operation. A timeout may leave the channel, or the underlying connection, in an inconsistent state. If the implementation cannot guarantee that bytes have not been read from or written to the channel, then it puts the channel into an implementation-specific *error state*. A subsequent attempt to initiate a read or write operation causes an unspecified runtime exception to be thrown.

Groups

As mentioned in the introduction to the chapter, the asynchronous API introduces a class named `AsynchronousChannelGroup`, which presents the concept of an *asynchronous channel group*, in which each asynchronous channel belongs to a channel group (the default one or a specified one) that shares a pool of Java threads. These threads receive instructions to perform I/O events and they dispatch the results to the completion handlers. The asynchronous channel group encapsulates thread pool and the resources shared by all the threads working for the channels. Also, the *channel* is in effect owned by the group, so if the group is closed, the channel is closed too.

Asynchronous channels are safe for use by multiple concurrent threads. Some channel implementations may support concurrent reading and writing but may not allow more than one read and one write operation to be outstanding at any given time.

Default Group

Besides the developer's created groups, JVM maintains a system-wide *default group* that is constructed automatically, useful for simple applications. When a group is not specified, or a `null` is passed instead, the asynchronous channels are bound, at construction time, to the default group. The default group may be configured by means of two system properties, the first of which follows:

```
java.nio.channels.DefaultThreadPool.threadFactory
```

Following is the description of this property from the official Java Platform SE 7 documentation for the AsynchronousChannelGroup class:

> *The value of this property is taken to be the fully-qualified name of a concrete ThreadFactory class. The class is loaded using the system class loader and instantiated. The factory's newThread method is invoked to create each thread for the default group's thread pool. If the process to load and instantiate the value of the property fails then an unspecified error is thrown during the construction of the default group.*

To paraphrase, this system property defines a java.util.concurrent.ThreadFactory to use instead of the default one.

The second system property is

java.nio.channels.DefaultThreadPool.initialSize

The official Java Platform SE 7documentation provides this description:

> *The value of the initialSize parameter for the default group. The value of the property is taken to be the String representation of an Integer that is the initial size parameter. If the value cannot be parsed as an Integer it causes an unspecified error to be thrown during the construction of the default group.*

In short, this system property specifies the thread pool's initial size.

Custom Groups

If the default group does not satisfy your needs, the AsynchronousChannelGroup class provides three methods for creating your own channel groups. For AsynchronousServerSocketChannel, AsynchronousSocketChannel, and AsynchronousDatagramChannel (unavailable as of this writing), the channel group is passed on creation in the open() method of each one. AsynchronousFileChannel differs from the other channels in that, in order to use a custom thread pool, the open() method takes an ExecutorService instead of an AsynchronousChannelGroup. Now, let's see what the advantages and disadvantages of each supported thread pool are; these characteristics will help you to decide which one is proper in your case.

Fixed Thread Pool

You can request a fixed thread pool by calling the following AsynchronousChannelGroup method:

```
public static AsynchronousChannelGroup withFixedThreadPool(int nThreads,
ThreadFactory threadFactory) throws IOException
```

This method creates a channel group with a fixed thread pool. You must specify the factory to use when creating new threads and the number of threads.

■ **Caution**   The life cycle in a fixed thread pool follows a simple scenario: a thread waits for an I/O event, completes I/O for the event, invokes a completion handler, and goes back to wait for more I/O events (the kernel dispatches events directly to these threads). When the completion handler terminates normally, the thread returns to the thread pool and waits for the next event. But if the completion handler does not complete in a timely manner, then it is possible to enter into an indefinitely blocking. If all threads "deadlock" inside a completion handler, then the application is blocked until a thread is available to execute again, and any new event will be queued until a thread is available. In the worst-case scenario, no thread can get free and the kernel can no longer execute anything. This issue may be avoided if you don't use blocking or long operations inside a completion handler. Also, you may use a cached thread pool or timeouts for avoiding this issue.

Cached Thread Pool

You can request a cached thread pool by calling the following `AsynchronousChannelGroup` method:

```
public static AsynchronousChannelGroup withCachedThreadPool(ExecutorService executor,
 int initialSize) throws IOException
```

This method creates an asynchronous channel group with a given thread pool that creates new threads as needed. You just need to specify the initial number of threads and an `ExecutorService` that creates new threads as needed. It may reuse previously constructed threads when they are available.

In this case the asynchronous channel group will submit events to the thread pool that simply invoke completion handlers. But if the thread pool simply invokes the completion handlers, then who does the hard work and performs the I/O operations? The answer is the *hidden thread pool*. This is a set of separate threads that waits for incoming I/O events. More precisely, the kernel I/O operations are handled by one or more invisible internal threads that dispatch events to a cached pool, which in turn invokes completion handlers.

The hidden thread pool is important because it greatly reduces the probability that the application will be blocked (it solves the fixed thread pool issue) and guarantees that the kernel will be able to complete its I/O operations. But we still have an issue, because the cached thread pool needs unbounded queuing, which can make the queue grow infinitely and cause `OutOfMemoryError`—so monitor the queue (avoid locking all the threads and avoid feeding the queue forever). Avoiding the use of blocking or long operations inside completion handlers is still a good idea.

Designated Thread Pool

You can also request a thread pool by calling the following `AsynchronousChannelGroup` method:

```
public static AsynchronousChannelGroup withThreadPool(ExecutorService executor)
throws IOException
```

This method creates an asynchronous channel group with a designated thread pool. The thread pool is provided through an `ExecutorService` object.

The `ExecutorService` executes tasks submitted to dispatch completion results for operations initiated on asynchronous channels in the group. Using this approach requires extra care when configuring `ExecutorService`—do at least two things here: provide support for *direct handoff* or *unbounded queuing* of submitted tasks, and never allow the thread that invokes the `execute()` method to invoke the task directly.

Shutting Down a Group

Shutting down a group can be accomplished by calling the `shutdown()` method or the `shutdownNow()` method. Calling the `shutdown()` method initiates the procedure of shutting down the group by marking the group as *shutdown*. Further attempts to construct a channel that binds to the group will throw `ShutdownChannelGroupException`. Once it is marked for shutdown, the group begins the *termination* process, which involves waiting for all the bound asynchronous channels to be closed (i.e., the completion handlers have run and the resources have been released).

You can block until the group terminates by calling the `awaitTermination()` method with a specified timeout—the blocking is in charge until the group terminates, the timeout occurs, or the current thread is interrupted, whichever happens first. You can check if a group has terminated by calling the `isTerminated()` method and you can check if it is shut down by calling the `isShutdown()` method. Keep in mind that the `shutdown()` method will not force to stop or interrupt threads that are executing completion handlers.

In addition, forcing a group to shut down can be accomplished by calling the `shutdownNow()` method, which will close all the channels in the group exactly as the `AsynchronousChannel.close()` method closes them. Keep in mind that calling this method will complete with the exception `AsynchronousCloseException` any outstanding asynchronous operations upon this channel. After a channel is closed, further attempts to initiate asynchronous I/O operations complete immediately with cause `ClosedChannelException`.

When a `ServiceExecutor` is specified, it is intended to be used exclusively by the resulting asynchronous channel group. Termination of the group results in the orderly shutdown of the executor service; if the executor service shuts down for some other reason, an unspecified behavior will occur.

■ **Note** In the case of an asynchronous channel for stream-oriented connecting sockets, there is also the possibility to shut down the connection for reading by calling the `shutdownInupt()` method (which will reject any further read attempts by returning the end-of-stream indicator, `-1`) and for writing by calling the `shutdownOutput()` method (which will reject any writing attempts by throwing a `ClosedChannelException` exception). Neither of these methods will close the channel.

ByteBuffer Considerations

As you know, `ByteBuffer`s are not thread-safe. Therefore, you must make sure that you do not access a byte buffer that is currently involved in an I/O operation. A nice solution for avoiding this issue is to use a `ByteBuffer` pool. When an I/O operation is oncoming, you get a byte buffer from the pool, perform the I/O operation, and then return the byte buffer to the pool.

Fixing this issue also fixes another issue regarding the out of memory errors. Memory requirements for buffers depend on the number of outstanding I/O operations, but using a pool will help you to reuse a set of buffers and avoid out of memory issues.

Introducing the ExecutorService API

The earlier discussion of groups referenced the `ExecutorService` API. If you are not familiar with this API, you should consult the official documentation, available at

`http://download.oracle.com/javase/7/docs/api/java/util/concurrent/ExecutorService.html`

This API is an important component of the Java concept of concurrency and multithreading, and it is beyond our aim to present it here since it is a large and complex API. I recommend that you also consult the "Java Concurrency/Multithreading" tutorial of Lars Vogel at `http://www.vogella.de/articles/JavaConcurrency/article.html` (published on May 17, 2011).

To give you a brief introduction, the Executor Framework provides a convenient way to create custom thread pools through the `java.util.concurrent.Executors` class (which contains factory and utility methods for different kinds of interfaces involved in the multithreading API, such as `java.util.concurrent.Executor` and `java.util.concurrent.ExecutorService`). This class contains methods such as `newFixedThreadPool()`, `newCachedThreadPool()`, and `newScheduledThreadPool()`.

Each of these methods creates a number (specified by developer or deduced by default implementation) of *worker* threads. The `ExecutorService` interface adds life cycle methods to the `Executor`, which enables shutting down the `Executor` (`shutdown()` method) and waiting for termination (`awaitTermination()` method). In many cases the Executor Framework works with `Runnable` tasks that do not return results, but when you expect your threads to return a computed result, you can use the `java.util.concurrent.Callable` interface, which makes use of generics to define the type of object returned. The result is computed inside the `Callable.call()` method, which should be overridden accordingly—this throws an `Exception` if the result cannot be computed. Each `Callable` task is submitted to the `Executor` (the `submit()` method) and it returns a `Future` representing the pending result; use this to check the result status and retrieve the result by calling the `get()` method.

Developing Asynchronous Applications

There are so many examples to develop and so many tests to perform to accomplish best scalability with the asynchronous channel API that an entire dedicated book would be required to cover all the details. Since we are covering the topic in a single chapter, we will cut straight to the stub applications, which should provide you with a source of inspiration to develop others.

We start this developing spree with the asynchronous file channel for reading, writing, and manipulating a file. You will see how to perform these I/O operations over a file based on both `Future` and `CompletionHander` forms. We'll then move on to the asynchronous channel for stream-oriented listening sockets and the asynchronous channel for stream-oriented connecting sockets.

Asynchronous File Channel Examples

The first step of any application that involves an asynchronous file channel is to create a new `AsynchronousFileChannel` instance for a file by calling one of the two `open()` methods. The easiest to use will receive the path of the file to open or create and, optionally, a set of options specifying how the file is opened, as shown next. This `open()` method will associate the channel with a system-dependent default thread pool that may be shared with other channels (the *default group*).

```
public static AsynchronousFileChannel open(Path file, OpenOption... options)
throws IOException
```

■ **Note** The set of options called in the preceding code are the StandardOpenOption enum constants previously described in both Chapter 4 and Chapter 7, so you should already be familiar with these options.

File Read and Future

The following code snippet creates a new asynchronous file channel for reading the file story.txt located in the C:\rafaelnadal\grandslam\RolandGaross directory (the file must exist):

```
Path path = Paths.get("C:/rafaelnadal/grandslam/RolandGarros", "story.txt");
AsynchronousFileChannel asynchronousFileChannel = AsynchronousFileChannel.
                                    open(path, StandardOpenOption.READ) ;
```

The file is prepared for reading, so we can start reading. This task is accomplished by the read() methods (there are two of them). Since we are interested in using the Future mode, we will use the following read() method:

```
public abstract Future<Integer> read(ByteBuffer dst, long position)
```

This method reads a sequence of bytes from this channel into the given buffer, starting at the given file position, and returns an object representing the pending result. Since we are in an asynchronous environment, this method just initiates the read and does not block the application. The following code shows you how to use it to read the first 100 bytes:

```
ByteBuffer buffer = ByteBuffer.allocate(100);
Future<Integer> result = asynchronousFileChannel.read(buffer, 0);
```

The pending result allows us to track the reading process status through the Future.isDone() method, which will return false until the read operation completes. Placing this call in a loop allows us to complete other tasks until the read completes:

```
while (!result.isDone()) {
    System.out.println("Do something else while reading ...");
}
```

When the read operation completes, the application flow exits the loop and the result can be retrieved by calling the get() method, which waits if necessary for the operation to complete. The result is an integer representing the number of read bytes, while the bytes are in the destination buffer:

```
System.out.println("Read done: " + result.isDone());
System.out.println("Bytes read: " + result.get());
```

Gluing everything together results in the following application:

```
import java.nio.ByteBuffer;
import java.nio.channels.AsynchronousFileChannel;
import java.nio.charset.Charset;
import java.nio.file.Path;
import java.nio.file.Paths;
import java.nio.file.StandardOpenOption;
import java.util.concurrent.Future;

public class Main {
```

```java
public static void main(String[] args) {
  ByteBuffer buffer = ByteBuffer.allocate(100);
  String encoding = System.getProperty("file.encoding");

  Path path = Paths.get("C:/rafaelnadal/grandslam/RolandGarros", "story.txt");
  try (AsynchronousFileChannel asynchronousFileChannel = AsynchronousFileChannel.open(path,
      StandardOpenOption.READ)) {

    Future<Integer> result = asynchronousFileChannel.read(buffer, 0);

    while (!result.isDone()) {
        System.out.println("Do something else while reading ...");
    }

    System.out.println("Read done: " + result.isDone());
    System.out.println("Bytes read: " + result.get());
  } catch (Exception ex) {
    System.err.println(ex);
  }
  buffer.flip();
  System.out.print(Charset.forName(encoding).decode(buffer));
  buffer.clear();
 }
}
```

The following is possible output of this application:

```
...

Do something else while reading ...

Do something else while reading ...

Do something else while reading ...

Do something else while reading ...

Read done: true

Bytes read: 100

Rafa Nadal produced another masterclass of clay-court tennis to win his fifth French Open
title ...
```

File Write and Future

The following code snippet creates a new asynchronous file channel for writing more bytes into the file
story.txt located in C:\rafaelnadal\grandslam\RolandGaross (the file must exist):

```
Path path = Paths.get("C:/rafaelnadal/grandslam/RolandGarros", "story.txt");
AsynchronousFileChannel asynchronousFileChannel = AsynchronousFileChannel.
                                      open(path, StandardOpenOption.WRITE) ;
```

The file is prepared for writing, so we can start writing. This task is accomplished by the write() methods (there are two of them). Since we are interesting in using the Future mode, we will use the following write() method:

```
public abstract Future<Integer> write(ByteBuffer src, long position)
```

This method writes a sequence of bytes to this channel from the given buffer, starting at the given file position, and returns an object representing the pending result. Since we are in an asynchronous environment, this method just initiates the write and does not block the application. The following code shows you how to use it to write some bytes starting from position 100:

```
import java.nio.ByteBuffer;
import java.nio.channels.AsynchronousFileChannel;
import java.nio.file.Path;
import java.nio.file.Paths;
import java.nio.file.StandardOpenOption;
import java.util.concurrent.Future;

public class Main {

 public static void main(String[] args) {

  ByteBuffer buffer = ByteBuffer.wrap("The win keeps Nadal at the top of the heap in men's
tennis, at least for a few more weeks. The world No2, Novak Djokovic, dumped out here in the
semi-finals by a resurgent Federer, will come hard at them again at Wimbledon but there is
much to come from two rivals who, for seven years, have held all pretenders at
bay.".getBytes());

  Path path = Paths.get("C:/rafaelnadal/grandslam/RolandGarros", "story.txt");
  try (AsynchronousFileChannel asynchronousFileChannel = AsynchronousFileChannel.open(path,
      StandardOpenOption.WRITE)) {

     Future<Integer> result = asynchronousFileChannel.write(buffer, 100);

     while (!result.isDone()) {
          System.out.println("Do something else while writing ...");
     }

     System.out.println("Written done: " + result.isDone());
     System.out.println("Bytes written: " + result.get());

 } catch (Exception ex) {
  System.err.println(ex);
 }
 }
}
```

This time the get() method returns the number of written bytes. The bytes are written starting with position 100 in the file. The application output will be as follows:

…

Do something else while writing ...

Do something else while writing ...

Do something else while writing ...

Written done: true

Bytes written: 319

As an exercise, try combining both applications into a single one for reading and writing asynchronously.

File Read and Future Timeout

As previously stated, the get() method waits if necessary for the operation to complete, after which it retrieves the result. This method also has a timeout version, in which we can specify precisely how long we can afford to wait. For this, we pass to the get() method a timeout and unit time. If the time expires, this method throws a TimeoutException and we can interrupt the thread to finish this task by calling the cancel() method with a true parameter. The following application reads the content of story.txt with a very short timeout:

```java
import java.nio.ByteBuffer;
import java.nio.channels.AsynchronousFileChannel;
import java.nio.file.Path;
import java.nio.file.Paths;
import java.nio.file.StandardOpenOption;
import java.util.concurrent.Future;
import java.util.concurrent.TimeUnit;
import java.util.concurrent.TimeoutException;

public class Main {

 public static void main(String[] args) {

  ByteBuffer buffer = ByteBuffer.allocate(100);
  int bytesRead = 0;
  Future<Integer> result = null;

  Path path = Paths.get("C:/rafaelnadal/grandslam/RolandGarros", "story.txt");

  try (AsynchronousFileChannel asynchronousFileChannel = AsynchronousFileChannel.open(path,
      StandardOpenOption.READ)) {

      result = asynchronousFileChannel.read(buffer, 0);
```

```
            bytesRead = result.get(1, TimeUnit.NANOSECONDS);

            if (result.isDone()) {
                System.out.println("The result is available!");
                System.out.println("Read bytes: " + bytesRead);
            }

    } catch (Exception ex) {
        if (ex instanceof TimeoutException) {
            if (result != null) {
                result.cancel(true);
            }
            System.out.println("The result is not available!");
            System.out.println("The read task was cancelled ? " + result.isCancelled());
            System.out.println("Read bytes: " + bytesRead);
        } else {
            System.err.println(ex);
        }
    }
  }
 }
}
```

This application has two possible outputs. First, if the time expires and the I/O operation does not complete, the output will be as follows:

```
The result is not available!

The read task was cancelled ? true //(or, false)

Read bytes: 0
```

If the I/O operation completes before the time expires, the output will be as follows:

```
The result is available!

Read bytes: 100
```

File Read and CompletionHandler

Now that you've seen a few examples of how the Future form works, it's time to see how a CompletionHandler can be written to read the story.txt content. After creating an asynchronous file channel for reading the content of the story.txt file, we call the second read() method of AsynchronousFileChannnel class:

```
public abstract <A> void read(ByteBuffer dst, long position, A attachment,
CompletionHandler<Integer,? super A> handler)
```

This method reads a sequence of bytes from this channel into the given buffer, starting at the given file position. Besides the destination buffer and the file position, this method gets the object to attach to the I/O operation (can be null) and the completion handler for consuming the result. Since we are in an asynchronous environment, this method just initiates the read and does not block the application. The following code shows you how to use it to read the first 100 bytes—you can locate the CompletionHandler as an anonymous inner class:

```java
import java.nio.ByteBuffer;
import java.nio.channels.AsynchronousFileChannel;
import java.nio.channels.CompletionHandler;
import java.nio.file.Path;
import java.nio.file.Paths;
import java.nio.file.StandardOpenOption;

public class Main {

 static Thread current;

 public static void main(String[] args) {

  ByteBuffer buffer = ByteBuffer.allocate(100);
  Path path = Paths.get("C:/rafaelnadal/grandslam/RolandGarros", "story.txt");

  try (AsynchronousFileChannel asynchronousFileChannel = AsynchronousFileChannel.open(path,
      StandardOpenOption.READ)) {

       current = Thread.currentThread();
       asynchronousFileChannel.read(buffer, 0, "Read operation status ...", new
       CompletionHandler<Integer, Object>() {

       @Override
       public void completed(Integer result, Object attachment) {
        System.out.println(attachment);
        System.out.print("Read bytes: " + result);
        current.interrupt();
       }

       @Override
       public void failed(Throwable exc, Object attachment) {
        System.out.println(attachment);
        System.out.println("Error:" + exc);
        current.interrupt();
       }
     });

     System.out.println("\nWaiting for reading operation to end ...\n");
     try {
         current.join();
     } catch (InterruptedException e) {
     }

     //now the buffer contains the read bytes
```

```
          System.out.println("\n\nClose everything and leave! Bye, bye ...");

    } catch (Exception ex) {
      System.err.println(ex);
    }
  }
}
```

The current thread was used just to discover when we should stop the application; in some cases, the flow may end the application before the completion handler consumes the result. You can choose instead to use a Thread.sleep() method, a System.in.read() method, or any other convenient approach.

Possible output follows:

```
Waiting for reading operation to end ...

Read operation status ...

Read bytes: 100



Closing everything and leave! Bye, bye ...
```

In other cases, you may see the waiting message after the CompletionHandler output, depending on how fast it consumes the result of the I/O operation.

The destination ByteBuffer may "arrive" into the CompletionHandler as the object attached to the I/O operation (when you do not have any attachments, just pass null). The following application decodes and displays the content of the destination ByteBuffer into the completed() method of CompletionHandler:

```java
import java.nio.ByteBuffer;
import java.nio.channels.AsynchronousFileChannel;
import java.nio.channels.CompletionHandler;
import java.nio.charset.Charset;
import java.nio.file.Path;
import java.nio.file.Paths;
import java.nio.file.StandardOpenOption;

public class Main {

  static Thread current;
  static final Path path = Paths.get("C:/rafaelnadal/grandslam/RolandGarros", "story.txt");

  public static void main(String[] args) {

    CompletionHandler<Integer, ByteBuffer> handler =
                      new CompletionHandler<Integer, ByteBuffer>() {

      String encoding = System.getProperty("file.encoding");
```

```
    @Override
    public void completed(Integer result, ByteBuffer attachment) {
      System.out.println("Read bytes: " + result);
      attachment.flip();
      System.out.print(Charset.forName(encoding).decode(attachment));
      attachment.clear();
      current.interrupt();
    }

    @Override
    public void failed(Throwable exc, ByteBuffer attachment) {
      System.out.println(attachment);
      System.out.println("Error:" + exc);
      current.interrupt();
    }
  };

  try (AsynchronousFileChannel asynchronousFileChannel = AsynchronousFileChannel.open(path,
      StandardOpenOption.READ)) {

      current = Thread.currentThread();
      ByteBuffer buffer = ByteBuffer.allocate(100);
      asynchronousFileChannel.read(buffer, 0, buffer, handler);

      System.out.println("Waiting for reading operation to end ...\n");
      try {
          current.join();
      } catch (InterruptedException e) {
      }

      //the buffer was passed as attachment
      System.out.println("\n\nClosing everything and leave! Bye, bye ...");

  } catch (Exception ex) {
    System.err.println(ex);
  }
 }
}
```

Possible output follows:

```
Waiting for reading operation to end ...



Read bytes: 100

Rafa Nadal produced another masterclass of clay-court tennis to win his fifth French Open
title ...
```

Closing everything and leave! Bye, bye ...

File Lock

Sometimes you need to acquire an exclusive lock on a channel's file before performing another I/O operation, such as reading or writing. AsynchronousFileChannel provides a lock() method for the Future form and a lock() method for CompletionHandler (both also have signatures for locking regions of a file, more details of which you can find in the official documentation at http://download.oracle.com/javase/7/docs/api/):

```
public final Future<FileLock> lock()
public final <A> void lock(A attachment, CompletionHandler<FileLock,? super A> handler)
```

The following application uses the lock() method with the Future form for locking a file. We will wait to acquire the lock by calling the Future.get() method, and, afterward, we will write some bytes into our file. Again, we call the get() method that will wait until the new bytes are written and, finally, release the lock. The file used is CopaClaro.txt, located in C:\rafaelnadal\tournaments\2009 (the file must exist).

```java
import java.nio.ByteBuffer;
import java.nio.channels.AsynchronousFileChannel;
import java.nio.channels.FileLock;
import java.nio.file.Path;
import java.nio.file.Paths;
import java.nio.file.StandardOpenOption;
import java.util.concurrent.Future;

public class Main {

  public static void main(String[] args) {

    ByteBuffer buffer = ByteBuffer.wrap("Argentines At Home In Buenos Aires Cathedral\n The
Copa Claro is the third stop of the four-tournament Latin American swing, and is contested on
clay at the Buenos Aires Lawn Tennis Club, known as the Cathedral of Argentinean tennis. An
Argentine has reached the final in nine of the 11 editions of the ATP World Tour 250
tournament, with champions including Guillermo Coria, Gaston Gaudio, Juan Monaco and David
Nalbandian.".getBytes());

    Path path = Paths.get("C:/rafaelnadal/tournaments/2009", "CopaClaro.txt");
    try (AsynchronousFileChannel asynchronousFileChannel = AsynchronousFileChannel.open(path,
        StandardOpenOption.WRITE)) {

      Future<FileLock> featureLock = asynchronousFileChannel.lock();
      System.out.println("Waiting for the file to be locked ...");
      FileLock lock = featureLock.get();
      //or, use shortcut
      //FileLock lock = asynchronousFileChannel.lock().get();
```

```
        if (lock.isValid()) {
            Future<Integer> featureWrite = asynchronousFileChannel.write(buffer, 0);
            System.out.println("Waiting for the bytes to be written ...");
            int written = featureWrite.get();
            //or, use shortcut
            //int written = asynchronousFileChannel.write(buffer,0).get();

            System.out.println("I've written " + written + " bytes into " +
                                      path.getFileName() + " locked file!");

            lock.release();
        }

    } catch (Exception ex) {
      System.err.println(ex);
    }
  }
}
```

Possible output follows:

```
Waiting for the file to be locked ...

Waiting for the bytes to be written ...

I've written 423 bytes into CopaClaro.txt locked file!
```

Moreover, an implementation of the lock() method with CompletionHandler may look like the
following:

```
import java.io.IOException;
import java.nio.channels.AsynchronousFileChannel;
import java.nio.channels.CompletionHandler;
import java.nio.channels.FileLock;
import java.nio.file.Path;
import java.nio.file.Paths;
import java.nio.file.StandardOpenOption;

public class Main {

 static Thread current;

  public static void main(String[] args) {

    Path path = Paths.get("C:/rafaelnadal/tournaments/2009", "CopaClaro.txt");

    try (AsynchronousFileChannel asynchronousFileChannel = AsynchronousFileChannel.open(path,
        StandardOpenOption.READ, StandardOpenOption.WRITE)) {

        current = Thread.currentThread();
```

```
asynchronousFileChannel.lock("Lock operation status:", new
                             CompletionHandler<FileLock, Object>() {

@Override
public void completed(FileLock result, Object attachment) {
 System.out.println(attachment + " " + result.isValid());

 if (result.isValid()) {
  //... processing ...
  System.out.println("Processing the locked file ...");
  //...
  try {
      result.release();
  } catch (IOException ex) {
    System.err.println(ex);
  }
 }
 current.interrupt();
}

@Override
public void failed(Throwable exc, Object attachment) {
 System.out.println(attachment);
 System.out.println("Error:" + exc);
 current.interrupt();
}
});

System.out.println("Waiting for file to be locked and process ... \n");
try {
    current.join();
} catch (InterruptedException e) {
}
System.out.println("\n\nClosing everything and leave! Bye, bye ...");

} catch (Exception ex) {
  System.err.println(ex);
}
}
}
```

The following is possible output:

```
Waiting for file to be locked and process ...



Lock operation status: true

Processing the locked file ...
```

Closing everything and leave! Bye, bye ...

■ **Note** AsynchronousFileChannel also provides the well-known tryLock() methods, but they are not associated with Future or CompletionHandler forms.

AsynchronousFileChannel and ExecutorService

So far, you've seen at work only the first AsynchronousFileChannel.open() method, which uses the default pool thread. It is time to see the second open() method at work, which allows us to specify a custom thread pool through an ExecutorService object. The syntax of this method is as follows:

```
public static AsynchronousFileChannel open(Path file, Set<? extends OpenOption> options,
ExecutorService executor, FileAttribute<?>... attrs) throws IOException
```

As you can see, this open() method gets the path of the file to open or create, a set of options specifying how the file is opened (optional), a thread pool (or null) as an ExecutorService (see "Introducing the ExecutorService API" above), and a list of file attributes to set atomically when creating the file (optional).

In our scenario, we want to develop an application that asynchronously fills up 50 ByteBuffers with bytes from random positions of the story.txt file. The capacity of ByteBuffers will also be random. Moreover, we want to use a custom group with a fixed thread pool of five threads.

We start by creating the thread pool through an ExecutorService:

```
final int THREADS = 5;
ExecutorService taskExecutor = Executors.newFixedThreadPool(THREADS);
```

We continue by passing the thread pool to the open() method, next to the file path and options:

```
private static Set withOptions() {
        final Set options = new TreeSet<>();
        options.add(StandardOpenOption.READ);
        return options;
}
AsynchronousFileChannel asynchronousFileChannel = AsynchronousFileChannel.open
                                        (path, withOptions(), taskExecutor);
```

Next, in a loop, we create 50 Callable *workers* (value-returning tasks) and override the call() method to create random-capacity byte buffers and fill them up with bytes from from random positions in the file—this is our computation. We submit each "worker" to the executor and store its Future into an ArrayList. Later, we will loop this list and call the get() method to retrieve the result from each byte buffer.

```
List<Future<ByteBuffer>> list = new ArrayList<>();
...
for (int i = 0; i < 50; i++) {
 Callable<ByteBuffer> worker = new Callable<ByteBuffer>() {
```

```
@Override
public ByteBuffer call() throws Exception {

ByteBuffer buffer=ByteBuffer.allocateDirect(ThreadLocalRandom.current().nextInt(100, 200));
asynchronousFileChannel.read(buffer, ThreadLocalRandom.current().nextInt(0, 100));

return buffer;
 }
};

 Future<ByteBuffer> future = taskExecutor.submit(worker);

 list.add(future);
}
```

Since we passed to the executor all the necessary tasks, we can shut it down so that it doesn't accept new tasks. It finishes all existing threads in the queue and terminates—in the meantime, we can count some sheep:

```
...
taskExecutor.shutdown();

while (!taskExecutor.isTerminated()) {
  //do something else while the buffers are prepared
  System.out.println("Counting sheep while filling up some buffers!
                      So far I counted: " + (sheeps += 1));
}
...
```

After counting sheep for awhile, the isTerminate() method returns true, and the results are just "out of the oven." Iterate the Future list and call the get() method to retrieve each result:

```
for (Future<ByteBuffer> future : list) {

 ByteBuffer buffer = future.get();

 ...
}
```

Done! Gluing everything together and adding boilerplate code and imports produces the following:

```
import java.nio.ByteBuffer;
import java.nio.channels.AsynchronousFileChannel;
import java.nio.charset.Charset;
import java.nio.file.Path;
import java.nio.file.Paths;
import java.nio.file.StandardOpenOption;
import java.util.ArrayList;
import java.util.List;
import java.util.Set;
import java.util.TreeSet;
import java.util.concurrent.Callable;
import java.util.concurrent.ExecutorService;
import java.util.concurrent.Executors;
```

```java
import java.util.concurrent.Future;
import java.util.concurrent.ThreadLocalRandom;

public class Main {

private static Set withOptions() {
        final Set options = new TreeSet<>();
        options.add(StandardOpenOption.READ);
        return options;
}

public static void main(String[] args) {

 final int THREADS = 5;
 ExecutorService taskExecutor = Executors.newFixedThreadPool(THREADS);

 String encoding = System.getProperty("file.encoding");
 List<Future<ByteBuffer>> list = new ArrayList<>();
 int sheeps = 0;

 Path path = Paths.get("C:/rafaelnadal/grandslam/RolandGarros", "story.txt");

  try (AsynchronousFileChannel asynchronousFileChannel = AsynchronousFileChannel.open(path,
      withOptions(), taskExecutor)) {

     for (int i = 0; i < 50; i++) {
         Callable<ByteBuffer> worker = new Callable<ByteBuffer>() {

           @Override
           public ByteBuffer call() throws Exception {
            ByteBuffer buffer = ByteBuffer.allocateDirect
                          (ThreadLocalRandom.current().nextInt(100, 200));
             asynchronousFileChannel.read(buffer, ThreadLocalRandom.current().nextInt(0,100));

             return buffer;
           }
         };

         Future<ByteBuffer> future = taskExecutor.submit(worker);
         list.add(future);
     }

     //this will make the executor accept no new threads
     // and finish all existing threads in the queue
     taskExecutor.shutdown();

     //wait until all threads are finished
     while (!taskExecutor.isTerminated()) {
            //do something else while the buffers are prepared
            System.out.println("Counting sheep while filling up some buffers!
                          So far I counted: " + (sheeps += 1));
     }
```

```
        System.out.println("\nDone! Here are the buffers:\n");
        for (Future<ByteBuffer> future : list) {

            ByteBuffer buffer = future.get();

            System.out.println("\n\n"+ buffer);
            System.out.println("_____");
            buffer.flip();
            System.out.print(Charset.forName(encoding).decode(buffer));
            buffer.clear();
        }

    } catch (Exception ex) {
        System.err.println(ex);
    }
  }
 }
}
```

The following is a fragment of possible output:

…

Counting sheep while filling up some buffers! So far I counted: 352

Counting sheep while filling up some buffers! So far I counted: 353

Counting sheep while filling up some buffers! So far I counted: 354

Done! Here are the buffers:

java.nio.HeapByteBuffer[pos=100 lim=100 cap=100]

---

d another masterclass of clay-court tennis to win his fifth French Open title ...

java.nio.HeapByteBuffer[pos=189 lim=189 cap=189]

---

nother masterclass of clay-court tennis to win his fifth French Open title ...

…

```
java.nio.HeapByteBuffer[pos=112 lim=112 cap=112]
```

```
y-court tennis to win his fifth French Open title ...
```

…

Asynchronous Channel Sockets Examples

Asynchronous channel sockets are the jewels of NIO.2. Developing an asynchronous client/server application is an interesting project for any Java developer who is focused on the networking applications field. The easiest approach for a better understanding of how to accomplish this task is to follow a straightforward set of steps accompanied by chunks of codes that will be glued together at the end of the discussion. We'll start with an asynchronous server based on the Future form.

Writing an Asynchronous Server (Based on Future)

We want to develop an asynchronous server that will echo to the client everything that it gets from it. During execution, the Future mode will be responsible for tracking the status of tasks such as accepting connections, reading bytes from the client, and writing bytes to the client.

Creating a New Asynchronous Server Socket Channel

The first step involves creating an asynchronous channel for a stream-oriented listening socket, which is accomplished with `java.nio.channels.AsynchronousServerSocketChannel`. More precisely, this task is accomplished by the `AsynchronousServerSocketChannel.open()` method, as shown here, in which the asynchronous server socket channel is bound to the default group:

```
AsynchronousServerSocketChannel asynchronousServerSocketChannel=
                        AsynchronousServerSocketChannel.open();
```

Keep in mind that a newly created asynchronous server socket channel is not bound to the local address. This will be accomplished in the following steps.

You can check if an asynchronous server socket is already open or has been successfully opened by calling the `AsynchronousServerSocketChannel.isOpen()` method, which returns the corresponding Boolean value:

```
if (asynchronousServerSocketChannel.isOpen()) {
    …
}
```

Setting Asynchronous Server Socket Channel Options

This is an optional step. There is no required option (you can use the default values), but we'll explicitly set a few options to show you how this can be done. More precisely, an asynchronous server socket channel supports two options: SO_RCVBUF and SO_REUSEADDR. We'll set them both, as follows:

```
asynchronousServerSocketChannel.setOption(StandardSocketOptions.SO_RCVBUF, 4 * 1024);
asynchronousServerSocketChannel.setOption(StandardSocketOptions.SO_REUSEADDR, true);
```

You can find out which options are supported for an asynchronous server socket channel by calling the inherited method supportedOptions():

```
Set<SocketOption<?>> options = asynchronousServerSocketChannel.supportedOptions();
for(SocketOption<?> option : options) System.out.println(option);
```

Binding the Asynchronous Server Socket Channel

At this point we can bind the asynchronous server socket channel to a local address and configure the socket to listen for connections. For this we call the AsynchronousServerSocketChannel.bind() method. Our server will wait for an incoming connection on localhost (127.0.0.1), port 5555 (arbitrarily chosen):

```
final int DEFAULT_PORT = 5555;
final String IP = "127.0.0.1";
asynchronousServerSocketChannel.bind(new InetSocketAddress(IP, DEFAULT_PORT));
```

Another common approach is to create an InetSocketAddress object without specifying the IP address, only the port (there is a constructor for that). In this case, the IP address is the *wildcard* address, and the port number is a specified value. The wildcard address is a special local IP address that can be used *only* for bind operations.

```
asynchronousServerSocketChannel.bind(new InetSocketAddress(DEFAULT_PORT));
```

In addition, there is one more bind() method that gets, in addition to the address to bind the socket to, the maximum number of pending connections:

```
public abstract AsynchronousServerSocketChannel bind(SocketAddress local,int pc) throws
IOException
```

The local address can also be automatically assigned if we pass null to the bind() method. You can also find out the bound local address by calling the AsynchronousServerSocketChannel.getLocalAddress() method, which is inherited from the NetworkChannel interface. This returns null if the asynchronous server socket channel has not been bound yet.

```
System.out.println(asynchronousServerSocketChannel.getLocalAddress());
```

Accepting Connections

After opening and binding, we finally reach the accepting milestone. We signal our impatience to accept new connections by calling the AsynchronousServerSocketChannel.accept() method, which initiates an asynchronous operation to accept a connection made to this channel's socket and returns a Future object to track the operation status. We call the Future.get() method, which returns the new connection on successful completion. In addition, you may want to use the isDone() method to check periodically the operation completion status. The returned connection is an instance of the

AsynchronousSocketChannel class, which represents an asynchronous channel for stream-oriented connecting sockets.

```
Future<AsynchronousSocketChannel> asynchronousSocketChannelFuture =
                                asynchronousServerSocketChannel.accept();
AsynchronousSocketChannel asynchronousSocketChannel = asynchronousSocketChannelFuture.get();
```

■ **Note** Trying to invoke the accept() method for an unbound server socket channel will throw a NotYetBoundException exception.

Once we have accepted a new connection, we can find out the remote address by calling the AsynchronousSocketChannel.getRemoteAddress() method:

```
System.out.println("Incoming connection from: " +
                asynchronousSocketChannel.getRemoteAddress());
```

Transmitting Data over a Connection

At this point the server and client can transmit data over a connection. They can send and receive different kinds of data packets mapped as byte arrays. Implementing the transmission (send/receive) is a flexible and specific process since it involves many options. For example, for our server we'll use ByteBuffers, keeping in mind that this is an echo server—what it reads from the client is what it writes back. Here is the transmitting code snippet:

```
final ByteBuffer buffer = ByteBuffer.allocateDirect(1024);
…
while (asynchronousSocketChannel.read(buffer).get() != -1) {

        buffer.flip();

        asynchronousSocketChannel.write(buffer).get();

        if (buffer.hasRemaining()) {
            buffer.compact();
        } else {
            buffer.clear();
        }
    }
```

The preceding read() and write() methods get a destination/source ByteBuffer, initiate a read/write operation, and return a Future<Integer> object for tracking the read/write operation status. Calling the get() method forces the application to wait until the operation is complete before returning the number of read/written bytes. First, we wait for incoming bytes to be read (this is what the server echoes). Second, we wait until the write operation ends, to avoid the case in which more bytes should be echoed and a thread initiates a new write operation before a previous write operation has completed, which ends with a WritePendingException exception. Since the application is "captured" inside read/write operations with the first client, it is unprepared to accept other connections until it has completely served the current client, which means that only one client can be served at a time. This is pretty rudimentary, and obviously not satisfactory for a server, but it is acceptable for our first asynchronous server.

Closing the Channel

When a channel becomes useless, it must be closed. To accomplish this, you can call the `AsynchronousSocketChannel.close()` method (this will not close the server for listening for incoming connections, it will just close a channel for a client) and/or the `AsynchronousServerSocketChannel.close()` method (this will close the server for listening for incoming connections; subsequent clients won't be able to locate the server any more).

```
asynchronousServerSocketChannel.close();
asynchronousSocketChannel.close();
```

Alternatively, we can close these resources by placing the code into the Java 7 *try-with-resources* feature. This is possible because the `AsynchronousServerSocketChannel` and `AsynchronousSocketChannel` classes implement the `AutoCloseable` interface. Using this feature will ensure that the resources are closed automatically.

Combining Everything into an Echo Server

Now we have everything we need to create our echo server. Putting together the preceding chunks of code and adding the necessary imports, spaghetti code, and so forth produces the following echo sever:

```java
import java.io.IOException;
import java.net.InetSocketAddress;
import java.net.StandardSocketOptions;
import java.nio.ByteBuffer;
import java.nio.channels.AsynchronousServerSocketChannel;
import java.nio.channels.AsynchronousSocketChannel;
import java.util.concurrent.ExecutionException;
import java.util.concurrent.Future;

public class Main {

 public static void main(String[] args) {

  final int DEFAULT_PORT = 5555;
  final String IP = "127.0.0.1";

  //create an asynchronous server socket channel bound to the default group
  try (AsynchronousServerSocketChannel asynchronousServerSocketChannel =
      AsynchronousServerSocketChannel.open()) {

     if (asynchronousServerSocketChannel.isOpen()) {

     //set some options
     asynchronousServerSocketChannel.setOption(StandardSocketOptions.SO_RCVBUF, 4 * 1024);
     asynchronousServerSocketChannel.setOption(StandardSocketOptions.SO_REUSEADDR, true);
     //bind the asynchronous server socket channel to local address
     asynchronousServerSocketChannel.bind(new InetSocketAddress(IP, DEFAULT_PORT));
```

```java
        //display a waiting message while ... waiting     clients
        System.out.println("Waiting for connections ...");
        while (true) {
                Future<AsynchronousSocketChannel> asynchronousSocketChannelFuture =
                                        asynchronousServerSocketChannel.accept();

            try (AsynchronousSocketChannel asynchronousSocketChannel =
                asynchronousSocketChannelFuture.get()) {

                System.out.println("Incoming connection from: " +
                                asynchronousSocketChannel.getRemoteAddress());

                final ByteBuffer buffer = ByteBuffer.allocateDirect(1024);

                //transmitting data
                while (asynchronousSocketChannel.read(buffer).get() != -1) {

                    buffer.flip();

                    asynchronousSocketChannel.write(buffer).get();

                    if (buffer.hasRemaining()) {
                        buffer.compact();
                    } else {
                        buffer.clear();
                    }
                }

                System.out.println(asynchronousSocketChannel.getRemoteAddress() +
                                " was successfully served!");

            } catch (IOException | InterruptedException | ExecutionException ex) {
                System.err.println(ex);
            }
        }
        } else {
            System.out.println("The asynchronous server-socket channel cannot be opened!");
        }

    } catch (IOException ex) {
        System.err.println(ex);
    }
  }
 }
}
```

You're likely still wondering about how to accept multiple clients. A simple solution is to wrap the preceding code into an ExecutorService. Every time a new connection is accepted and the get() method returns it as an AsynchronousSocketChannel channel, we write a "worker" meant to maintain or close the "conversation" with the client. Afterward, the worker is submitted to the executor and a new connection is prepared to be accepted. If an unexpected error occurs, then we shut down the executor and wait to terminate. The following application modifies the preceding one so that it accepts multiple clients at the same time:

```java
import java.io.IOException;
import java.net.InetSocketAddress;
import java.net.StandardSocketOptions;
import java.nio.ByteBuffer;
import java.nio.channels.AsynchronousServerSocketChannel;
import java.nio.channels.AsynchronousSocketChannel;
import java.util.concurrent.Callable;
import java.util.concurrent.ExecutionException;
import java.util.concurrent.ExecutorService;
import java.util.concurrent.Executors;
import java.util.concurrent.Future;

public class Main {

 public static void main(String[] args) {

  final int DEFAULT_PORT = 5555;
  final String IP = "127.0.0.1";
  ExecutorService taskExecutor=
                Executors.newCachedThreadPool(Executors.defaultThreadFactory());

  //create asynchronous server socket channel bound to the default group
  try (AsynchronousServerSocketChannel asynchronousServerSocketChannel =
                                  AsynchronousServerSocketChannel.open()) {

     if (asynchronousServerSocketChannel.isOpen()) {

       //set some options
       asynchronousServerSocketChannel.setOption(StandardSocketOptions.SO_RCVBUF, 4 * 1024);
       asynchronousServerSocketChannel.setOption(StandardSocketOptions.SO_REUSEADDR, true);
       //bind the server socket channel to local address
       asynchronousServerSocketChannel.bind(new InetSocketAddress(IP, DEFAULT_PORT));

       //display a waiting message while ... waiting clients
       System.out.println("Waiting for connections ...");

       while (true) {
        Future<AsynchronousSocketChannel> asynchronousSocketChannelFuture =
              asynchronousServerSocketChannel.accept();

        try {
           final AsynchronousSocketChannel asynchronousSocketChannel =
                                      asynchronousSocketChannelFuture.get();
           Callable<String> worker = new Callable<String>() {

             @Override
             public String call() throws Exception {

             String host = asynchronousSocketChannel.getRemoteAddress().toString();
```

```java
                System.out.println("Incoming connection from: " + host);

                final ByteBuffer buffer = ByteBuffer.allocateDirect(1024);

                //transmitting data
                while (asynchronousSocketChannel.read(buffer).get() != -1) {

                        buffer.flip();

                        asynchronousSocketChannel.write(buffer).get();

                        if (buffer.hasRemaining()) {
                            buffer.compact();
                        } else {
                            buffer.clear();
                        }
                }

                asynchronousSocketChannel.close();
                System.out.println(host + " was successfully served!");
                return host;
                }
              };

              taskExecutor.submit(worker);

          } catch (InterruptedException | ExecutionException ex) {
            System.err.println(ex);

            System.err.println("\n Server is shutting down ...");

            //this will make the executor accept no new threads
            // and finish all existing threads in the queue
            taskExecutor.shutdown();

            //wait until all threads are finished
            while (!taskExecutor.isTerminated()) {
            }

            break;
          }
        }
      } else {
        System.out.println("The asynchronous server-socket channel cannot be opened!");
      }

  } catch (IOException ex) {
    System.err.println(ex);
  }
 }
}
}
```

Writing an Asynchronous Client (Based on Future)

Now let's develop a client for our echo server. Suppose we have the following scenario: The client connects to our server, sends a "Hello!" message, and then keeps sending random numbers between 0 and 100 until the number 50 is generated. When the number 50 is generated, the client stops sending and closes the channel. The server will echo (write back) everything it reads from the client. The steps for implementing the client for this scenario are discussed next.

Creating a New Asynchronous Socket Channel

The first step is to create an asynchronous channel for stream-oriented connecting sockets bound to the default group. This is accomplished with the **java.nio.channels.AsynchronousSocketChannel** class. More precisely, this task is accomplished by the **AsynchronousSocketChannel.open()** method, as follows:

```
AsynchronousSocketChannel asynchronousSocketChannel = AsynchronousSocketChannel.open();
```

Keep in mind that a newly created asynchronous socket channel is not connected. You can check if an asynchronous server socket is already open or has been successfully opened by calling the **AsynchronousSocketChannel.isOpen()** method, which returns the corresponding Boolean value:

```
if (asynchronousSocketChannel.isOpen()) {
    …
}
```

Setting Asynchronous Socket Channel Options

An asynchronous socket channel supports the following options: SO_RCVBUF, SO_REUSEADDR, TCP_NODELAY, SO_KEEPALIVE, and SO_SNDBUF. Some of them are shown here:

```
asynchronousSocketChannel.setOption(StandardSocketOptions.SO_RCVBUF, 128 * 1024);
asynchronousSocketChannel.setOption(StandardSocketOptions.SO_SNDBUF, 128 * 1024);
asynchronousSocketChannel.setOption(StandardSocketOptions.SO_KEEPALIVE, true);
```

You can discover the supported options for an asynchronous server socket channel by calling the inherited method **supportedOptions()**:

```
Set<SocketOption<?>> options = asynchronousSocketChannel.supportedOptions();
for(SocketOption<?> option : options) System.out.println(option);
```

Connecting the Asynchronous Channel's Socket

After opening an asynchronous socket channel (and optionally binding it), you should connect to the remote address (the server-side address). The intention to connect is signaled by calling the **AsynchronousSocketChannel.connect()** method and passing to it the remote address as an instance of **InetSocketAddress**, as follows (remember that our echo servers runs on 127.0.0.1, port 5555):

```
final int DEFAULT_PORT = 5555;
final String IP = "127.0.0.1";
Void connect = asynchronousSocketChannel.connect
                                  (new InetSocketAddress(IP, DEFAULT_PORT)).get();
```

247

This method initiates an operation to connect to this channel. The method returns a Future<Void> object representing the pending result. The Future's get() method returns null on successful completion.

Transmitting Data over a Connection

The connection has been established, so we can start transmitting data packets. The following code sends the "Hello!" message, and then sends random numbers until the number 50 is generated. The following read() and write() methods get a destination/source ByteBuffer, initiate a read/write operation, and return a Future<Integer> object for tracking the read/write operation status. Calling the get() method will wait until the operation is complete and returns the number of read/written bytes. Using the get() method with the write() method will avoid the case in which more bytes should be written and a thread initiates a new write operation before a previous write operation has completed, which ends with a WritePendingException exception.

```
ByteBuffer buffer = ByteBuffer.allocateDirect(1024);
ByteBuffer helloBuffer = ByteBuffer.wrap("Hello !".getBytes());
ByteBuffer randomBuffer;
CharBuffer charBuffer;
Charset charset = Charset.defaultCharset();
CharsetDecoder decoder = charset.newDecoder();
...
asynchronousSocketChannel.write(helloBuffer).get();

while (asynchronousSocketChannel.read(buffer).get() != -1) {

    buffer.flip();

    charBuffer = decoder.decode(buffer);
    System.out.println(charBuffer.toString());

    if (buffer.hasRemaining()) {
        buffer.compact();
    } else {
        buffer.clear();
    }

    int r = new Random().nextInt(100);
    if (r == 50) {
        System.out.println("50 was generated! Close the asynchronous socket channel!");
        break;
    } else {
    randomBuffer = ByteBuffer.wrap("Random number:".concat(String.valueOf(r)).getBytes());
    asynchronousSocketChannel.write(randomBuffer).get();
    }
}
```

Closing the Channel

When a channel becomes useless, it must be closed. To accomplish this, you can call AsynchronousSocketChannel.close(), and the client will be disconnected from the server:

```
asynchronousSocketChannel.close();
```

Again, the Java 7 *try-with-resources* feature may be used for automatically closing.

Combining Everything into a Client

Now we have everything we need to create our client. Putting together the preceding code chunks and adding the necessary imports, spaghetti code, and so on will provide us the following client:

```
import java.io.IOException;
import java.net.InetSocketAddress;
import java.net.StandardSocketOptions;
import java.nio.ByteBuffer;
import java.nio.CharBuffer;
import java.nio.channels.AsynchronousSocketChannel;
import java.nio.charset.Charset;
import java.nio.charset.CharsetDecoder;
import java.util.Random;
import java.util.concurrent.ExecutionException;

public class Main {

  public static void main(String[] args) {

    final int DEFAULT_PORT = 5555;
    final String IP = "127.0.0.1";
    ByteBuffer buffer = ByteBuffer.allocateDirect(1024);
    ByteBuffer helloBuffer = ByteBuffer.wrap("Hello !".getBytes());
    ByteBuffer randomBuffer;
    CharBuffer charBuffer;
    Charset charset = Charset.defaultCharset();
    CharsetDecoder decoder = charset.newDecoder();

    //create an asynchronous socket channel bound to the default group
    try (AsynchronousSocketChannel asynchronousSocketChannel =
                         AsynchronousSocketChannel.open()) {

        if (asynchronousSocketChannel.isOpen()) {

            //set some options
            asynchronousSocketChannel.setOption(StandardSocketOptions.SO_RCVBUF, 128 * 1024);
            asynchronousSocketChannel.setOption(StandardSocketOptions.SO_SNDBUF, 128 * 1024);
            asynchronousSocketChannel.setOption(StandardSocketOptions.SO_KEEPALIVE, true);
            //connect this channel's socket
            Void connect = asynchronousSocketChannel.connect
                    (new InetSocketAddress(IP, DEFAULT_PORT)).get();
```

```java
            if (connect == null) {

                System.out.println("Local address: " +
                                    asynchronousSocketChannel.getLocalAddress());

                //transmitting data
                asynchronousSocketChannel.write(helloBuffer).get();

                while (asynchronousSocketChannel.read(buffer).get() != -1) {

                    buffer.flip();

                    charBuffer = decoder.decode(buffer);
                    System.out.println(charBuffer.toString());

                    if (buffer.hasRemaining()) {
                        buffer.compact();
                    } else {
                        buffer.clear();
                    }

                    int r = new Random().nextInt(100);
                    if (r == 50) {
                        System.out.println("50 was generated! Close the asynchronous
                                                        socket channel!");
                        break;
                    } else {
                        randomBuffer = ByteBuffer.wrap("Random
                                    number:".concat(String.valueOf(r)).getBytes());
                        asynchronousSocketChannel.write(randomBuffer).get();
                    }
                }

            } else {
                System.out.println("The connection cannot be established!");
            }

        } else {
            System.out.println("The asynchronous socket channel cannot be opened!");
        }

    } catch (IOException | InterruptedException | ExecutionException ex) {
        System.err.println(ex);
    }
  }
 }
}
```

Testing the Echo Application (Based on Future)

Testing the application is a simple task. First, start the server and wait until you see the message "Waiting for connections ...". Continue by starting the client and check out the output. The following is possible serve output:

```
Waiting for connections ...

Incoming connection from: /127.0.0.1:49578

Incoming connection from: /127.0.0.1:49579

Incoming connection from: /127.0.0.1:49580

/127.0.0.1:49579 was successfully served!

Incoming connection from: /127.0.0.1:49581

/127.0.0.1:49580 was successfully served!

/127.0.0.1:49578 was successfully served!

/127.0.0.1:49581 was successfully served!
```

The following is some possible client output:

```
Hello !

Random number:78

Random number:72

Random number:29

Random number:77

Random number:35

Random number:0

...

50 was generated! Close the asynchronous socket channel!
```

Writing an Asynchronous Server (Based on CompletionHandler)

Next, we want to develop the same echo asynchronous server using the `CompletionHandler` mode instead of the `Future` mode. Actually, we will mix them together, by letting the `CompletionHandler` mode deal with the connection's acceptance operation and letting the `Future` mode deal with read/write operations. We open the asynchronous server socket channel, set its options, and bind it in the exact same manner as we did earlier. Next we focus on signaling the desire to accept connections. For this, we call the `accept()` method:

```
public abstract <A> void accept(A attachment,
CompletionHandler<AsynchronousSocketChannel,? super A> handler)
```

This method gets the object to attach to the I/O operation (which can be `null`) and the completion handler that is invoked when a connection is accepted (or the operation fails). The result passed to the completion handler is the `AsynchronousSocketChannel` to the new connection.

We implement the `CompletionHandler` as an anonymous inner class and override its methods. Now, the `completed()` method of the completion handler is responsible for maintaining and closing the "conversation" with the connected client. For this we use the same `read()` and `write()` methods as earlier and use the same approach. The `failed()` method of the completion handler should be called only if the operation of accepting connections fails—we just throw an exception and get ready to accept another connection.

Once a connection is accepted, we immediately get ready for a new one by invoking the `accept()` method from the `completed()` and `failed()` methods, as follows (this is the first line of code):

```
asynchronousServerSocketChannel.accept(null, this);
```

Finally, there is one more aspect to take care off. Since this is an asynchronous application, the flow will "traverse" the entire application and exit so fast that not even a single connection can be established or served, which is not good, because we want the server to wait and serve clients for a long time. Thus, we have to add some code to make the flow "hang in the air," such as by adding a `Thread.sleep()` method or a `System.in.read()` method or by joining the main thread and waiting until it dies or something else. We'll choose the `System.in.read()` method for this example.

Here is the `CompletionHandler` asynchronous server:

```
import java.io.IOException;
import java.net.InetSocketAddress;
import java.net.StandardSocketOptions;
import java.nio.ByteBuffer;
import java.nio.channels.AsynchronousServerSocketChannel;
import java.nio.channels.AsynchronousSocketChannel;
import java.nio.channels.CompletionHandler;
import java.util.concurrent.ExecutionException;

public class Main {

 public static void main(String[] args) {

   final int DEFAULT_PORT = 5555;
   final String IP = "127.0.0.1";

   //create an asynchronous server socket channel bound to the default group
   try (AsynchronousServerSocketChannel asynchronousServerSocketChannel =
       AsynchronousServerSocketChannel.open()) {
```

```java
if (asynchronousServerSocketChannel.isOpen()) {

 //set some options
 asynchronousServerSocketChannel.setOption(StandardSocketOptions.SO_RCVBUF,4 * 1024);
 asynchronousServerSocketChannel.setOption(StandardSocketOptions.SO_REUSEADDR, true);
 //bind the server socket channel to local address
 asynchronousServerSocketChannel.bind(new InetSocketAddress(IP, DEFAULT_PORT));

 //display a waiting message while ... waiting clients
 System.out.println("Waiting for connections ...");

 asynchronousServerSocketChannel.accept(null, new
                          CompletionHandler<AsynchronousSocketChannel, Void>() {

  final ByteBuffer buffer = ByteBuffer.allocateDirect(1024);

  @Override
  public void completed(AsynchronousSocketChannel result, Void attachment) {

   asynchronousServerSocketChannel.accept(null, this);

   try {
       System.out.println("Incoming connection from: " + result.getRemoteAddress());

       //transmitting data
       while (result.read(buffer).get() != -1) {

               buffer.flip();

               result.write(buffer).get();

               if (buffer.hasRemaining()) {
                   buffer.compact();
               } else {
                   buffer.clear();
               }
       }
   } catch (IOException | InterruptedException | ExecutionException ex) {
     System.err.println(ex);
   } finally {
     try {
         result.close();
     } catch (IOException e) {
       System.err.println(e);
     }
   }
  }

  @Override
  public void failed(Throwable exc, Void attachment) {
   asynchronousServerSocketChannel.accept(null, this);
```

```
            throw new UnsupportedOperationException("Cannot accept connections!");
          }
      });

      // Wait
      System.in.read();

      } else {
        System.out.println("The asynchronous server-socket channel cannot be opened!");
      }

  } catch (IOException ex) {
    System.err.println(ex);
  }
 }
}
```

Writing an Asynchronous Client (Based on CompletionHandler)

The client for our server can also be implemented with a CompletionHandler for dealing with the connection request operations. For this, we will call the following connect() method:

```
public abstract <A> void connect(SocketAddress remote, A attachment,
CompletionHandler<Void,? super A> handler)
```

This method gets the remote address to which this channel is to be connected, the object to attach to the I/O operation (can be null), and the completion handler that is invoked when the connection is successfully established or not.

We implement the CompletionHandler as an anonymous inner class and override its methods. Now, the completed() method of the completion handler is responsible for maintaining and closing the "conversation" with the server. For this we use the same read() and write() methods as earlier and use the same approach. The failed() method of the completion handler should be called only if the operation of connecting fails—in this case, the channel is closed.

Here is the CompletionHandler asynchronous client:

```
import java.io.IOException;
import java.net.InetSocketAddress;
import java.net.StandardSocketOptions;
import java.nio.ByteBuffer;
import java.nio.CharBuffer;
import java.nio.channels.AsynchronousSocketChannel;
import java.nio.channels.CompletionHandler;
import java.nio.charset.Charset;
import java.nio.charset.CharsetDecoder;
import java.util.Random;
import java.util.concurrent.ExecutionException;

public class Main {

 public static void main(String[] args) {
```

```java
final int DEFAULT_PORT = 5555;
final String IP = "127.0.0.1";

//create an asynchronous socket channel bound to the default group
try (AsynchronousSocketChannel asynchronousSocketChannel =
        AsynchronousSocketChannel.open()) {

    if (asynchronousSocketChannel.isOpen()) {

        //set some options
        asynchronousSocketChannel.setOption(StandardSocketOptions.SO_RCVBUF, 128 * 1024);
        asynchronousSocketChannel.setOption(StandardSocketOptions.SO_SNDBUF, 128 * 1024);
        asynchronousSocketChannel.setOption(StandardSocketOptions.SO_KEEPALIVE, true);

        //connect this channel's socket
        asynchronousSocketChannel.connect(new InetSocketAddress(IP, DEFAULT_PORT), null,
                    new CompletionHandler<Void, Void>() {

            final ByteBuffer helloBuffer = ByteBuffer.wrap("Hello !".getBytes());
            final ByteBuffer buffer = ByteBuffer.allocateDirect(1024);
            CharBuffer charBuffer = null;
            ByteBuffer randomBuffer;
            final Charset charset = Charset.defaultCharset();
            final CharsetDecoder decoder = charset.newDecoder();

            @Override
            public void completed(Void result, Void attachment) {
             try {
                System.out.println("Successfully connected at: " +
                        asynchronousSocketChannel.getRemoteAddress());

                //transmitting data
                asynchronousSocketChannel.write(helloBuffer).get();

                while (asynchronousSocketChannel.read(buffer).get() != -1) {

                        buffer.flip();

                        charBuffer = decoder.decode(buffer);
                        System.out.println(charBuffer.toString());

                        if (buffer.hasRemaining()) {
                            buffer.compact();
                        } else {
                            buffer.clear();
                        }

                        int r = new Random().nextInt(100);
                        if (r == 50) {
                            System.out.println("50 was generated! Close the asynchronous
                                                        socket channel!");
                            break;
```

255

```
                } else {
                    randomBuffer = ByteBuffer.wrap("Random
                                    number:".concat(String.valueOf(r)).getBytes());
                    asynchronousSocketChannel.write(randomBuffer).get();
                }
            }
        } catch (IOException | InterruptedException | ExecutionException ex) {
            System.err.println(ex);
        } finally {
            try {
                asynchronousSocketChannel.close();
            } catch (IOException ex) {
                System.err.println(ex);
            }
        }
    }

    @Override
    public void failed(Throwable exc, Void attachment) {
     throw new UnsupportedOperationException("Connection cannot be established!");
    }
});

System.in.read();

        } else {
            System.out.println("The asynchronous socket channel cannot be opened!");
        }

    } catch (IOException ex) {
        System.err.println(ex);
    }
 }
}
```

Testing the Echo Application (Based on CompletionHandler)

Testing the application is a simple task. First, start the server and wait until you see the message "Waiting for connections ...." Continue by starting the client and checking out the output. The following is possible server output:

```
Waiting for connections ...

Incoming connection from: /127.0.0.1:50369

Incoming connection from: /127.0.0.1:50370

Incoming connection from: /127.0.0.1:50371
```

```
Incoming connection from: /127.0.0.1:50372
```

The following shows possible client output:

```
Hello !

Random number:19

Random number:54

Random number:28

Random number:59

Random number:34

Random number:60

…

50 was generated! Close the asynchronous socket channel!
```

Using Read/Write Operations and CompletionHandler

In the previous examples, we have managed the read/write operations through the Future mode. If you want to associate a CompletionHandler with a read/write operation, then you can use the next AsynchronousSocketChannel read() and write() methods:

- The first read() method initiates an operation that reads a sequence of bytes from this channel into a subsequence of the given buffers (known as an *asynchronous scattering read*). The operation must end in the specified timeout:

```
public abstract <A> void read(ByteBuffer[] dsts, int offset, int length, long timeout,
TimeUnit unit, A attachment, CompletionHandler<Long,? super A> handler)
```

- This method initiates an operation that reads a sequence of bytes from this channel into the given buffer:

```
public final <A> void read(ByteBuffer dst, A attachment, CompletionHandler<Integer,? super
A> handler)
```

- This method initiates an operation that reads a sequence of bytes from this channel into the given buffer. The operation must end in the specified timeout:

```
public abstract <A> void read(ByteBuffer dst,long timeout, TimeUnit unit, A attachment,
CompletionHandler<Integer,? super A> handler)
```

Analogue to these methods, but for writing operations, we have one method for *asynchronous gathering write*:

```
public abstract <A> void write(ByteBuffer[] srcs, int offset, int length, long timeout,
TimeUnit unit, A attachment, CompletionHandler<Long,? super A> handler)
```

And we have two more methods for writing a sequence of bytes to this channel from the given buffer:

```
public final <A> void write(ByteBuffer src, A attachment,
CompletionHandler<Integer,? super A> handler)
```

```
public abstract <A> void write(ByteBuffer src, long timeout, TimeUnit unit,
A attachment, CompletionHandler<Integer,? super A> handler)
```

Writing an Asynchronous Client/Server Based on Custom Group

The previous client/server applications were developed by using the default group. We can specify a custom group as an AsynchronousChannelGroup object passed to the AsynchronousServerSocketChannel.open() method and/or AsynchronousSocketChannel.open() method. First, we create a custom group. This example creates a cached thread pool with the initial size of one thread:

```
AsynchronousChannelGroup threadGroup = null;
…
ExecutorService executorService = Executors
                .newCachedThreadPool(Executors.defaultThreadFactory());
try {
    threadGroup = AsynchronousChannelGroup.withCachedThreadPool(executorService, 1);
} catch (IOException ex) {
  System.err.println(ex);
}
```

The following example creates a fixed thread pool with exactly five threads:

```
AsynchronousChannelGroup threadGroup = null;
…
try {
    threadGroup = AsynchronousChannelGroup.withFixedThreadPool(5,
                                        Executors.defaultThreadFactory());
    } catch (IOException ex) {
      System.err.println(ex);
}
```

And, the threadGroup can be passed to the asynchronous channel for stream-oriented listening sockets—if the group is shut down and a connection is accepted, then the connection is closed, and the operation completes with an IOException exception and causes ShutdownChannelGroupException:

```
AsynchronousServerSocketChannel asynchronousServerSocketChannel =
AsynchronousServerSocketChannel.open(threadGroup);
```

When a new connection is accepted, the resulting AsynchronousSocketChannel will be bound to the same AsynchronousChannelGroup as this channel.

Or the `ThreadGroup` can be passed to the asynchronous channel for stream-oriented connecting sockets—if the group is shut down and a connection is active, then the connection is closed, and the operation completes with an `IOException` exception and causes `ShutdownChannelGroupException`:

```
AsynchronousSocketChannel asynchronousSocketChannel =
AsynchronousSocketChannel.open(threadGroup);
```

Now you can modify the preceding applications for using custom groups.

Tips

The applications presented in this chapter are fine for educational purposes but not for a production environment. If you need to write applications for a production environment, then it is a good idea to keep in mind the following tips.

Use Byte Buffer Pool and Throttle Read Operations

Consider the scenario in which an `AsynchronousSocketChannel.read()` method reads from thousands of clients and creates thousands of `ByteBuffer`s. The method is able to read from a large number of slow clients for a while, but eventually it is overwhelmed by the huge number of clients arriving. You can avoid this by applying a trick: use a byte buffer pool and throttle read operations. In addition, there may be a danger here of running out of memory if your byte buffer grows too large, so you must be mindful of memory consumption (perhaps adjust Java heap parameters such as `Xms` and `Xmx`).

Use Blocking Only for Short Reading Operations

For the next scenario, suppose that an `AsynchronousSocketChannel.read()` method is reading from clients in `Future` mode, which means that the `get()` method will wait until the read operation completes, thus blocking the thread. In this scenario, you must make sure you do not lock your thread pool, especially if you are using a fixed thread pool. You can avoid this scenario by using blocking only for short reading operations. Using timeouts can also be a solution.

Use FIFO-Q and Allow Blocking for Write Operations

Focusing now on write operations, consider the scenario in which an `AsynchronousSocketChannel.write()` method writes bytes to its client without blocking—it initiates the write operation and moves on to other tasks. But, moving on to other tasks may cause the thread to invoke the `write()` method again, and the completion handler has not yet been invoked by the previous write call. Bad idea! A `WritePendingException` exception will be thrown. You can fix this issue by making sure that the completion handler `complete()` method is invoked before a new write operation is initiated. For this, use a first-in first out queue (FIFO-Q) for the byte buffers and write only when the previous `write()` has completed. So, use FIFO-Q and allow blocking for write operations.

Refer to the "ByteBuffers Considerations" section, earlier in this chapter, also.

Writing an Asynchronous Datagram Application

As of this writing, the `AsynchronousDatagramChannel` class is no longer available (it existed in Java 7 DRAFT ea-b89), so this discussion is included just in case it reappears in the future. If it does, this class will follow the same trend as the AsynchronousServerSocketChannel and AsynchronousSocketChannel classes: it will provide two open() methods (one for the default group and one for custom groups), a bind() method, and a connect() method. It will also have dedicated methods for read/write operations: a set of send()/receive() methods for connectionless case, and a set of read()/write() methods for connection case. All read/write operations will be asynchronous and will provide support for Future and CompletionHandler modes.

ASYNCHRONOUSDATAGRAMCHANNEL

This class was introduced in and then removed from earlier, unstable versions of Java 7. There is a chance it will show up in later releases, so some guidelines for its main features are presented here.

The AsynchronousDatagramChannel class represents an asynchronous channel for datagram-oriented sockets. This channel supports asynchronous opening and read/write operations (through send()/receive() methods for unconnected channels, and read()/write() methods for connected channels). That means that these operations can be tracked by Future and CompletionHandler mechanisms. On the other hand, this channel implements NetworkChannel for binding and setting/getting socket options and implements MulticastChannel for joining multicast groups.

If you work with an asynchronous datagram channel in the future, you must be careful to take into account the following aspects:

- An attempt to connect a channel may cause a ClosedChannelException exception if this channel is closed.

- An attempt to invoke an I/O operation upon an unconnected channel will cause a NotYetConnectedException exception to be thrown.

- Closing an asynchronous datagram socket channel by explicitly calling the inherited close() method (from the AsynchronousChannel interface) causes all outstanding asynchronous operations on the channel to complete with the AsynchronousCloseException exception. After a channel is closed, further attempts to initiate asynchronous I/O operations complete immediately with cause ClosedChannelException. In addition, the inherited MulticastChannel.close() method is available for closing the channel.

The following snippet of code was copied verbatim from the official documentation available for Java 7 DRAFT ea-b89, to give you a general idea of what may be available in the future:

```
final AsynchronousDatagramChannel dc = AsynchronousDatagramChannel.open()
    .bind(new InetSocketAddress(4000));

// print the source address of all packets that we receive
dc.receive(buffer, buffer, new CompletionHandler<SocketAddress,ByteBuffer>() {
  public void completed(SocketAddress sa, ByteBuffer buffer) {
    System.out.println(sa);
    buffer.clear();
    dc.receive(buffer, buffer, this);
```

```
    }
    public void failed(Throwable exc, ByteBuffer buffer) {
        ...
    }
});
```

Summary

In this chapter, you learned how to work with the NIO.2 asynchronous channel API. After a brief introduction to the differences between synchronous I/O and asynchronous I/O, you received a detailed overview of this API structure. After that, you saw theory put into practice, starting with the `java.nio.channels.AsynchronousChannel` interface, which extends a channel with asynchronous I/O operations support. The three classes that implement this interface for asynchronous operations over files and sockets were then presented: `AsynchronousFileChannel`, `AsynchronousSocketChannel`, and `AsynchronousServerSocketChannel`. The currently unavailable `AsynchronousDatagramChannel` class was also described in this chapter, just in case it reappears in the future. The chapter also introduced the `AsynchronousChannelGroup`, including the notion of the asynchronous channel group. The chapter wrapped up with a few tips regarding developing asynchronous-based applications.

CHAPTER 10

Important Things to Remember

The first parts of this chapter offer some information that is good to know, or at least hear about. This information didn't fit neatly into any of the previous chapters, and you probably won't use it very soon, but it may be helpful someday. The following topics are covered:

- Refactoring `java.io.File` code
- Working with the ZIP file system provider
- Considerations about custom file system providers

We finish this chapter (and the book also) with a set of NIO.2 milestone methods that were presented and used in the book. Every time you need a quick reminder or overview of these methods, you can easily leaf through the last pages of the book for them.

Refactoring java.io.File Code

If you have developed a few applications based on `java.io.File`, then you should be familiar with the most common methods of this class. But, if you've developed more than a few applications based on `java.io.File`, then you should be familiar with not only its methods, but also its methods' drawbacks. For example, many of these methods don't throw exceptions when they fail, there is no real support for symbolic links, metadata access is inefficient, file-renaming across platforms is inconsistent, some methods don't scale, and so on—all of which should sound pretty familiar to many senior Java developers, and pretty scary for juniors.

While juniors will sprightly jump to Java 7 (which fixes these drawbacks and is a breath of fresh air in this area), seniors must take some precious time to refactor existing code to support Java 7 (or more precisely, `java.nio.file` classes).

The first milestone of refactoring `java.io.File` code may be considered the conversion of `File` objects into `java.nio.file.Path` objects through the `java.io.File.toPath()` method:

```
File file ...;
Path path_from_file = file.toPath();
```

After conversion, you can exploit the `Path` features.

However, while this is the easiest solution, it may not always satisfy your needs. Sometimes you will need to rewrite your file I/O code and align code to `java.nio.file` classes, and for this you can use the one-by-one correspondence between the two APIs. Table 1-1 shows this correspondence.

Table 1-1. Correspondence Between java.io.File and java.nio.file

Javadoc Description	java.io.File	java.nio.file	Chapter
Class name correspondence	`java.io.File`	`java.nio.file.Path`	Chapter 1
Tests this abstract pathname for equality with the given object	`File.equals(Object)`	`Path.equals(Object)`	Chapter 1
Compares two abstract pathnames lexicographically	`File.compareTo(File)`	`Path.compareTo(Path)`	Chapter 1
Returns the absolute pathname string of this abstract pathname	`File.getAbsolutePath()`	`Path.toAbsolutePath()`	Chapter 1
Returns the absolute form of this abstract pathname	`File.getAbsoluteFile()`	`Path.toAbsolutePath()`	Chapter 1
Returns the canonical pathname string of this abstract pathname	`File.getCanonicalPath()`	`Path.toRealPath(LinkOption...)` `Path.normalize()`	Chapter 1
Returns the canonical form of this abstract pathname	`File.getCanonicalFile()`	`Path.toRealPath(LinkOption...)` `Path.normalize()`	Chapter 1
Constructs a `file:` URI that represents this abstract pathname	`File.toURI()`	`Path.toUri()`	Chapter 1
Tests whether the file denoted by this abstract pathname is a normal file	`File.isFile()`	`Files.isRegularFile(Path, LinkOption ...)`	Chapter 4
Tests whether the file denoted by this abstract pathname is a directory	`File.isDirectory()`	`Files.isDirectory(Path, LinkOption...)`	Chapter 4
Tests whether the file named by this abstract pathname is a hidden file	`File.isHidden()`	`Files.isHidden(Path)`	Chapter 4
Tests whether the application can read the file denoted by this abstract pathname	`File.canRead()`	`Files.isReadable(Path)`	Chapter 4
Tests whether the application can modify the file denoted by this abstract pathname	`File.canWrite()`	`Files.isWritable(Path)`	Chapter 4

Javadoc Description	java.io.File	java.nio.file	Chapter
Tests whether the application can execute the file denoted by this abstract pathname	File.canExecute()	Files.isExecutable(Path)	Chapter 4
Tests whether the file or directory denoted by this abstract pathname exists	File.exists()	Files.exists(Path, LinkOption ...) Files.notExists(Path, LinkOption ...)	Chapter 4
Creates the directory named by this abstract pathname	File.mkdir()	Files.createDirectory(Path, FileAttribute<?> ...)	Chapter 4
Creates the directory named by this abstract pathname, including any necessary but nonexistent parent directories	File.mkdirs()	Files.createDirectories(Path, FileAttribute<?> ...)	Chapter 4
Atomically creates a new, empty file named by this abstract pathname if and only if a file with this name does not yet exist	File.createNewFile()	Files.createFile(Path, FileAttribute<?> ...)	Chapter 4
Returns an array of strings naming the files and directories in the directory denoted by this abstract pathname	File.list() File.listFiles()	Files.newDirectoryStream(Path)	Chapter 4
Returns an array of strings naming the files and directories in the directory denoted by this abstract pathname that satisfy the specified filter	File.list(FilenameFilter) File.listFiles(FileFilter) File.listFiles(FilenameFilter)	Files.newDirectoryStream(Path, DirectoryStream.Filter<? super Path>) Files.newDirectoryStream(Path, String)	Chapter 4
The length of the file denoted by this abstract pathname	File.length()	Files.size(Path)	Chapter 4
Deletes the file or directory denoted by this abstract pathname	File.delete()	Files.delete(Path) Files.deleteIfExists(Path)	Chapter 4
Renames the file denoted by this abstract pathname	File.renameTo(File)	Files.move(Path, Path, CopyOption)	Chapter 4

Javadoc Description	java.io.File	java.nio.file	Chapter
Sets the owner or everybody's execute permission for this abstract pathname	File.setExecutable(boolean, boolean)	Files.setAttribute(Path, String, Object, LinkOption...)	Chapter 2
Sets the owner or everybody's read permission for this abstract pathname	File.setReadable(boolean, boolean)	Files.setAttribute(Path, String, Object, LinkOption...)	Chapter 2
Marks the file or directory named by this abstract pathname so that only read operations are allowed	File.setReadOnly()	Files.setAttribute(Path, String, Object, LinkOption...)	Chapter 2
Sets the owner or everybody's write permission for this abstract pathname	File.setWritable(boolean, boolean)	Files.setAttribute(Path, String, Object, LinkOption...)	Chapter 2
Returns the time that the file denoted by this abstract pathname was last modified	File.lastModified()	Files.getLastModifiedTime(Path path, LinkOption... options)	Chapter 2
Sets the last-modified time of the file or directory named by this abstract pathname	File.setLastModified(long)	Files.setLastModifiedTime(Path, FileTime)	Chapter 2
Creates an empty file in the default temporary-file directory, using the given prefix and suffix to generate its name	File.createTempFile(String, String)	Files.createTempFile(String prefix, String suffix, FileAttribute<?>... attrs)	Chapter 4
Creates a new empty file in the specified directory, using the given prefix and suffix strings to generate its name	File.createTempFile(String, String, File)	Files.createTempFile(Path dir, String prefix, String suffix, FileAttribute<?>... attrs)	Chapter 4
Returns the size of the partition named by this abstract pathname	File.getTotalSpace()	FileStore.getTotalSpace()	Chapter 2
Returns the number of unallocated bytes in the partition named by this abstract path name	File.getFreeSpace()	FileStore.getUnallocatedSpace()	Chapter 2

Javadoc Description	java.io.File	java.nio.file	Chapter
Returns the number of bytes available to this virtual machine on the partition named by this abstract pathname	`File.getUsableSpace()`	`FilesStore.getUsableSpace()`	Chapter 2
Lists the available file system roots	`File.listRoots()`	`FileSystem.getRootDirectories()`	Chapter 4
Random access file	`java.io.RandomAccessFile`	`java.nio.channels.SeekableByte Channel`	Chapter 7
Requests that the file or directory denoted by this abstract pathname be deleted when the virtual machine terminates	`File.deleteOnExit()`	Replaced by the `DELETE_ON_CLOSE` option	Chapter 4
Combines two paths	`new File(parent, "new_file")`	`parent.resolve("new_file")`	Chapter 1

This table will make your code transition from Java 5 or 6 to Java 7 much easier.

Working with the ZIP File System Provider

Conforming to NIO.2, a file system concerns the generic notion of a container that's capable of managing and accessing the file system objects. A file system object is typically a file store (e.g., on Windows we usually have `C:`, `D:`, and `E:` file stores, and we refer to them as partitions), but it can be a directory or a file as well.

Based on this approach, the NIO.2 API introduced in Java 7 the ability to develop a custom file system provider that can be used to manage file system objects. Moreover, it provides an implementation of a custom file system provider—the *ZIP File System Provider (ZFSP)*—that can be used as-is, and/or can be the inspiration point to develop other custom file system providers. The ZFSP treats a ZIP/JAR file as a file system and provides the ability to manipulate the contents of the file. The ZFSP creates one file system for each ZIP/JAR file.

In this section, you will see how to use the ZFSP to create a ZIP file system (the `C:\rafaelnadal\tournaments\2009\Tickets.zip` archive will become a ZIP file system) and to copy a file named `AEGONTickets.png` from the new ZIP file system in the `C:\rafaelnadal\tournaments\2009\` directory as `AEGONTicketsCopy.png`.

First, we create a simple `HashMap` that contains the configurable properties of a ZIP file system created by the ZFSP. Currently, there are two properties that can be configured:

- `create`: The value can be `true` or `false`, but of type `java.lang.String`. If the value is `true`, the ZFSP creates a new ZIP file if it does not exist.

- `encoding`: The value is a `java.lang.String` indicating the encoding scheme (e.g., UTF-8, US-ASCII, ISO-8859-1, etc.). UTF-8 is the default.

Therefore, we can indicate that the ZIP file exists and the needed encoding is ISO-8859-1 like so:

```
Map<String, String> env = new HashMap<>();
env.put("create", "false");
env.put("encoding", "ISO-8859-1");
```

For creating a new ZIP file system or obtaining a reference to an existing one, we use the factory methods of the java.nio.file.FileSystems class. Create a ZIP file system by specifying the path of the ZIP/JAR file. This can be accomplished by using the JAR URL syntax defined in the java.net.JarURLConnection class:

```
URI uri = URI.create("jar:file:/C:/rafaelnadal/tournaments/2009/Tickets.zip");
FileSystem ZipFS = FileSystems.newFileSystem(uri, env);
```

In addition, there are two more newFileSystem() methods for accomplishing this step:

```
public static FileSystem newFileSystem(Path path, ClassLoader loader) throws IOException
public static FileSystem newFileSystem(URI uri, Map<String,?> env, ClassLoader loader) throws
IOException
```

Now that we have an instance of a ZIP file system, we can invoke the methods of the java.nio.file.FileSystem and java.nio.file.Path classes to perform operations such as copying, moving, and renaming files, as well as modifying file attributes. We want to copy the AEGONTickets.png entry out of the archive. The following code will do that for us:

```java
import java.io.IOException;
import java.net.URI;
import java.nio.file.FileSystem;
import java.nio.file.FileSystems;
import java.nio.file.Files;
import java.nio.file.Path;
import java.nio.file.Paths;
import java.util.HashMap;
import java.util.Map;

public class Main {

 public static void main(String[] args) throws IOException {

    //set zip file system properties
    Map<String, String> env = new HashMap<>();
    env.put("create", "false");
    env.put("encoding", "ISO-8859-1");

    //locate file system with java.net.JarURLConnection
    URI uri = URI.create("jar:file:/C:/rafaelnadal/tournaments/2009/Tickets.zip");

    try (FileSystem ZipFS = FileSystems.newFileSystem(uri, env)) {
        Path fileInZip = ZipFS.getPath("/AEGONTickets.png");
        Path fileOutZip = Paths.get("C:/rafaelnadal/tournaments/2009/AEGONTicketsCopy.png");

        //copy AEGONTickets.png outside the archive
        Files.copy(fileInZip, fileOutZip);
```

```
        System.out.println("The file was successfully copied!");
        }
    }
}
```

If everything worked fine, then you will see the following message, and the file
AEGONTicketsCopy.png should exist in C:\rafaelnadal\tournaments\2009 directory.

```
The file was successfully copied!
```

Considerations on Developing a Custom File System Provider

In the preceding section, you saw how to use a custom file system provider. If you decide to try to write
your own custom file system provider, then it is a good idea to take into account the considerations
listed in this section. For one, you must know that the main class that supports this kind of attempt is
java.nio.file.spi.FileSystemProvider. A custom file system provider will implement this class as a
factory for java.nio.file.FileSystem instances. A file system provider is identified by a URI scheme
such as file, jar, memory, or cd, and a file system's URI has a URI scheme that matches the file system
provider's URI scheme.

Therefore, implementing a custom file system provider requires writing at least two classes and
keeping in mind a set of mandatory steps.

Creating a Custom File System Provider Class

You can create such a class by following these steps:

1. Extend the java.nio.file.spi.FileSystemProvider class.

2. Define a URI scheme for the provider (the getScheme() method should return
   this URI scheme).

3. Create an internal cache for managing the provider's created file systems.

4. Implement the newFileSystem() and getFileSystem() methods for creating a
   file system and for retrieving a reference to an existing file system.

5. Implement the newFileChannel() or the newAsyncronousFileChannel()
   method, which returns a FileChannel object that allows a file to be read or
   written in the file system.

Creating a Custom File System Class

Create such a class by following these steps:

1. Extend the java.nio.file.FileSystem class.

2. Implement the methods of the file system according to your needs (you may
   need to define the number of roots, read/write access, file stores, etc.).

For more details, you may want to take a closer look at official documentation, at http://download.oracle.com/javase/7/docs/technotes/guides/io/fsp/filesystemprovider.html.

Useful Methods

We have almost finished our NIO.2 journey. This last section covers some useful methods that are ready to help you in any NIO.2 application.

Default File System

You've seen how to get the default file system many times in this book, but we're putting this so you can easily access this information if you forget. Getting the default file system is accomplished through the `FileSystems.getDefault()` method:

```
FileSystem fs = FileSystems.getDefault();
```

File Stores

Getting the file system file stores is another well-covered subject in the book, but for a quick reminder, come here. Here's the required code:

```
for (FileStore store: FileSystems.getDefault().getFileStores()) {
    ...
}
```

Path of a File

Here's how to get the path of a file:

```
Path path = Paths.get("...");
Path path = FileSystems.getDefault().getPath("...");
Path path = Paths.get(URI.create("file:///..."));
Path path = Paths.get(System.getProperty("user.home"), "...");
```

Path String Separator

As you know, a path string separator is OS dependent. To retrieve the `Path` string separator for the default file system, you can use one of the following approaches:

```
String separator = File.separator;
String separator = FileSystems.getDefault().getSeparator();
```

Summary

In this chapter you learned how to convert code based on the `java.io.File` class into code based on the `java.nio.file.Path` class. Also, you learned how to use the ZIP file system provider and some information on creating a custom file system provider. The chapter (and the book) ends with the most used snippets of codes from the book.

INDEX

■ ■ ■

A

Access control list (ACL)
  AclEntry class, 24, 26
  AclEntry.Builder object, 26, 27
  AclFileAttributeView interface, 23
  Files.getAttribute() method, 24
  Files.getFileAttributeView() method, 23
Asynchronous channel API, 215
  asynchronous channel sockets
    asynchronous client (*see*
      Asynchronous client)
    asynchronous datagram
      application, 259, 261
    asynchronous server (*see*
      Asynchronous server)
    byte buffer pool and throttle read
      operations, 259
    custom group, 258
    echo application test (*see* Echo
      application test)
    FIFO-Q, 259
    production environment
      applications, 259
    read/write operations and
      CompletionHandler mode, 257
    short reading operation blocking,
      259
    write operation blocking, 259
  asynchronous I/O (*see* Asynchronous
    I/O)
  AsynchronousFileChannel class (*see*
    AsynchronousFileChannel class)

Asynchronous client
  CompletionHandler mode, 254–256
  future mode, 247
    AsynchronousSocketChannel.close(
) method, 249
    AsynchronousSocketChannel.conne
      ct() method, 247
    channel creation, 247
    client creation, 249, 250
    data transmission, 248
    options setting, 247
Asynchronous I/O
  asynchronous channels, 216
    AsynchronousFileChannel, 218
    AsynchronousServerSocketChannel,
      219
    AsynchronousSocketChannel, 219,
      220
  AsynchronousChannelGroup, 220
  ByteBuffers, 223
  complete result and
    CompletionHandler interface, 217
  custom groups
    cached thread pool, 222
    designated thread pool, 222
    ExecutorService function, 221
    fixed thread pool, 221
    shutdown() method, 223
  default group, 220, 221
  ExecutorService API, 224

pending result and future class, 216, 217

vs. synchronous I/O, 215, 216

Asynchronous server
  CompletionHandler mode, 252, 254
  future mode
    AsynchronousServerSocketChannel. accept() method, 241, 242
    AsynchronousSocketChannel.close() method, 243
    channel binding, 241
    channel creation, 240
    data transmission, 242
    echo server, 243–246
    options setting, 241

AsynchronousFileChannel class
  ExecutorService object, 236–239
  file lock, 233, 234, 236
  file read
    CompletionHandler class, 229, 231, 233
    future mode, 225, 226
    future Timeout, 228, 229
  file write and future mode, 226, 227
  open() method, 224

B

ByteBuffer
  ancestor methods, 139, 140
  components, 135
  properties, 136–139

C

completed() method, 217
Custom file system provider
  class creating, 269
  system class creation, 269

D

deleteIfExists() method, 102

Directories, 43
  delete() method, 70, 71
  entire content list, 49, 50
  file system root directories, 47, 48
  Files.copy() method, 71–74
  Files.newDirectoryStream() method, 49
  glob pattern content list, 50, 51
  move() method, 74, 75
  new directory creation, 48, 49
  Path class, 43
  temporary directory (*see* Temporary directory)
  user-defined filter, 51, 52

E

Echo application test
  CompletionHandler mode, 256, 257
  future mode, 251
ExecutorService interface, 224

F, G

FileChannel
  benchmarking, 159–165
    FileChannel.transferTo() *vs.* FileChannel.transferFrom() *vs.* FileChannel.map() method, 165
    Files.copy() method, 166
    non-direct buffer *vs.* FileChannel.transferTo() *vs.* Path to Path method, 167
    non-direct *vs.* direct buffer, 165
  file locking, 154–157
  file mapping, 153, 154
  FileChannel.open() method, 152
  files copying
    direct/non-direct ByteBuffer, 157, 158
    FileChannel.map() method, 158, 159
    FileChannel.transferFrom() method, 158
    FileChannel.transferTo() method, 158

Files, 43
  accessibility, 44–46
  buffer, 53
  delete() method, 70, 71
  exists() method, 44
  Files.copy() method, 71–74
  Files.newBufferedWriter() method, 58
  Files.write() method, 54
  isSameFile() method, 46
  isSomething method, 43
  move() method, 74, 75
  new file creation, 54
  newBufferedReader() method, 58, 59
  newBufferedWriter() method, 58
  newInputStream() method, 60, 61
  newOutputStream() method, 60
  notExists() method, 44
  Path class, 43
  readAllBytes() method, 56, 57
  readAllLines() method, 57
  StandardOpenOption class, 53
  stream, definition, 53
  temporary files (see Temporary file)
  visibility, 47
  writing bytes, 55
  writing lines, 56
Files.copy() method, 104
Files.move() method, 107, 109
File search application
  complete search program, 94–102
  FileVisitor tool, 81, 82
  glob pattern, 84–88
  search by content
    ArrayList, 88
    Excel files, 91, 92
    PDFs, 89, 90
    PowerPoint files, 92, 93
    searchText() method, 88
    Text files, 93, 94
    Word document, 90, 91
  search by name, 82, 84
Future.get() method, 217
Future.isCancelled() method, 216
Future.isDone() method, 216

H, I

Hard link
  creation, 38, 39
  differences/similarities, 35, 36

J, K

Java.io.file code, 263–267

L

lock() method, 233–235

M

Metadata file attributes, 11
  default file system, 12
  FileStore.supportsFileAttributeView()
    method, 13
  java.nio.file.attribute package, 11
  NIO.2 (see NIO.2 group)

N, O

NetworkChannel
  bind() method, 170
  socket options
    IP_MULTICAST_IF, 171
    IP_MULTICAST_LOOP, 171
    IP_MULTICAST_TTL, 171
    IP_TOS, 171
    SO_BROADCAST, 171
    SO_KEEPALIVE, 171
    SO_LINGER, 171
    SO_RCVBUF, 172
    SO_REUSEADDR, 172
    SO_SNDBUF, 172
    TCP_NODELAY, 172
NIO.2 application
  default file system, 270
  file path, 270
  file stores, 270

path string separator, 270
NIO.2 group, 11
  ACL (*see* Access control list)
  basic attribute method, 15, 16
  BasicFileAttributeView, 13
  DOS file system, 16, 17
  file owner system
    FileOwnerAttributeView interface,
     18
    FileOwnerAttributeView.getO
     wner() method, 19
    FileOwnerAttributeView.setOwner()
     method, 18, 19
    Files.getAttribute() method, 20
    Files.setAttribute() method, 19
    Files.setOwner() method, 18
    UserPrincipal interface, 18
  file store attribute
    FileStore abstract class, 27
    FileStoreAttributeView class, 30
    FileSystem.getFileStores() method,
     28, 29
    Path object, Files.getFileStore()
     method, 29
  getAttribute(), single attribute, 14, 15
  POSIX attribute
    Files.getAttribute() method, 23
    permissions() method, 22
    PosixFileAttributes class, 21
    setGroup() method, 22
    Unix, 21
  readAttributes(), bulk attributes, 13, 14
  supportsFileAttributeView() method,
    30, 31
  user-defined attribute operation
    file.description attribute, 31
    names and value sizes, 32
    UserDefinedFileAttributeView.delet
     e() method, 33
    UserDefinedFileAttributeView.read(
) method, 32, 33
    write() method, 32
  UserDefinedFileAttributeView
    interface, 30

P, Q

Packets, 169
Path class
  conversion
    file, 7
    real path, 6
    relative absolute path, 6
    string path, 6
    URI path, 6
  definition
    absolute path, 2
    relative file store root, 3
    shortcuts, 3
    URI, 4
    working folder, 3
  getDefault(), 1
  getFileSystem(URI uri), 2
  getting information
    file/directory name, 5
    name elements path, 5
    parent path, 5
    path root, 5
    subpath, 5
  name element iterating, 10
  newFileSystem() methods, 1
  path combining, 7
  path comparing, 9
  path construction, 8
postVisitDirectory() method, 79
preVisitDirectory() method, 78, 79

R

Random access files (RAFs), 135
  block-oriented I/O system, 140
  ByteBuffer (*see* ByteBuffer)
  FileChannel (*see* FileChannel)
  Java 7, 135
  SeekableByteChannel interface
    features, 140
    file attributes, 144, 145
    newByteChannel() method, 141
    old ReadableByteChannel interface,
     145

old WritableByteChannel interface,
146
position() and position(long)
method, 146–152
reading a file, 141, 142
writing a file, 143, 144
stream-oriented I/O system, 140
Recursive programming technique, 77
factorial calculation, 77
file copy application, 104, 106
file delete application, 102, 104
file search application (*see* File search
application)
FileVisitor.postVisitDirectory() method,
79
FileVisitor.preVisitDirectory() method,
78, 79
FileVisitor.visitFile() method, 78
FileVisitor.visitFileFailed() method, 79
FileVisitResult enum, 78
move files application, 107, 109
SimpleFileVisitor class, 79, 80
walkFileTree() method, 80, 81

S

SimpleFileVisitor class, 79, 80
Socket, 169
StringTokenizer class, 88
Symbolic link
checking, 39, 40
command line creation, 36
creation, 36, 38
definition, 35
differences/similarities, 35, 36
target checking, 41
target locating, 40

T

TCP client
block writing, 179
close() method, 181
configuring blocking mechanisms, 179
data transmission, 180
putting together, 181
setting() option, 179
socketchannel connect() method, 180
SocketChannel.open(), 179
TCP server/client applications
blocking TCP server
accept() method, 175
bind() method, 174, 175
buffering, 176
close() method, 177
configuring mechanisms, 174
data transmitting, 176
echo server, 177, 178
I/O connection, 177
new creation, 173
setting options, 174
blocking *vs.* non-blocking mechanisms,
173
echo testing, 183
non-blocking
accept() method, 185
client writing, 190–193
I/O operation, 184
selection keys,sets, 185
selectionKey.OP_ACCEPT, 184
selectionKey.OP_CONNECT, 184
selectionKey.OP_READ, 184
selectionKey.OP_WRITE, 184
selector methods, 186
selector.wakeup() method, 185
server writing, 187–190
testing, 193
telephone connection, 172
Temporary directory
createTempDirectory() method, 62, 63
deletion
deleteOnExit() method, 65, 66
Shutdown-Hook, 63–65
Temporary file
createTempFile() method, 66, 67
deletion
DELETE_ON_CLOSE option, 69, 70
deleteOnExit() method, 68, 69
Shutdown-Hook, 67, 68

TimeoutException function, 217
Transmission control protocol (TCP), 169

U

UDP server/client application
    DatagramChannel.connect() method,
        202
    DatagramChannel, IOException, 204
    DatagramChannel.read() method, 202
    datagramChannel.write() method, 202
    datagram–oriented socket channel
        bind() method, 196
        ByteBuffer, 196
        creation, 195
        data packets transmission, 196–197
        data receive() method, 197
        datagramChannel.close(), 198
        setting option, 196
    multicasting
        block/unblock key, 206
        blocking and unblocking datagrams,
            212
        check validity key, 206
        client writing, 210–212
        close() method, 206
        descriptions and definitions, 205
        drop key, 206
        find out local interfaces, 208
        first join() method, 205
        get channel key, 206
        get group key, 206
        get network interface key, 206
        get source address key, 206
        multicast channel interface, 205
        Network interface, 207
        second join() method, 205
        testing, 213
        UDP server/client application, 208–
            210
    send() and receive() methods, 199
    testing echo application, 201
    together server, 198
User datagram protocol (UDP), 169

V

visitFileFailed() method, 79

W, X, Y

walkFileTree() method, 80, 81
Watch service API
    directory tree
        CREATE event, 120
        HashMap, 122–24
        registerPath() method, 121
        registerTree() method, 120, 121
        visitFileFailed() method, 120
    event modifier, 112
    event types, 112
    implementing
        creation, 112
        event type and count, 116
        file name retrieving, 117
        gluing, 118, 119
        incoming events, 114
        key back, 117
        pending events, 115
        registering objects, 112
        watch key, 114, 115
        WatchService.close() method, 118
    printer tray system
        DELETE event, 130
        HashMap loop, 130
        Print class, 129
        Print thread, 130
        testing, 133
        thread termination, 129
    video camera, 125–128
    watchable object, 112
    watcher, 112

Z

ZIP file system, 267–269
ZIP file system provider (ZFSP), 267

Made in the USA
San Bernardino, CA
20 April 2014